Enchanted

Remembrances

1838-1925

THE LIFE OF A SUNDAY'S CHILD

෴

SUSANNE SCHMALTZ

Revised and Translated from the German
with Love by Her Great-Grandniece

INGE KISTLER

EVANSTON PUBLISHING, INC.
EVANSTON, ILLINOIS 60201

Beglückte Erinnerungen was originally published in 1926 by Verlag
Deutsche Buchwerkstätten, Dresden

Enchanted Remembrances
© 1994 by Inge Kistler

EVANSTON PUBLISHING, INC.
1571 SHERMAN AVENUE, ANNEX C
EVANSTON, IL 60201

Printed in the U.S.A.

10 9 8 7 6 5 4 3 2 1

ISBN: 1-879260-29-8

ACKNOWLEDGMENTS

I am deeply grateful to the many people who have helped me bring this project to fruition. Special thanks go to Margaret Shaklee for her constructive comments upon reading the first draft of my translation, and to Don and Antje Draganski for their assistance in identifying many of the references. Anthony Green and Mary Houlgate took meticulous care in proofreading the manuscript. Ellen Pullin, always ready to help when I need her, prepared the map displaying the amazing journey remembered in these pages.

I cannot omit mentioning my debt to Klaus Geitel of *Die Welt,* whose exuberant description of the book in 1963 convinced me that interest in her story would not be limited to the descendants of Susanne Schmaltz. Finally, I acknowledge with deep gratitude the support of my husband who encourages me in whatever I pursue.

-Inge Kistler
June, 1994

TABLE OF CONTENTS

Hiller - Friedrich Devrient - Russian Easter - Move to Kamenny-Ostrov - Count Alexander Keyserling - Summer in Oranienbaum - Peter Petrovich Semenov - Mikluko Maclay - Nihilism, Student Kitchens - Franco-Prussian war - Visit to Hamburg - Return to the Palais Michel - Story of the Madman in York Cathedral - Death of the Grand Duchess Helene.

ILLUSTRATIONS

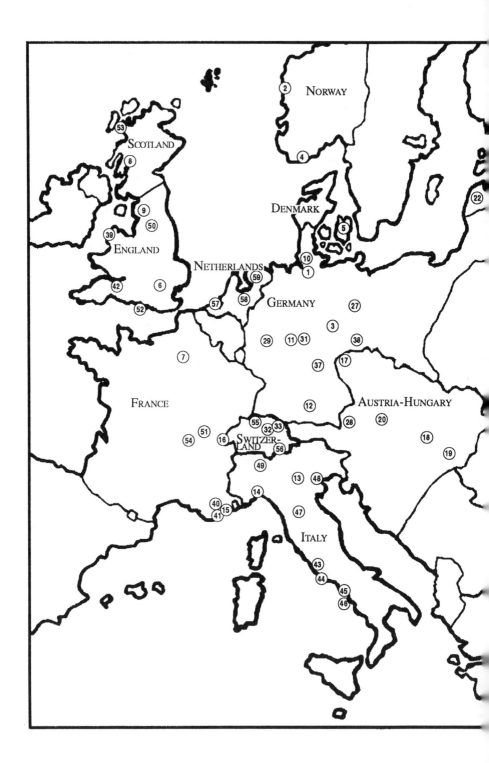

1. Hamburg
2. Bergen
3. Leipzig
4. Kristiansand
5. Copenhagen
6. London
7. Paris
8. BuchananCastle (Loch Lomond)
9. Windermere (Westmoreland)
10. Kiel
11. Eisenach
12. Munich
13. Verona
14. Genoa
15. Nice
16. Geneva
17. Karlsbad
18. Budapest
19. Temesvar
20. Vienna
21. St. Petersburg
22. Courland
23. Moscow
24. Ryazan Province
25. Reval (Yervacant and Raykuell)
26. Chernigov
27. Berlin
28. Gmunden
29. Soden (near Frankfurt)
30. Novgorod
31. Weimar
32. Davos
33. Ragaz
34. Bucharest
35. Sinaia
36. Kamenets-Podolskiy
37. Bayreuth
38. Dresden
39. Castle Carnarvon (Wales)
40. Antibes
41. Grasse
42. Kings Weston (near Bristol)
43. Rome
44. Porto D'Anzio
45. Naples
46. Capri
47. Florence
48. Venice
49. Como
50. Kirkstall (near Leeds)
51. Cluny
52. Ventnor (Isle of Wight)
53. Island Skye
54. Vichy
55. Zurich
56. St. Moritz (Engadin)
57. Vlissingen (Flushing)
58. Wageninen
59. Heerde

Suzanne Schmaltz at 29

GROWING UP

During a lively conversation in an English country house someone threw out the question whether we would like to relive our lives in exactly the same way. Everyone rejected this; I, however, affirmed the proposition with the reasoning that the brightly shining episodes of my life far outweighed the dark moments, and that I would and should gladly accept the latter into the bargain.

℘

I was born into an old Saxon family. My father, Dr. Moritz Ferdinand Schmaltz, was a distinguished preacher even as a young man. His first position was as pastor in the beautifully situated town of Wehlen in "Saxon Switzerland." After only two years, in 1816, he was called to the Evangelical (Lutheran) church in Vienna and married my mother, the eighteen-year-old Concordia Hänsel from Pirna.

The congregation loved and befriended its young preacher, and the young couple spent an idyllic time in Vienna.

They took an active interest in the arts. At that time, the great tragic actress, Sophie Schröder, was at the Burgtheater. Her extremely talented daughter, the singer Wilhelmine Schröder (later famous as Wilhelmine Schröder-Devrient), delighted my parents. My mother told me how Karl Devrient lifted his bride high up while he sang "You are the loveliest Viennese girl I have ever seen!" in the delightful musical, *The Viennese in Berlin,* by Heinrich Marschner. The enthusiastic Viennese audience responded with thunderous applause.

In Vienna my mother gave birth to two daughters. After only two years the lovely stay came to an end because my father followed a call to the "Dreikönigskirche" (Church of the Three Kings) in Dresden-Neustadt. In the beautiful "Florence on the Elbe" my father soon enjoyed a life as blessed as in Vienna. My parents' house was on the main street; however, in the summer they lived in a house in the country with a big garden, at the upper end of

Alaun Street where several large trees from that time are still standing.

The congregation loved my father and held him in high esteem. The church was overflowing when he preached. One of his sermons gave Friedrich August II, King of Saxony, cause for a political speech in which he quotes my father, "trust begets trust." This incident is mentioned by Büchmann in his *Geflügelte Worte, (Famous Quotations)*.

Among my parents' friends was General Raabe, who was well known around town for his eccentricity. The Countess Elisa von der Recke was another frequent visitor in their home and flamboyantly approached my father for advice. My mother thought that she too was quite eccentric, insisting, for example, that she wanted to be buried without a coffin, just lying on a board. I suspect this wish was not granted.

My father was a helper and comforter to all, far beyond his own congregation. He was passionate and God-fearing, freethinking but pious and kind, and with all his scholarship he was a considerate teacher of the young students.

Six children were born in Dresden. In spite of her delicate constitution, my mother wholeheartedly attended to her family and to the congregation as well. She was a loving wife, cheerful, enlightened, and well suited to keeping husband and children happy.

During this time my father received calls to become court preacher to the Grand Duke of Oldenburg, to serve the German St. Petri Church in St. Petersburg, and to become Senior Pastor at St. Katherine's in Hamburg, all of which he declined.

After fifteen infinitely happy years a cloud appeared on the horizon. My father's health had suffered from too much work and responsibility. Therefore, he could not refuse a second call to Hamburg, this time to the St. Jakobi Church. In 1833 my parents moved with their seven children — one had died in Dresden — to Hamburg. Representatives of the governing body of the church greeted them in Bergedorf with a large reception and then led them into the city.

My father, as "Senior" clergyman, had to ordain the new graduates and conduct the Latin colloquium preceding the ordination. As "Scholarch" he also had to attend the annual exams at the

"Gymnasien" and other schools. His sermons were printed every week.

In 1836 my oldest sister died of typhus, called "nerve fever" in those days. My mother suffered deeply at this loss and became very depressed. Then I came into the world in Hamburg, on Thursday, April 19, 1838, as "consolation child."

Joyful and sunny was my childhood. I grew up loved by parents, brothers, and sisters. At birth I was already an aunt since my oldest sister was married by this time. All my brothers and sisters were musical and filled the air with songs. By age five I was singing myself, "Reich mir die Hand, mein Leben," (La ci darem la mano) from Mozart's *Don Giovanni*.

Early on, I was taken along to the opera, and I remember my embarrassment when I expressed my delight with Auber's *Les Diamants de la Couronne* and my mother had to whisper "quiet" into my ear. Unforgettable also are the afternoons when my mother sat with me on the sofa and told Bible stories in her own, warm, poetic way. How indignant I became that Joseph's brothers would sell him, and how happy when he later gained a high position; again, how I resented it that Jacob deceived his father.

Not far from us lived an English family whose five-year-old son was my friend. One day we were running together through the meadow by our house to a pond. At its edge was a lovely flower which my friend wanted to pick, but he could not reach it. "I will get it for you," I said almost motherly, stretched out my arm, and fell in the water. I can still feel the heaviness which grasped my limbs. I believed that the water nymphs, about whom my nanny had told me, were pulling me down. I tried to hold on to the grass, but it kept tearing; my little friend stood like a silent spectator. Miraculously enough, I saved myself and ran home, crying and covered with black slime. I was greeted with open arms and hugged by my family who had already been looking for me.

That same year my sister Therese married Pastor Gotthard Ritter who was serving a congregation in Groden near Kuxhaven. He was called as Deacon to the St. Petri Church in Hamburg two years later.

My father's birthday was on June 18. This was always a special day for us. On the 17th I would ride with my mother to the famous gardener, Booth. We selected fuchsias and geraniums in his hothouse and carried them home in our carriage. Then we would tie garlands for the next day's joyous celebration.

Christmas was another wonderful festival in our home in which my married sister, her husband, and their three sons took part. At first we had to wait in the dark. Then —what an impressive contrast —the door was opened to the brightly illuminated hall revealing the tree. How happy we all were, Father, Mother, children, servants. Everyone had his own table of gifts arranged with so much poetic feeling and love.

Other memories are of evenings when my father, his duties completed, read to us from the works of Sir Walter Scott, whom my mother greatly admired. I still see him coming down with his candlestick. In those days there were no lights in the hallways and it was quite a trip from his study upstairs down to us by way of large and small stairways. Our house was, in fact, quite strange and was said to be haunted. Once, at night, we were aroused by a terrible rumbling noise. The servants were awakened too, and my father went with them through the whole house. At the foot of the stairs on the third floor they found a big parish register which had been on the table in the hall. How it happened to fall down we never discovered. The book was very heavy and the cat could not have pushed it off. Other than this incident, we noticed nothing of ghosts. —The big staircase of our house is now supposed to be in the museum in Hamburg as an architectural masterpiece.

My mother often was homesick for the beautiful city of Dresden. Our house was opposite the gate to the Jakobi church. Above the entrance were skulls and skeletons chiselled into stone and underneath the words, "memento mori." That was certainly in strong contrast to the cheerful main street in Dresden where the band of the main guard passed our house every day.

My father loved flowers and managed to get a profusion of hyacinths, narcissi, daffodils, etc., to bloom every year for my mother's birthday on March 16. The apartment became a flower garden. Later in the spring we would move into the country.

My school years were enjoyable and stimulating since there were only twelve children in the class. Even then we did not lack small social events as was the custom for children in our circle. Thus my teenage years arrived quickly.

My mother, Concordia Hänsel Schmaltz

My father, Dr. Moritz Ferdinand Schmaltz

About this time (1850), the youngest of my sisters, who was eight years older than I, married, and it grew lonely in the big house. My mother became sickly and had to stay in bed frequently. The relationship between us was so close that I could keep no secret from her. One day I was invited to a friend's house. It happened that this was the first and only time that I had to stay after school. I did not know my French vocabulary. My friend suggested that she stay with me and take me to her home afterwards. "That way, no one will ever know," she said. But I could not have enjoyed our afternoon together without first confessing this humiliation to my mother. We ran home and I went up to my mother's bed, told her everything and felt relieved.

Even at that time I often experienced the feeling of intense loneliness which has accompanied me throughout my life. But I did not let it depress my spirits. I remember the winter blessed by the preparation for my confirmation. My father did this himself for his daughter, even though in Hamburg the confirmation is customarily performed not by the senior pastor but by the three deacons who are engaged at his church.

The evenings of our confirmation lessons were magical evenings. The lamp stood on the round table where I and two other young girls were waiting in anticipation. The mothers of the other participants were great admirers of my father and had requested that their daughters join my confirmation lessons. The door opened and my father entered in his official robes. In this moment he was not the loving father but only the minister who wants to transfer Christianity into the lives of those given into his care. He accomplished this with great imagination and understanding. Discussing the details of life in the light of Christ's words, he gave us a source of strength for our lives. His black eyes were shining with love of God and men at such times. He selected these words as my confirmation text: "All your life, have God before your eyes and in your heart, and take care that you suffer no evil nor act against God's commandments." (Tob IV. 6) The confirmation took place in our hall. A small altar had been set up and the path was strewn with rosebuds.

Unfortunately, we three friends were not to remain together later in life. One of my friends died after a short, but happy marriage;

the other, daughter of a landowner, remained in the country and led an active, beneficial life.

After my confirmation I spent much time on music. I practiced piano for four hours a day, so that my excellent teacher, Mr. Grund, the conductor of well-attended concerts in Hamburg, was quite satisfied.

Shortly after my sixteenth birthday I lost my mother. She died on May 7, 1854, when she was 56 years old. It was a hard time for us. At the urging of my sisters who were married and living in Bergen, my father and I went to visit them. We spent a quiet summer in beautiful Norway. Since I was not prepared to marry in Bergen also, I returned to Hamburg with my father.

We now engaged a housekeeper. A lady who had once been confirmed by my father in Dresden and held great admiration for him, was pleased to take good care of him.

Here I would like to make an observation. One should not give a young lady a companion of incredible ugliness. It was torture for me to sit across from her. I simply could not look at her.

Thus, knowing that my father was well taken care of, I was delighted to accept an invitation from my sister Klara in Leipzig. I spent three wonderful months there and became close friends with my niece, Mathilde Hoffmann, who was only one and a half years younger than I.

In Leipzig I took piano lessons from Professor Ernst Ferdinand Wenzel, to whom Brahms dedicated one of his compositions. Through him I gained admission to the performances at the conservatory and the rehearsals of the Gewandhaus concerts. Professor Wenzel was unusually stimulating and perceptive. He wrote into my album the following verse:

> *Der beste Lehrer kann dich nicht umgestalten,*
> *er kann dich entwickeln, du musst dich entfalten.*

> *The best teacher cannot change your mold,*
> *he can nourish you, but you must unfold.*

I have often experienced the truth of these words.

At our first encounter he asked me how much I expected to practice. I said, "two hours a day." He flared up. "You might as well look out the window for two hours. You must practice four hours!" On November 10th there was a great celebration for Schiller's birthday and we watched the parade from the window at the home of friends. Naturally, my practicing suffered. Wenzel noticed it at once. When he commented on this fact, I replied playfully, "I practiced for two hours and looked out of the window for two hours, that makes four." Instead of laughing he became furious and I took care not to be so impertinent in the future.

He really had an uncontrolled temper. An English lady, also his student, once got him so upset that he threw the burning lamp into the grand piano. Terrified, she shouted, "But Mr. Wenzel, if you are so violent, I cannot play." Whereupon he answered, "I, violent? I am like a lamb."

At Christmas I returned to Hamburg where my sister Therese was now living quite close to our house. To her I fled when I could not stand the presence of my father's housekeeper. She was my favorite sister and did everything in her power to replace the loss of my dearly beloved mother.

Soon I traveled again to Bergen to be with my sister, Doris Dahl, who had just had her second child. One evening we were talking about the great fire in Hamburg in 1842. I did not remember it, but my sister told me much about it. That same night I was suddenly awakened and saw the whole room lit up in a red glow; at the same moment the old Norwegian nurse stormed into my room; "Quick, get up, the house is burning!" As fast as I could, I threw on some clothes and tumbled down the wooden stairs to the vestibule where my sister, her husband and the children were waiting for me, ready to flee. We ran across the market-square to my elder sister, Selma Dahl, whose house, built on piles, lay across from us. From here we watched how the fire reached one room after the other. Friends were kind enough to save for me a picture of Jenny Lind whose singing had made a deep impression on me.

In that night 173 houses burnt to the ground, all made of wood. The fire had started in the house next to ours, and, as we heard later, was arson.

We moved to a country house situated in the mountains with a magnificent view. Here I became acquainted with the writings of

Fredrika Bremer. I read *Neighbors*, *Strife and Peace*, and *Diary*. I was so inspired by these books that one day I wrote to her in neighboring Sweden, and poured out my heart. I received a charming response from her expressing her joy at my youthful exuberance, closing with the words, "Such children are my children, and such a child still lives in my breast, although more than sixty years have pressed their heavy hand on it." I wished I could have met her, but she traveled to America soon afterwards. Later, in Dresden, I became acquainted with an American lady, Mary Howitt, who translated Fredrika Bremer's works into English for America. Recently, Selma Lagerlöf celebrated this remarkable woman in her story *Fredrika*. I placed my letter from her in my just established "art collection."

In late summer I was drawn home once again. Originally I had planned to travel on the ship "Norge," but I decided to stay one more week. On this voyage the Norge sank near Christiansand; several men and only one woman were saved. Thus I escaped death by water twice and death by fire once. For what purpose? Probably because, along with some hardships, life had many wonderful things in store for me.

The figures we meet in our lives are strung together like the links of a chain made from different metals, be it gold, silver, platinum, iron, or tin.

Back in Hamburg, I found my father deep in the intellectual pursuits which alone could sustain him in the grief over my mother's death. Therefore, I did not see much of him. But one evening, busy in the garden with his beloved flowers, he spoke to me of his interest and his joy in my love of music, and he thought I should continue my lessons with Wenzel in Leipzig.

So I travelled again to my sister, Klara Hoffmann, and stayed past Christmas. Leipzig offered an extraordinary variety of interesting things. My brother-in-law, as member of the Church Council, had much contact with the university professors. Coffee houses (where the unmarried unfortunately always had to sit in a separate room), social evenings, and balls followed one another. On one such evening Gustav Freytag appeared. I was overjoyed to have him as my neighbor at the table. I expressed, perhaps in somewhat childish fashion, my delight over *Soll und Haben* which had excited me recently; he answered, "Ein Buch ist nur der Abklatsch der Empfindungen." (A book is only the poor imitation of experience.) This sobered me up a little, but later I understood the meaning of his words.

I enjoyed Wenzel's teaching as much as before. I also got to know Moscheles and his family. He, whose beautiful etudes are still being played, did not mind playing dance music for us. Once he made a real production for us. He said we were travelers, sightseeing in Monte Carlo. In the concert hall a Beethoven quartet was being performed. Now we heard an Andante, exquisitely played by Moscheles. Gradually these sounds became mingled with weaker notes which, he said, were coming across from a distant ballroom. According to his instructions we walked forward; the dance music became louder, the classical music softer until we heard a waltz upon our arrival in the ballroom. This was indeed a feat.

I also became acquainted with David, the concertmaster of the Gewandhaus Orchestra. The whole orchestra consisted of artists, conducted by Maestro Rietz, but to see David among them and to watch him move his bow with such enthusiasm was a pleasure all its own. I became a member of the chorus (Gesangverein) after passing the audition. I enjoyed even the audition because Rietz had so much wit and understanding.

The time in Leipzig passed quickly. It was a typical adolescent period, full of joy and hope. In deep gratitude I remember today all those, long gone, who helped to provide this beautiful time for me and who experienced it with me.

Now I was ready to go home where I no longer minded the appearance of the housekeeper. I had learned to appreciate her good qualities. My beloved sister Therese did everything to accommodate my youthful expectations. She arranged receptions for young people in her home and played indefatigably for our dancing. I spent many enjoyable hours in her home. My father, too, neglected nothing in his power to create a beautiful home for me, the motherless child. Many scholars and clergymen from out of town came to our house, and I could not hear enough of the interesting discussions around the table. I did not like it at all when domestic duties required my attention and I had to leave the guests.

A famous preacher from Breslau, who had been called to the Nikolai Church, once told me, "I have noticed that one can tease you," and he delighted in doing so in full measure. The expression "taking offense" is not in my dictionary. I have always tried not to dwell on insults. "Forget it," is my motto. With it I fared very well in this world, won many friends throughout my life, and, what is more important, have kept them.

Johannes Ronge, the founder of the German-Catholic Congregation, was one of the people visiting us. Although my father did not agree with Ronge, he welcomed him kindly. Ronge put his hand on my head and blessed me, which was not particularly comfortable for me at that time, but for which I am now grateful. The Ronge's family situation provided the subject for lively conversation. The wife of a wholesale manufacturer obtained a divorce because of him and went with him to England. However, she visited her first husband often in Hamburg and remained on good terms with him. Her sister later married the well known Carl Schurz who rescued the poet Gottfried Kinkel from prison.

It was an idyllic life that I led. My dear father put no restrictions on me. I supervised the household only to the extent that I decided what we would eat and went over the expenses with the cook. It was particularly pleasant that I only had to associate with people whom I found congenial. Only good friends visited our house. Sunday evenings were set aside for relaxing family get-togethers. My sister Therese would come with her husband, and after supper we played whist. My father and my brother-in-law had done so much talking in their ministry that a harmless card game was real relaxation for them.

I decided to form a club with three girlfriends, one of whom, Agnes Rindelaub, later became the wife of my brother Paul. My love for the theatre had been awakened by my mother's tales of her time in Vienna, and I transferred this now to my companions. We memorized the roles for different plays and performed them for our entertainment. The best location for this undertaking was the home of Oberbürgermeister (Lord Mayor) and police commissioner Binder whose daughter was a member. I had two friends, Franziska and Camilla Meier, who did not belong to this club. Their parents, Senator and Mrs. Meier, were celebrating their silver wedding anniversary that year, and this occasion gave us the bold idea to perform *Der Freischütz*. Naturally, we only had a piano for the orchestral music and accompaniment, but it was played by a competent pianist. I sang Agathe, all the other roles were sung by friends of ours. Although simply done without any scenery, it was a successful evening and a great pleasure for the anniversary celebrants.

In the spring we heard from Bergen that my brother-in-law who had just recovered from typhus, needed a rest in the country, and my sister asked me to help with his care.

On the trip to Bergen I had very pleasant company. It so happened that I was the only lady, and the Captain as well as the other gentlemen did everything to make my journey pleasant. Until we reached Christiansand I hid in my cabin and paid Neptune his tribute. From then on the voyage was wonderful except for a short stretch, called "Jedderen," where every passenger became seasick. In later times, a railroad was installed so that the travellers could avoid the unpleasant stretch and get back on the ship at Stavanger. I took all my meals on deck, and the men danced Norwegian folk dances and sang Norwegian songs for me. The scenery of the Norwegian fjords is unforgettable. Once in a while we would pass an isolated farm. When we passed one such settlement, we noticed two old people waving with big sheets. We knew they were greeting one of our passengers, a man with a dark tan, who was also waving and who called with breaking voice, "My beloved Norge." He had been away for thirty years and was now returning to the home of his childhood. The ship slowed down, a small boat came, and trembling with emotion he climbed in. We continued our trip, but the moving scene of the man, overcome with emotion, running into the arms of his old parents, amidst the magnificent surroundings, stayed with me to this day.

Soon we approached Bergen where my two sisters were waiting for me at the pier. They were married to two brothers. The older one, Selma, had seven children. The younger one, Doris, to whom I was going, had three.

Now began a quiet, pleasant time, wholly dedicated to the care of my brother-in-law. Initially he was so weak that he could only take a few steps, and only if he was leaning on one of us. But he recovered quickly, and in August I could leave my sister, my mind at ease.

I found my father more absorbed in his work than ever. He was getting ready to publish a new edition of his book, *Für Jünglinge and Jungfrauen*, (For young men and women), which

12

made great demands on his time. Nevertheless, our Sunday evenings remained reserved as before for our small family gatherings.

My father, earlier in his life an ardent visitor of the theatre, no longer paid homage in this temple of the arts, but my sister and her husband went frequently to the Thalia Theater which even then, under Maurice, had become an excellent training ground for actors. It happened often that the Burgtheater in Vienna called its actors from here, as was the case with Dawison. Fine comedies starring the ingenue, were performed. Strangely, this type of performance has almost disappeared today, and the actors of these roles have moved to different fields. The humor of those days has also taken a different turn. Real geniuses in that field were Nestroy, Gern, Helmerding, Engel, Gustav Räder, etc., who only had to walk on stage to have the audience break out in uproarious laughter. I saw Engel as "Wirt" in Lessing's *Minna von Barnhelm* —a delightful accomplishment. Then there were such charming, innocent plays as, for instance, *Ein Stündchen in der Schule* (An Hour At School), in which the comedian Wilde, a splendid actor, appearing casually in a dressing gown and holding a long pipe, had the audience alternately crying and laughing. I cannot forget him in his song:

> *Die Menschen sind Scholaren,*
> *das Schicksal klopft sie fürchterlich,*
> *und selbst die brav und fleissig waren*
> *erhalten oft den schlimmsten Strich.*

> *Women and men are pupils*
> *beaten by fate without end,*
> *even those who behave and study*
> *oft reap the worst punishment.*

The so-called "Posse" (farce) was simple and sometimes touching. The plays of Ferdinand Raimund were very successful. His *Verschwender* (Spendthrift) and *Alpenkönig und Menschenfeind* (King of the Alps and Misanthrope) are still being staged.

Offenbach led in a new direction: the operetta. So far, one had enjoyed the minor comedies with music, such as *Luzifers Töchter* (Lucifer's Daughters), *Einen Jux will er sich machen* (He Wants

13

to Have Some Fun), or *Die Wiener in Berlin*, charming musicals of which the latter two have enjoyed recent revivals. At that point only Offenbach's harmless *Le mariage aux lanternes* had appeared. But now followed *La Belle Helene*, *La Vie Parisienne*, and many others which presented vice as quite alluring. The public was so delighted with these piquant novelties that the earlier, harmless musicals were squeezed out.

A new star arose on the horizon of the Thalia theater with the eighteen-year-old ingenue, Friederike Gossmann. She won the hearts of the audiences. As Gretchen Western in the comedy *Erziehungsresultate* (The Results of Education), she was so convincing in the role of the simple girl brought up in the country, that we went home totally enraptured. The oftener we saw her, the greater became our desire to get to know her personally. We achieved our goal faster than expected. On my sister's birthday Miss Friederike Gossmann was suddenly announced.

Two of my sister's friends had arranged this surprise. The two Misses von Melle had written to the artist of my sister's admiration for her, and asked her if she would appear at her house as "birthday present." This wonderful surprise was a gift for me too, for "Tiffi," as we called her, and I became close friends, and this friendship was the source of much joy for us all. My brother-in-law , who knew Goethe's writings well and was a great admirer of the poet, followed the development of the theater with lively interest. He expressed the farsighted and, for a clergyman, uncommon opinion that a pastor should make every effort to open his home to artists as a refuge. "When this is not done, such gifted people will look for relaxation elsewhere and may easily go astray," he said. "And what a pleasure it is for us clergymen, to be able to further such talent." Friederike Gossmann later made reference to these words. Under a picture of herself as "Grille" which she presented to him she wrote; "I needed the advice and help of a God-fearing person, and I think when I came to you, Pastor Ritter, I was in the right place." How true that was. In word and deed my sister and her husband stood by her and remained true to her beyond her death. Friederike Gossmann was sometimes accused of playing herself. But that was the beauty in this unaffected being, a fresh spring welled up inside her and enlivened everything. Her deep sensitivity was demonstrated in her performance of Birch-Pfeiffer's

Grille, which she, so to speak, created. It seems strange to me that there is no place for her kind of talent in today's comedies.

The following year she was called to the Burgtheater in Vienna where she excited the greatest enthusiasm. She sent me the first flowers she received, and continued in similar ways to remain a true friend. She became the darling of the Viennese public, but after a short time she married Count Anton Prokesch-Osten, son of the Austrian Ambassador in Constantinople. I had the pleasure of seeing her again in Duesternbrook near Kiel where her first child was born. Later on they moved to Gmunden and lived in a charming villa. We saw each other often and I could enjoy the blossoming of her family.

After a trip to Leipzig with my father during the summer, I gave myself totally to my music the following winter. Then, as now, concerts played an important part in the cultural life of Hamburg. And so I heard Jenny Lind. She sang, "O könnt ich fliegen mit Tauben dahin" from the *Lobgesang* by Mendelssohn with such incredible feeling that she brought tears to our eyes. The lovely song by Taubert, "Vöglein, was singst du im Lande so laut," with all the trills of the nightingale, the lark, etc. received rapturous applause. My adoration of this great artist remained undiminished throughout her life.

I also started to attend the symphony concerts with my two close friends, Franziska and Camilla Meier. Since we young girls understandably desired to catch a glimpse behind the scenes we stole into a rehearsal one day. It happened that the great violinist, Joachim, was there not only as soloist but also as conductor. He was rehearsing the First Serenade by Brahms, who was still very young at that time. I had as yet no idea how deeply he would touch my life. Joachim excited us, and the words he used to inspire the orchestra, "Rüstig vorwärts" (boldly forward) became our motto for our life and our seal. Our enthusiasm for the young composer, however, knew no bounds, and we were determined to do what we could to help pave his way. All three of us felt like his Maecenices.

Brahms' Serenade had not yet been printed, and we wanted to accomplish its publication. We went, each alone, to the large music dealers and music publishers with the question whether the Serenade had been printed and was for sale. Of course, everywhere we got the same negative reply. Then, one day I received a letter in large handwriting, signed, Johannes Brahms. It said, he had tried to interest the music publishers in his Serenade, but these "mercenary souls" refused. So he is turning to young ladies, "flower souls." His suggestion was to publish the Serenade by selling shares at 100 Mark per share, and he was counting on our kind support. —Excited and delighted I rushed to my sister who was having coffee with her husband. "You will buy one right away, won't you?" I shouted. My sister, almost choking with repressed laughter, answered, "What is today's date?" It struck me like lightning, "The first of April!" Furious, I threw the letter into the stove; my sister, equally fast, pulled it back out with the fire tongs. My splendid brother-in-law, great preacher, helper of the poor, father of his congregation, intelligent, and endowed with a great sense of humor, had allowed himself this April Fools' Day trick on me. Once again, I was the object of a prank. My gullibility made me an easy prey for such jokes.

Not long afterwards the Serenade appeared in print. Whether we three friends had any hand in it I cannot say. In any case, I was now playing it daily four-handed with one of the other admirers. We called ourselves "Brahmans," read about their customs in the encyclopedia and imitated them in our enthusiasm, even though they had really nothing to do with Johannes Brahms.

My most ardent wish now was to take piano lessons from Brahms. But an hour's lessons was then very expensive, five marks. The uncle of my brother-in-law came to my aid. He offered to pay for my piano lessons with Brahms which would take place twice a week in his house. That was a great and wonderful gift for me. Brahms was short, blond, and had big, expressive blue eyes. He was usually very quiet. During the lessons he was clear and precise in what he wanted and expected. Basically, I was quite afraid of him, and when I saw him from the window, coming along, the ribbon on his little hat blowing in the breeze, I began to tremble in anticipation. I had to summon all my strength when I was playing. The last movement of a Beethoven sonata was particularly difficult for me and I never played it fast enough for him, so that he urged me on, "Fix, immer fix!" (Quick, ever quick!) This induced me later to present him as a farewell gift a gold pen in a silver penholder with the engraving, "Fix, immer fix!" To that he responded, "Yes, now I shall always compose quickly."

Johannes Brahms at the time of the Hamburg Women's Chorus

Brahms' Monument, Resselpark, Vienna, with the "little spirit"

I also took harmony lessons from him which required much concentration. In his corrections of my work he could be quite sarcastic and I feared his remarks a little. Once in a while he would become talkative. On such an occasion he told me how he played four-handed with Robert Schumann when Schumann was already mentally ill. "He noticed every mistake," Brahms said. "He was friendly, but woe me, if I hit a wrong note." I learned more about Schumann through Miss Annette Preusser with whom I had become acquainted in Leipzig. The Schumanns once stayed in her house as guests. She told me that the beginning of Schumann's insanity manifested itself in that he constantly heard a single note, and only found peace when one of his daughters played the piano. Clara Schumann had asked Miss Preusser not to send a knife with his breakfast in the morning since she had noticed disturbing symptoms in her husband.

One day Brahms had to go from my lesson straight to the rehearsal for a symphony concert where he was to play his D-minor piano concerto. "It is extremely difficult," he said, "I have had to practice terribly." "Well, that is really strange," I replied, "Then you cannot compose as you want. It is as if a little spirit blows it into you?" "Yes," he laughed, "and sometimes even a great spirit. But with me it was probably a little one." Naturally, I was awfully embarrassed.

Brahms was well versed in literature and art and had expressed an interest in paintings. Therefore, the aunt of my brother-in-law, a lovely, delicate woman, thought I should take him to her drawing-room and show him the portrait of a relative, painted by a well-known artist. No sooner said than done. We went in and stood in front of the picture. The aunt explained it to him; he stood silently in front of it and did not say a word. We remained there for quite a long time until I, rather disconcerted, finally suggested, "Hadn't we better go?" Whereupon we returned quietly to the music room and sat down at the piano without a word.

At the same time, August 1859, a small women's chorus was founded in Hamburg with Brahms as director, and I was invited to participate. This choral singing became a source of great joy for all participants. We gathered once a week in the evening alternately at the participants' homes. Brahms composed new pieces or arranged old folksongs for us in three parts; since there were twelve members, each voice had four singers.

I remember one particularly beautiful evening in the spring. We sang, as always, a capella, standing in the moonlight under an apple tree in bloom, Brahms in the middle, conducting:

> *Der Holdseligen, sonder Wank,*
> *sing' ich fröhlichen Minnesang;*
> *denn die Reine,*
> *die ich meine,*
> *winkt mir minniglich: Habe Dank.*

> *To the lovely one, boldly*
> *I sing joyful love songs.*
> *Since the pure maid*
> *whom I address*
> *beckons lovingly: Take my thanks!*

One evening, Joachim joined us after he had given a thrilling performance of the Beethoven violin concerto. He and Brahms were close friends and he did much for Brahms. He was exceptionally knowledgeable in literature and a supporter of the Romantic school. He talked with me at length about Achim von Arnim, Brentano, and others. I was told later that he was in love with Bettina von Arnim's daughter, Gisela; however, she married the art historian Hermann Grimm in Berlin, and Joachim married Amalie Schneeweiss. She entranced her audiences with her beautiful alto voice.

After our musical evenings with Brahms we often walked home singing, dropping off the members one by one. Brahms was composing his "Marienlieder" at this time, and we sang them in the Petri church. Each of us was given a medallion with the inscription "Hamburger Frauenchor," which we considered sacred. Nevertheless, I lost mine after many years, along with the watch to which it was attached, and I never found either one again.

The famous singer, Julius Stockhausen, became conductor of the Grundsche Singakademie of which I was already a member. We performed Haydn's *Jahreszeiten*, (The Seasons). It was a treat to sing under Stockhausen's direction, and I was all fired up for the performance. At the dress rehearsal in the section "Herbst" (Fall) when we were singing, "Nun lasst uns fröhlich sein," I miscounted one measure and shouted "Juchhee!" in full voice into the audience. Terribly ashamed I went to Stockhausen and begged him to forgive me. He, however, laughed and said; "I wish I had more such enthusiastic singers in my chorus."

Later on we performed *Paradies und Peri* by Robert Schumann, and I was supposed to sing the part of the "Jungfrau." As much as I like to sing and love to accompany myself on the piano, it is impossible for me to sing in an auditorium where everyone is staring at me. I explained this to Maestro Grund who was conducting the work. His objection, a favorite then as now, "My dear, just think they are all heads of cabbage!" was in vain. I remained firm. I have never been able to take it when everyone is staring at me.

In the summer of 1859 my father and I made our last trip together to Copenhagen where my brother, Paul Ferdinand Schmaltz, held the position of pastor at the German St. Petri church. He was married to my best friend from our club in Hamburg, Agnes Rindelaub. The time with these two people, who were so dear and close to us, was joyful and harmonious. I stayed with my father in the charming Klampenborg. The magnificent blue sound and the island Hven lay in front of us. Here Tycho Brahe had once made his studies of astronomy. Behind us, for miles and miles, stretched the zoo whose beauty I enjoyed thoroughly. At Klampenborg I became acquainted with the great Danish character actor, Phister. Every day we walked together in the woods. His stories made these walks highly interesting. His first wife was the daughter of the famous Danish poet Oehlenschläger, and his daughter from this marriage and I became good companions. His second marriage also seemed to be very happy. A lovely poem, which he dedicated to me, was unfortunately among the many valuable documents and priceless souvenirs which were in a trunk that got lost in Russia.

One day Phister insisted on bringing me to the stage of the empty Hoftheater. I was to recite something. He claimed I was made for his art, but again I was gripped by that unexplainable panic. "No, I can't!" I called, "I shall never have the courage to appear in public, so we better forget it." We left the theater without having accomplished his mission, but we remained friends, and I like to think of those days.

My conscientious father never took more than four weeks vacation, and so we returned to Hamburg where he was literally overburdened with work. He began to think seriously of retiring from his position. However, there were always new duties which induced him to stay a little longer. I continued my piano lessons with Brahms with great joy. Once he came to us with some of his songs which I sang for him. My sister resumed the evening receptions at her home, and often we danced there. In the middle of all this gay social life came the Christmas celebration which, as always, took place in our home. Of this particular Christmas I have incredibly beautiful memories because it was the last one with my father. The piles of official business, the Sunday sermons which were still being printed, began to affect my father's health. He still spoke with fiery eloquence from the pulpit, was still available for all who sought advice or help, and he still gathered the young divinity students around him to further them in their careers. But his beautiful black eyes had lost their sparkle. He was often tired and spoke then with me about my mother whom he had loved so tenderly. These were lovely hours for me, but they were also those when worry filled my heart. The change in his condition was noticeable. A second physician I consulted urged him to retire. But before he could do so, he became so weak that he had to stay in bed. We were still hopeful, but after five days, on February 15, 1860, he passed on.

My sister in Hamburg and her husband, who were both so very close to me, immediately took me into their house which now became my home. The first weeks passed very quietly; I dropped all my activities except my lessons and singing with Brahms. Those were the bright stars in these dark days. Although my sister's home offered me everything a comfortable home should be, I began to think seriously about my future. I definitely did not want to accept their generosity on a continuing basis. It was decided to have a family conference in which my brother from Copenhagen, my brother-in-law from Leipzig, and even one brother-in-law from Norway participated. These four well-meaning brothers declared it would be best if I spent three months a year with each of them. The Church Council member from Leipzig said it would be very pleasant, but he wished I would curtail my love for music and arts somewhat. The brother from Copenhagen assured me that the children would be delighted to have an aunt. The Norwegian and the Hamburger were also looking forward to my stay, and everyone was very disappointed when I declared; "I thank you all sincerely, but I do not accept your kind offers. I want to see the world."

There followed a rather hard fight with each one of the participants. Finally my brother-in-law Ritter agreed with me; however, he and my sister insisted; "Our house will remain your home for ever. Your room will be yours, you need never announce your coming in advance."

I now began to look for employment. I wrote to a lady in London who ran a boarding-school for young girls. She answered that she did not have an opening at the moment, but if I wanted to accept a position as teacher, then her friend, Miss Johnson, would engage me at once for German and Music in her boarding school. I, who had never taken an exam, got scared at the thought of working as a teacher, but my brother and sister assured me that I could do anything I wanted to do. So I accepted. Miss Johnson wrote that I would get a vacation every three months, which pleased the Ritters very much and me even more. Parting from Brahms was very hard for me, and only the prospect of continuing my lessons during the summer vacation consoled me.

INTO THE WORLD

Early in May in the year 1860, I took a ship directly from Hamburg to London. Upon my arrival I took a cab and within half an hour I arrived at a beautiful villa with a garden surrounded by a high wall.

Miss Johnson herself received me. She was still beautiful with brown eyes, sparkling white teeth, lightly graying hair, and an imposing figure. Right away she acquainted me with my duties which were totally different from the customs in our schools. There was no German class; instead I had sessions with only two students at a time, and I was to teach only German reading, translating, and speaking. I had to arrange the sessions and match the students which was quite difficult since each set of students had to have three lessons a week, and there were approximately twenty girls in age from fifteen to twenty years. It was the same with the piano lessons, except that here I had one student at a time. It was a severe test of my patience, sometimes enough to drive me mad, but I always managed to keep my composure and continue the lesson. At eight o'clock we had breakfast. Then the "classes" began, if you can call them that, and lasted until eleven o'clock, followed by a long walk which took an hour and a half. At twelve thirty we changed for dinner, which was set for one o'clock. After dinner came free time in the garden or in one's room. I used this time to take English lessons from one of the students who was almost the same age as I.

From four to six o'clock we again had lessons scheduled. Then it was tea time, with innumerable sandwiches, followed by homework. When that was finished there was more free time until the simple supper. At nine o'clock the students went to bed. I myself ate supper at nine thirty with Miss Johnson and her friend who was also teaching. It consisted of bread and butter, cheese, and lettuce which was eaten dipped in salt and tasted delicious. The meals were very healthy and I was never sick there.

On Sundays the young girls always wore silk. We went to church twice and were otherwise free, but letter writing was out, and only "Sunday books" were allowed to be read. I often took my writing materials to the attic and up there I wrote my letters to relatives and friends. The young girls were charming, friendly, and polite.

When Miss Johnson was teaching, I stayed in the room and wrote, but I also listened. She had a peculiar method. Every student had, among other things, a book called "Generalities" which consisted of individual questions which the students had to answer in written form with the help of the encyclopedia. Miss Johnson would follow the book and give each student a good mark for a correct answer. The funny thing about it was the mixture of questions; for instance: 1. "How is cheese made?" 2. "When did Elizabeth live and how long did she reign?" 3. "Which flower blooms in February?" This method, obviously, was a bit superficial, but it was amusing, and the girls had a lot of trouble in looking up the answers.

History was taught in a different style. The girls had to read several pages a day in the text book and then relate the contents.

Approximately four weeks had passed peacefully in this way when Miss Johnson announced one Sunday; "Next Tuesday is an exam which will be administered by Dr. Kinkel."

I was frozen with fright, for I had not been able to make much progress in those few weeks, and prior to my coming, the German lessons had been completely neglected. The dreaded day arrived. The girls sat at a long table and at the head were two chairs for the examiner and me. The door opened and in came a tall, manly figure. It was Gottfried Kinkel, the poet, the author of *Otto der Schütz,* he who was banished and could not yet return to Germany. I was trembling with fear, which, unfortunately, was only too justified. He began by analyzing sentences: transitive, intransitive verbs, imperative sentences, etc. The girls had no idea and Kinkel announced this quite openly and expressed the hope that it would go better next year.

He took his leave, and Miss Johnson, somewhat disturbed, followed him and urged me to stay upstairs. But nothing could be farther from my mind. I ran down the stairs and told Kinkel what the situation had been at my arrival, and that I had only been there a few weeks, and that I was not even asked to teach grammar. I was beside myself.

Kinkel's beautiful, stern face became friendly, and smiling he said to Miss Johnson; "This excited young lady has explained everything. She is in no way to be reprimanded."

Quite composed, I bade him farewell, and he asked me to visit him. Now my ambition was aroused, and instead of leaving at the end of July, as I had intended, I accepted Miss Johnson's offer to stay for another whole year, for I wanted to erase this disaster from the memory of all participants.

I began to seriously use an English-German grammar, studying mornings and evenings in bed until the summer holidays, which I spent as always with my sister in Hamburg.

During those six weeks I continued my lessons with Brahms. We had become close friends, and at the end he took no payment, but said, "These were conversations between friends." That was when I gave him the already mentioned silver penholder with the engraving "Fix, immer fix." Shortly afterwards he left Hamburg and chose Vienna for his residence. Before we parted he composed a song for me and presented the beautiful, handwritten manuscript to me. Unfortunately, it too was in the trunk which was lost in Russia, but Brahms included it later in a collection of his songs.

Mein Schatz ist nicht da,
ist weit überm See,
und so oft ich dran denk',
tut mir's Herze so weh.

Schön blau ist der See,
und mein Herz tut mir weh,
und mein Herz wird nicht g'sund
bis mein Schatz wiederkummt.

My love is not here,
Is far across the sea,
And when I think of that,
My heart is in pain.

Oh, blue is the sea,
But my heart is in pain,
And my heart won't get well,
Till my love shall return.

છ

*"Mein Schatz is nicht da," originally written by Brahms for
Susanne Schmaltz. This version is from Franziska Meier's book. Ref. 11*

After my vacation I returned to Miss Johnson's school. I now had the great pleasure of being a frequent visitor in Gottfried Kinkel's house. His first wife, Johanna, had died, and his second wife idolized her husband. For this reason, the two daughters and the son from the first marriage were often left to themselves. I became the fourth partner in this club, and spent lovely evenings with my friends. Sadly, the oldest, Johanna, died of scarlet fever. Since the son, Gottfried, was busy studying for his exams, Adele and I were left to each other and formed a close friendship which lasted all our lives. Later, she married a Mr. von Asten, and the marriage was unfortunately very unhappy. But in those days there was nothing but cheerfulness in our get-togethers. In youthful exuberance, we played writing games which brought forth such hearty laughter that Kinkel came down to see what was going on. That was a special joy for us. In spite of his white hair, his heart had remained young, and he would join in our game for a short time, while his beautiful dark eyes took on a strange gleam. Occasionally his deep-seated longing for his country was clearly revealed. I remember a time when his daughter was playing "Arabia, my homeland" from *Oberon*. Tears welled up in his eyes, and he said, "My Germany, my fatherland."

In Germany I had been given a letter of introduction to Mrs. Sterndale Bennett. Her husband had studied with Mendelssohn and was conductor of the big, public concerts in London. Later he was knighted, Sir William Sterndale Bennett. His wife was one of those rare persons of a delicate, sensitive, good-hearted, and even-tempered nature. As a result of a fire in her home she was not well herself, but was always ready to help where there was a need.

She always welcomed me warmly and stood ready to assist me. Often, she gave me tickets to the wonderful concerts which her husband was conducting. An unforgettable pleasure was an invitation to a reading by Charles Dickens. When he changed his voice to represent the different characters he had created and distorted his face to present the schoolmaster Squeers, there was no end to the laughter. He has been gone for a long time, and in recent years his works have not been read as much as they deserve. He did his country an inestimable service by exposing great social ills. Among other things he achieved better care for the sick. The change was initiated by the amusing and simultaneously distressing description of the attendant (nurses were unknown at that time) in *David Copperfield,* who tortures the sick people in her care. The reader enjoys the description because it is seasoned with wonderful humor. The attendant keeps quoting the words of her nonexistent friend, Mrs."Arris" (Harris) to reinforce her own words.

After thirteen weeks of serious work I travelled home to Hamburg for Christmas. The children's holiday joy cheered us up, while we were still missing our father very much. My vacations lasted four weeks, and I returned to the boarding school for the continuation of my work at the end of January.

My favorite relaxation was the association with Kinkel. At one time the poet told us how his friend, Carl Schurz, dressed as an organ grinder, had saved him from prison. His homesickness grew from day to day until he moved to Switzerland where he was at least among German-speaking people.

I made the acquaintance of another refugee, by the name of Zerffy. It was rather interesting to get to know the lives and dealings of these German exiles, who managed to entertain guests in spite of their artistic slovenliness and their lack of money. Of course, one could not have any expectations, and sometimes one had to close both eyes, yet, I have to be grateful for their hospitality, even if I preferred visiting Kinkel's house which was filled with poetry and intelligence.

The work in preparation for the exam now demanded all my energy. I did not want to leave Miss Johnson without preparing the students for an honorable exam. Finally the day had arrived. As the year before, the girls sat at a long table, on the side on a little elevation, Miss Johnson, and at the end the two chairs for the examiner and me. Just as in the previous year, Kinkel entered and took his place at the upper end of the table. As before, my heart was beating fast, but soon I calmed down. The girls wanted to prove their ability and the answers came like clockwork. They really answered every question correctly and enthusiastically. At the end of the exam Kinkel expressed his great satisfaction, saying, in his experience there had rarely been such a good exam. If our friendship had some influence on his judgment I cannot say.

Now it was time to go home for a while. After a warm, affectionate parting, I boarded an English ship for Copenhagen to visit my brother's family. The voyage was horrible. Kattegat and

Skagerrak deserve their bad reputation. Seasickness and fear of drowning took hold of me, and left me only when the ship entered the sound. My brother Paul and his wife, Agnes, gave me a warm welcome. We spent a beautiful autumn together. I remember with special fondness the hours at dusk, when we sat down in three comfortable rocking chairs in the big dining room and exchanged memories. Occasionally we took lovely excursions, for instance to the castle Fredensborg where the Tsar of Russia visited his Danish relatives every year in order to enjoy a trouble-free life for a short time. I became a member of the "Singakademie" of Copenhagen which was directed by Niels Gade. The audition with him was most amusing. He spoke fluent German with a Danish accent, and had a wonderful sense of humor. The musical evenings under his direction were extremely stimulating. We were practicing the choruses with solo voices from Mendelssohn's opera fragment, *Loreley*, and were singing it in Danish, which improved my knowledge of that language. I had learned Norwegian quite well during my stays in Bergen, and since Danish has the same written language but different pronunciation, the conversation went very well. Gade himself accompanied the rehearsals on the piano, frequently reaching into the ever present bag of candy sitting on top, the gift of a lady admirer.

After the performance, which was a great success, Gade invited me to his villa, which was in a beautiful spot, right on the sound. Here he allowed his delicious sense of humor to run free. At the coffee table he suddenly asked me in his best German; "Fräulein Schmaltz, was sagen Sie ssu meine Couleur?" (Miss Schmaltz, what do you say about my "couleur?"), because he had a very ruddy complexion. What was I supposed to say except, "I think it is very beautiful." This aroused great merriment.

ৎ৲

After the delightful stay in Copenhagen, I returned to my home in Hamburg. I was ready to return to England because I had become fond of the country and its people, and I would have liked to work for a family. Before taking any further steps, however, I interrupted my stay and travelled for a week to my sister in Leipzig. There I met a lady who was governess in the house of the Duchess of Somerset and was vacationing in Leipzig. She expressed such satisfaction with her profession and her situation that I proclaimed, "I want to go to a Duchess in England too!" Everyone laughed and said, that is not so easy.

Back in Hamburg, I seriously discussed my further steps with the Ritters. Fluent in English, I desired to achieve the same competence in French. To this end I wrote to the director of a boarding school, Madame Rey, who had been recommended to me, and requested admission. She accepted me as a so-called "private pupil." I financed the stay with her and also my further sojourn in Paris with the inheritance from my father, which naturally then shrunk considerably.

In October, 1861, my cab stopped in front of a huge house in Paris on the Rue de Batailles, where Madame Rey and all her students, five hundred in number — all French girls — lived. We private pupils came from Germany, England, America, etc. The French girls slept in large halls; we foreigners had each our own, if quite small, room. We also had our separate dining room, and, as I must mention, excellent food. Here Madame St. Hilaire ruled, a slim blonde, who sometimes insulted us by addressing us as "jeune personne." In spite of all the privileges which we private pupils enjoyed, we were still treated as children. At nine in the morning the very robust, stately Madame Rey appeared and seated herself on her "throne." Then we had to pass her, single file, and place a kiss on her rather fat cheek. With me this procedure consisted of a whiff, whereupon Madame always said, "Qu'elle est difficile a menager cette jeune demoiselle!" (How difficult it is to deal with this young lady.) This remark was primarily a reference to my refusal to wear wool sweaters, as she requested.

Then began the lessons, which I attended with only a few of the foreigners. Even though the instructions were sometimes boring, I learned a lot from them. Walks and lessons alternated; after supper we were completely free. Then two or three English ladies came to my room, and we often performed hilarious comedies. The "audience" sat on my bed, and loud laughter could be heard from my room.

To continue my musical studies I took piano lessons from Stephen Heller. He became famous through his compositions, especially his "Tarantella" and his etudes, which are still a valuable tool in piano lessons. At that time, everyone was playing the "Tarantella," now it is out of fashion. I remember one day when he was suffering from a terrible toothache and had a big scarf wrapped around his head with the ends sticking up like rabbit ears. He looked so funny that I could hardly control myself. Nevertheless, I suppressed my urge to laugh and we began our four-handed playing and brought it to a conclusion without incident. The fee for the lesson was one Louis d'or and had to be paid each time. This caused me such embarrassment, that I usually hid the gold piece somewhere. I heard later that he often spent a long time to find it.

I had the audacity to introduce myself to Madame Viardot-Garcia to obtain voice lessons. She received me very kindly but told me at once that she only trained artists for the stage and concerts, and then added in good German; "Nun singen Sie mir mal etwas." (Now sing something for me.) I sat down at the grand piano and sang one German folk song after the other. She leaned against the instrument, listened amused and always said; "Now one more." After half a dozen of such songs, she suggested her student, Madame Orville, who was staying with her, as my teacher. Madame Viardot also invited me to her weekly Saturday evening musicales. I was beginning to achieve more freedom from Madame Rey, and she allowed me to go out on these evenings.

I now had to start practicing diligently. For this purpose, Madame Rey's establishment provided twenty-five pianos in little cells which opened onto a long corridor. The noise in the corridor was earshattering when all twenty-five pianos were in use.

The evenings at Madame Viardot-Garcia were extremely entertaining. At first we would sing several choruses as practice for a performance for the guests who would come later. When we were learning something new, I was often asked to sing it for the others because, according to Madame Viardot, "The Germans sing already in the cradle." The guests belonged to the social elite of Paris. Among them was the beautiful Princess Orloff, née Princess Troubetzkoy, who won my greatest admiration. Her fiancé had lost an eye in the Crimean war, which left him severely disfigured. He wanted to release her from her commitment, but she remained true to her love and married him. He would appear at Madame Viardot's with a black scarf covering a quarter of his face while his wife radiated beauty and at the same time simplicity. I still see her before me in a grey, closely fitted, high collar moiré dress, a single diamond the only jewelry. The lovely blond color of her hair and the penetrating eyes which expressed such goodness have remained unforgettable for me. Bismarck later became well acquainted with her and admired her very much. I also became acquainted with Miss Tochterow, the niece of Prince Troubetzkoy, and both of them would often take me along to visit the attractions of Paris.

The Russian writer Ivan Turgenev was living at Madame Viardot's. He had such a tremendous admiration for her that he hardly dared approach her and, for instance, did not even ask for fuel to heat his room.

In addition to the invitation to Madame Viardot-Garcia's soirées, I also received a request to attend the Thursday Evenings at Mr. and Mrs. Damcke's. Stephen Heller had introduced me to them. At Damcke's, many young people gathered and we spent joyful hours in their house. Here I heard Désirée Artot sing the "Habañera" from *Carmen* and a mazurka by Chopin. She was just beginning to appear publicly. After such artistic performances there would be dancing, which was welcomed by the young people.

Stephen Heller was being called to England by his friend, the popular pianist Charles Hallé, who was there conducting the concerts he made famous. Just at this moment, Clara Schumann was coming to Paris for six weeks, and she accepted me as her student. At the first lesson she frightened me terribly; confident though nervous, I played something by Mozart for her, when she grabbed me by the arm and exclaimed, "What are you doing?" She had a totally different method of teaching than Heller, but I made considerable progress under her guidance. I was always invited to her soirées, where I got to know her as the charming hostess. I became friends with her daughter Marie, and the two of us often shopped for the fruit juice which Mrs. Schumann served her guests. These soirées were highly stimulating. Madame Claus-Scavardy, the famous pianist, Julius Stockhausen, and others enlivened the parties. Sometimes Mrs. Schumann would give recitals. One time she played with another German pianist on two pianos the Variations by her husband. Another time she played the A Minor piano concerto by Schumann with orchestral accompaniment; she also played

Bach. These rare experiences were the high points of my stay in Paris.

Since I wanted to perfect my French conversation before leaving Paris in late spring, I left the boarding school of Madame Rey and took a room with a friendly, outgoing widow, Madame Roger. At last I had the freedom I desired and took advantage of it by going on excursions into the surrounding area with my English friend, Mary Rymer. During that period unmarried young ladies in France did not live alone in hotels or go sight-seeing by themselves. We knew how to get around that. We turned our rings around to make them look like wedding bands, and when others were listening, we would talk about our husbands. We visited the beautiful, historic Fontainebleau where the moss-covered carps of stone may have witnessed Napoleon's farewell speech which he delivered there. We strolled through the surrounding woods in all directions. Another time we went to St. Germain, which Louis XIV began to loathe because from here he could see the cathedral of St. Denis, the burial place of the French kings. We admired the old courtyard but were amazed not to meet a soul. We looked for the doorkeeper but found none. Then I discovered a partially open door leading to a winding staircase which we ascended quickly. On the first floor we found a long, bright hall with numerous high, wide doors. One of them had a bunch of keys hanging in the lock. We entered and came into a flight of high, old rooms which once must have been beautifully furnished but were now empty. The wallpaper was hanging down and everything was dusty. Above a side door were the words, "Appartements de Jacques II," where the wall coverings were also hanging in pieces. We were ready to inspect these rooms which Louis XIV had made available to the fugitive English King James II and had even provided him with a considerable sum of Louis d'ors in a basket on the table. At that moment a thundering voice roared from a distance. I turned around and flew down the stairs, taking two steps at once. My poor friend, however, could not run so fast, and was grabbed by the guard who showered her with terrible threats. As fast as possible we escaped to a nearby inn where we enjoyed a lovely view and fortified ourselves with a snack accompanied by Bordeaux wine. Here we found out that the castle, on orders of Louis Napoleon, was to be turned into a museum, and that we were lucky to have had the chance to glimpse the historic rooms in their original condition.

By chance, we witnessed the funeral of Halévy, the composer of *La Juive*, on Montmartre and saw Offenbach and Gounod at close range. In contrast to the other artists, the latter made a very cultured impression. A short time later, we saw the wife of Louis Napoleon, Empress Eugénie, driving slowly in an open carriage down the Champs Elysées. She was most beautiful. The famous court painter, Winterhalter, captured her features faithfully in a very lovely portrait.

Paris was smiling and delightful at that time. Exquisite flowers were displayed by the vendors in the streets. The meadows and woods in the outskirts were full of charming flora. But as big and beautiful as Paris and nature were, so small and insignificant became my wallet. It had to be filled.

For this purpose I planned to go back to England, but not without first seeing my family again. I stayed two weeks with my sister in Leipzig. A student ball happened to fall into this period, which gave me a chance to see many old friends and make some new acquaintances. Among the latter was a student from Kassel who, even though he stuttered, was so interesting in his conversation that he held my attention all evening. During the flower cotillion he presented me with a myrtle stem which pleased me so much that I took it with me on my trip. I spent another ten days at home with the Ritters in Hamburg, and then I traveled on a big steamship directly to London.

SECOND STAY IN ENGLAND

During my last three months in London I had made the acquaintance of three sisters. They were living alone with a housekeeper because they had lost their parents early, and they had invited me to come now for an extended visit. The trip was lovely, and as we were approaching Greenwich, church bells were ringing. I heard a gentleman's voice behind me saying; "This is a friendly greeting England is offering you." As I stepped out of the coach, my myrtle from Leipzig fell into a coal chute and I was very sad at this loss.

I hurried to my friends who welcomed me with open arms. Who can describe my surprise the next morning, when a gentleman asked to see me and I recognized in him the friendly interpreter of the pealing of the bells. He was holding my myrtle stem in his hand and had come to return it to me.

I spent three most enjoyable weeks. We four young ladies, without any supervision, thought it best to lead a discreet life, and therefore, we did not invite any further visits from the gentleman, who had taken such kind trouble to restore my loss. After a week of relaxation and pleasant companionship, I thought it my duty to begin looking for employment. I turned to the same agent who had procured the position with the Duchess of Somerset for the lady I met in Leipzig. The first referral came to naught, and I waited another week.

I used this time to follow up on an introduction to the family Goschen, which I had received in Leipzig. Georg Joachim Göschen had been the editor of the works of Goethe. His descendant, George Joachim Goschen (he had crossed out the "umlaut" and called himself Goschen), was now living in London. The Lord Goschen who was the English ambassador in Berlin and left Germany at the declaration of war in 1914 was one of his descendants.

Mrs. Goschen immediately responded to my letter with an invitation to lunch. I took the train to Rockhampton. In front of the splendid country home a servant received me, led me into the elegant vestibule and from there into a big salon where the family was assembled. They welcomed me graciously, and we sat around the fireplace until we were called to lunch. In spite of the hospitality

I felt a little strange, and it was like a warm breeze from Germany when Miss Annette Preusser took me up to her room after the meal. She was a friend of the family whom I knew from Leipzig. She showed a keen interest in me and my desire to be useful in this world, so that I felt my heart warming up. When she even expressed her readiness to welcome me as a guest in her country home in Westmoreland whenever I would announce my coming, England no longer seemed foreign. Cheerful and encouraged, I returned to my friends in the afternoon.

A week later I went back to the employment agent. This time she told me of a position with the Duchess of Montrose. To my objection, "You've probably sent countless numbers of applicants there," she replied, "Not every governess is suited for this."

I dressed in a simple but pretty Parisian suit and took a hansom, which was the most common carriage in England at that time, with the driver's seat in the back. I asked the driver to wait in front of the house.

A servant in powdered wig and livery with yellow velvet trousers received me in the vestibule. What did I see? A long row of ladies seated on chairs and benches who wanted to apply for the position as governess. The servant, however, followed my request to introduce me at once. I entered the spacious salon where I was met by a young lady. We had a long, pleasant conversation. She could not have been the Duchess, and so I was not surprised when she said, "I will call my mother."

An imposing blonde in a white negligée with pink ribbons appeared and asked me several questions. When she asked for letters of recommendation, I could produce none and gave Lady Sterndale Bennett as my only reference. "I'll have to think about it," the Duchess said, and I replied cordially but still rather impertinently, "I believe you first want to interview all the ladies who are waiting in the vestibule." "Indeed, no," she said blushing but smiling. Naturally, the whole conversation took place in English.

I took my leave, but hardly had I taken my seat in the hansom when the footman came running and asked me to return to the Duchess.

"I have thought about it," she said, "I will engage you for my little eight year old daughter in Scotland and want you to come to us in eight days. But first I would like you to accompany my daughter, whom you just met, to Windsor where she has to pay a visit."

I was immediately ready to accompany Lady Violet Graham, who was going to visit the daughter of the Belgian ambassador, and we became better acquainted on the drive. During her short stay, I strolled through the magnificent park of Windsor. Then I accompanied her home and we parted for eight days. After this week I travelled by night train to Sterling and from there to my destination, Buchanan Castle.

At the small station, an open carriage, a break, was waiting for me, and an adorable little girl, Lady Alma Graham, was standing beside it. She was to become my student for several years. English children of high nobility keep the family name, even if the father receives higher titles associated with different names, be it through inheritance or as reward for faithful service. That explains why Alma Graham was the name of the daughter of the Duke of Montrose.

We drove through a beautiful park and stopped in front of an impressive castle, which, with its many towers resembled a small town. On top of one of the towers, stood a tall figure, forged by an artist's hand: the watchman. We walked through the vestibule, decorated with plants, and then through a marvellous hall. Carpets and bearskins covered the floors. On one wall were life-size pictures of the Duke and Duchess in court-dress. On the other side hung the portrait by van Dyck of Charles I on horseback and next to it a portrait of the great Marquess of Montrose, the loyal supporter and defender of Charles I, whose life ended at the scaffold. We climbed the splendid staircase and arrived in the wing of the castle which we would occupy by ourselves.

Here was my very beautiful, large room with a view of the park. Alma's room was the next one. Then followed the one of the old attendant, Mrs. Stone. The school room was a few steps higher, in another wing which offered a magnificent view of the Scottish lake, Loch Lomond, and the high mountains behind it in violet hues from the blooming heather. I was practically overcome by all the beauty which surrounded me and praised my fate from the bottom of my thankful heart for having brought me to this position.

Buchanan, 1993 (photograph by Manfred Bartnick)

The oldest son, the Marquis of Graham, was still at Eton, the school of the English aristocracy. The youngest son, Ronald, called Ronnie, was eleven years old and had his own tutor, a so-called "Oxonian," which meant, he was studying at Oxford. The oldest daughter, Lady Agnes Murray, was married and lived near Stirling.

We had our breakfast at 8:30 in the school room, and then we went outside. Only from 11:00 till luncheon did we have lessons. In the afternoon we drove into the mountains in a small car reserved for our use. What a pleasure that was! The beauty of nature, the lake so close, and the magnificent mountains! In the evening, after tea, I usually played a game with Alma and read to her from a book in English. However, she was so intelligent that she soon caught on to German and learned it. Right in the beginning, when I described the three definite articles and gave man, woman, and child as examples, she came up to me on Sunday morning and said in English; "Do you hear the church bells? That must mean: der die das, man, woman, child go to church." A few months later she already had tried to write poetry in German. I read with her *Das Tagebuch dreier Kinder* (The Diary of Three Children) by the then popular but now forgotten woman writer, Stein. This book fascinated her so much that she learned German very quickly.

At eight o'clock Alma went to bed and then I received a truly Lucullian meal, which was served in the school room.

It was the custom in England's aristocratic families that the governess would have luncheon with the whole family but would stay in her room in the evening. When the Duchess later discovered that I was musical, I had to come down in the evenings. Since this required getting into formal attire, I did not find it very convenient, but I spent some very enjoyable evenings and met interesting people on these occasions.

Sundays we regularly drove to church where the Duke, as church patron, had his own chair. The Scottish Presbyterian service is quite simple, without organ. The old presenter who added ornamentation to the hymns often provoked my laughter so that I had to suppress it with my handkerchief. The preacher, Mr. Mackintosh, was a scholar and his sermons contained beautiful insights. By a strange coincidence he had lived with a pastor in my home town, Hamburg, for a year to learn German. This established a connection for us. He was a kind man. His intelligent, beautiful, vivacious, witty, and yet unassuming wife made her parsonage into a real paradise where I was always welcome.

After Alma had gone to sleep at eight o'clock, watched over by her Mrs. Stone, Jimmy Mitchell, actually a farmer but our driver for the small car, came and took me to the Mackintosh's. There, over tea and delicious scones, a Scottish tea cake, interesting discussions developed. The topic might derive from the books which the pastor ordered from a famous library in London. After tea I often sat down at the piano and played and sang German folksongs. Promptly at 10:30 the faithful Jimmy picked me up.

In late fall the Duke's family traveled to London and I stayed alone with Alma and the servants. It was not at all lonesome because the Mackintoshes came often in the evening or we would go there. We also knew other pastor's families whose churches likewise belonged to the castle. Some of them had grown daughters and consequently arranged social events.

At the Mackintosh's on Loch Lomond, however, I felt most comfortable. "Isn't it wonderful to be alive," the charming pastor's wife said to me one evening when we had finished playing croquet, and the mountains shone in a most unusual coloration as the sunset illuminated the heather on the slopes and the nearby lake shimmered in its deep, dark blue. I agreed heartily.

In November the Duke himself spent several weeks at Buchanan Castle and took Alma from Saturday to Monday to his daughter, Lady Agnes Murray. I used these three days for a visit to Miss Annette Preusser. She had a charming home in beautiful Westmoreland. I have often been amazed by the fact that many English people travel abroad to see beautiful scenery without knowing their own beautiful county, Westmoreland. Miss Preusser's property was situated on a lake, which was surrounded by mountains and lovely forests. I felt extremely happy there, and the three days passed quickly. I returned to Scotland filled with gratitude.

Since both Ronnie and Alma were musical and had lovely voices, there was much music making in our schoolroom. After the Duke had left again we prepared a special festivity for the Christmas holidays. Together with Mr. Oldham, the tutor, I hit upon the idea to fix up the old puppet theater which was in a sad state of neglect. We completed the characters of the theater by drawing and painting several more puppets for Cinderella. During the holidays we invited the complete and quite numerous staff to the performance. The dear Mackintoshes came too, and it was a successful evening.

At the end of the Christmas holidays the tutor returned to Oxford and the two brothers to their schools. We had another month by ourselves. We visited the poor, and brought the old women pheasants — pheasants, which are such a delicacy in Germany! Since the gardener gave us complete freedom, we decorated our wing with pots of exquisite, blooming plants. We also grew hyacinths in glasses; in short, our rooms took on a lovely appearance.

By now, March had arrived and we had to think about the move to London. We were sorry that we had to leave our dear friends, the Mackintoshes. In London, however, we settled in the aristocratic Belgrave Square and soon got used to the new situation.

The lessons continued in regular sequence, interrupted by walks in Hyde Park. On Saturdays, half a holiday in England, we always planned something special.

In good weather we usually drove to Richmond or Kew Gardens. These wonderful botanical gardens contain the most exquisite and rarest plants. At that time, there was a palm in the conservatory which had grown so tall that the roof had to be raised. Unfortunately, this did not have the desired effect. Since heat rises and the room was well heated, the palm slowly dried up. In rainy weather we often visited the Royal Polytechnic institution where we tried to be educated and amused by lectures and scientific demonstrations. We were particularly intrigued by the big diving bell and asked for an explanation of its use.

My pupil went to bed at eight o'clock like all English children, and I was free to visit my friends whose number had increased considerably. I was also free when it happened that Alma went to the country with her family for a whole day. I took advantage of one such holiday to take my letter of introduction from Mrs. Clara Schumann to Jenny Lind.

I took the train to Wimbledon where the singer lived with her husband, Otto Goldschmidt, and their children. Camellia Japonica, the lovely plant with red blossoms, had grown up to the roof of the beautiful villa and gave it a charming appearance. I stood in front of it, my heart beating fast. I was an enthusiastic admirer of Jenny Lind's great vocal art and indeed her whole personality. Now my most ardent wish, to meet the artist personally, was to be fulfilled.

She received me at once and asked many questions about Mrs. Schumann. I told her about my piano lessons in Paris, the delightful soirees, and the concerts Clara Schumann gave. But I was mindful of the warning by Clara Schumann, "Never express the desire to hear her sing!" and did not touch on the subject of her singing. Suddenly she said to me; "I have no idea why you came here." I felt the blood rising to my head. "Why?" I exclaimed, "because I adore you, and it was my most ardent wish to get to know you! But if you don't like it, I'm very sorry." She suddenly became very friendly and said, "I don't want to be worshipped like that, but take your coat and hat off, rest a little, and stay for lunch. My little daughter will show you the garden."

The little four-year-old Jenny showed me everything, even the vegetable garden, and was generally very talkative. I had calmed down, and when we were called to the luncheon I was happy to be allowed to take a seat next to the great artist. She still had the lovely blond hair, and her big, blue eyes had kept their sparkle. The wall across from me was covered with a magnificent fresco: Christ standing by the shore while the two disciples pull their net out of the water.

We talked a great deal about Andersen. I owned his complete works, and Jenny Lind talked about her great admiration for him. I said, that I loved his *Story of My Life* especially. When she expressed her preference for this book too, my rash remark, "That surprises me," was countered with a puzzled, "Why?" "Because in this work Andersen expresses his high esteem for you." She looked at me and was silent.

After the luncheon I went back into the garden, and when I returned to the room later, Otto Goldschmidt was in the salon. Since he is also from Hamburg, we had several points of contact to explore. Soon afterwards, Jenny Lind came in and — oh, wonder! oh, joy! — she said; "Otto, I would like to go through a few songs with you." Now she sang several songs by Mendelssohn, among them a spring song, and she was just as enrapturing as in her younger days.

I was in seventh heaven. This feeling of bliss was even heightened when she abruptly turned to me with a warm, motherly expression on her face, "I have to go now and bathe my baby." I looked at some of the numerous books and pictures which were lying on the table, and said "good bye" when she returned. She went out into the front yard and picked a large bouquet of those beautiful red flowers for me.

Jenny Lind later rented the property of Miss Preusser in Windermere in Westmoreland and lived there for a while. She also spent an extended period in Dresden.

Many years later, when I happened to be in London after a long absence, I heard her at a concert in an unusual way. It was unusual for me, because I heard her free while ticket prices were extremely high. It was a hot summer day. The doors to the concert hall and the ticket office were still closed. A mass of people was waiting in the street at Hanover Square. I joined in, and behind me the number of art lovers grew astronomically. We stood there for about half an hour, I in my thin summer dress with my sovereign in my hand, ready for the opening of the box office. But I never reached it. When the doors opened, there was a horrible crush. I could move neither left nor right but was propelled forward, up the stairs, and into the hall, where I, with beating heart and torn dress but overjoyed, took an unreserved seat.

Jenny Lind was still singing beautifully. Her rendition of Haydn's "My mother bids me bind my hair" and several Mendelssohn duets, among them the spring song, which she performed with another singer, are unforgettable for me and received enthusiastic applause. I was overpowered and moved to tears of joy. What great, surpassing artistry! Once more I shed tears for her, but of a different kind, when I read the news of her death. Devout, as she had lived, so she died.

I was deeply sorry that this pure soul, who had once turned her back to the stage for religious reasons, has been defamed by a stage play. People who had known her all her life, the witnesses who told me about her development and her strict philosophy of life, would be equally outraged if they were still alive.

જ

Remembering Goethe's words from his poem "Der Schatzgräber" (The Digger for Treasure), "Work during the day, guests in the evening," I devoted my daytime hours to my highly gifted little Alma. The London season had been moved to the summer because Parliament was in session through July, and the Duke, as a Peer, had a seat in the House of Lords. Therefore, Alma and I also stayed in London. The heat was almost unbearable. We often drove to Battersea Park, took a boat, rowed out on the little lake and stopped at a spot where the trees on the shore gave shade for our boat. There we enjoyed the refreshments we had brought along, and I read to my pupil from her favorite book, *Das Tagebuch dreier Kinder.* In August everyone went to the country for hunting.

The following spring we spent two weeks with the widowed Lady Amely Foley, the Duke's sister. It was an enjoyable stay. Lady Amely, an aristocratic lady of the old school, treated me with exceptional cordiality. For the evening meal she always appeared in beautiful, low-cut gowns whose splendour was enhanced by precious jewels — sapphires, emeralds, rubies, or diamonds — even when we were eating by ourselves. I still see the old lady in front of me. After the meal she would sit at the piano, erect and majestic, playing an "old tune," which, as she explained to me, Blondel, the friend of the imprisoned Richard the Lionheart, had played for him under his window.

Then she wanted to hear me. Since I was singing only folk songs from memory at that time, I entertained her with some in German, Norwegian, and French. Finally she asked me to sing one in Russian. Here I was in a real quandary. I knew only the melody of the "Red Sarafan" but not the words, and I knew only two words in Russian, "Matushka" and "Gortchakov." I bravely began the Russian song using as text the two words alternately and was rewarded with generous applause.

From Lady Amely Foley's castle we could take lovely walks through the woods and up the mountains. Once we had an adventure that still gives me chills when I think of it.

Lady Amely had a keen interest in our excursions through the surroundings of her estate, Stoke Edith Park, and one warm, sunny morning she suggested a hike to a little woods where primroses were already in bloom. She made a sketch of the path for us. The trail first went uphill and then straight along the rim of the mountain through wooded and cleared areas. Twice we had to climb over a so-called stile, steps over the fences which provide a barrier between fields for the cattle. After about an hour and a half we reached our destination and sat down on the soft moss, surrounded by spectacular yellow primroses. It was a delightful morning. After we had rested a while and refreshed ourselves, we started on the way back and marched happily along. Suddenly we saw a man coming out of the bushes, some distance from us. He was wearing an unusual white gown and was walking slowly forward. Consequently we slowed our steps. It seemed that he had noticed us, for he turned around, walked backwards and did not take his eyes off us. I took Alma firmly by the hand and when she asked what I would do if he came towards us, I said, "I'll throw the milk bottle at his head." What good would this defense have done? Back to civilization was my only thought. The man in the white robe made such a sinister impression, that even though I had no reason to suspect anything evil, I felt an unspeakable anxiety at being exposed to this strange person with my charge all alone.

At the end of the trail was the first stile. To our dismay we saw that the man did not go across but was waiting for us. We quickly decided to turn right. Fleeing through undergrowth and shrubs we reached a higher, parallel trail bordered by a low wall. Quietly we crept forward. Suddenly a big rock came flying over the wall, fortunately at some distance from us. Now an enormous fear took hold of us, and we turned right and ran through the woods down hill a great distance until we were totally exhausted. We rested quietly under a tree. I thought, if he comes, I'll scream so loud that someone will hear us in the house we had seen on our way up. After half an hour we moved on. I took my direction from the sun, and we finally reached the second stile, not far from that house. As we climbed over the stile we again saw the terrifying figure at some distance, walking towards the house. We succeeded in reaching the house in a frantic gallop and were welcomed with sympathy by the farmer's family. It was not long before one of the five servants arrived whom Lady Amely had sent out to look for us when we had not returned by six o'clock in the evening. He had not seen the stranger.

With torn clothes and loose hair we arrived at the castle. Lady Amely greeted us with joyous relief. Mrs. Stone, the old attendant, described for us the excitement at the castle when we had not returned at the expected hour. She herself had thought that Alma had fallen into the water and that I was afraid to come home.

Since Lady Amely was patroness in four parishes, she invited the four clergymen to dinner with the request to make inquiries about the occurrence. One of the clergymen brought the news that the man had escaped from the insane asylum but had been caught and returned. The adventure did not do us any harm, but Lady Amely had the experience of the "Reiter und der Bodensee" (a ballad by Gustav Schwab about a horseman who died of fright after realizing that he crossed Lake Constance in the fog), for from then on she worried terribly about all the things that could have happened if we had fallen into the hands of the mad man.

Then followed another delightful summer in Scotland. I made the suggestion to the Duke that he build a little house for Alma with a garden for flowers and vegetables. The proposal met with approval. Carpenters brought wood and other building materials and in a very short time the most adorable house was built, all at ground level, to the left a kitchen and to the right a living room.

The Duchess provided us with all accessories, and Alma herself painted the outside in a bright color, which she enjoyed very much. We planted climbing roses and called the little house "rose cottage." A little railroad was installed: rails were laid from the castle to the cottage, and on these rails two cars for two persons each could transport us quickly down there. Here we prepared tea and baked delicious cakes. Mr. Atkins, the new tutor, and Ronnie helped us. A goat would later pull the cars, filled with dirty dishes, back to the castle. We spent delightful hours in the rose cottage, but occasionally we became annoyed because so many visitors to the castle wanted to have tea with us. This bothered especially Mr. Atkins, because he had to cut the fire wood and bring it to the cottage.

When the time for hunting arrived, we often joined in. The Duke's people, who wore his tartan of blue, green, and white, would meet us and row us across the lake in the boats which were prepared for us. At the islands we got out and accompanied the gentlemen into the woods where they were shooting pheasants and partridges. Towards evening we went home rather tired but always with plenty of game.

In the spring we moved back to London. That year I lost my dear, unforgettable friend, Lady Sterndale Bennett.

Four years passed this way with work and relaxation alternating. Particularly enjoyable were the visits to Windermere where Miss Preusser always received me with the same kindness.

Now I longed to return to my homeland. I wished I could have taken Alma with me, but that was impossible for various reasons. She married a nobleman at a very young age. I saw her again as Marchioness of Breadalbane on several occasions. She remained childless, but she established a home for boys with her own money. Her old attendant, Mrs. Stone, was the supervisor. The common notion that the children of convicts inherit the bad tendencies of their parents was not borne out. For instance, she had the experience that the two sons of a man who had been executed for murder became useful members of society through the good upbringing and education in her home. Here, at least, heredity did not seem to dominate.

TO KIEL, NICE, AND KARLSBAD

I settled in with my beloved sister and brother-in-law and en-joyed a delightfully relaxing time. Pastor Ritter, my brother-in-law, always stimulated us to new thoughts with his conversations. He was a prominent preacher and applied his Christian faith to every aspect of the human condition. It sometimes happened that people who had had a falling out came to him after the sermon to tell him they had been reconciled. He was a friend of the poor, and he received every petitioner, no matter who he might be. Pastor Ritter did not have special office hours but was available any time. My sister was a great help in his efforts. In the morning at break-fast, they always discussed which persons in need would be given aid in the course of the day. The rich were his friends too. He would visit his parishioners in their villas on the Elbe to solicit their assistance in his work for the poor, while my sister and I waited in the garden of a small restaurant. It was lovely. The big ocean freighters with goods from all parts of the world passed by while my sister and I recalled childhood memories. In the evening we played a few hands of robber whist for relaxation, which Pastor Ritter spiced with his delightful humor.

During this visit I became acquainted with a friend of the Ritters, Mrs. Mathilde Arnemann, who was a benefactor of man-kind, in the true sense of those words. She helped many a person to achieve success in his or her field, be it through assistance with money or by bringing her protégé to the attention of people in influential positions. For example, she once was so impressed with the intelligence of a gardener who led her through a hot house, that she brought about his admission to university studies. He be-came a famous professor of medicine.

No one in need came to her in vain. She had once been very rich, but after the death of her husband, who had already lost ev-erything while he was still alive, she moved into a small house with a straw roof in the village of Ottensen, near Hamburg. When I went to visit her, I had to walk through the Ottensen cemetery which strangely enough was crossed by the Danish customs bound-ary. Regularly, the customs officer would jump out from behind the grave of Klopstock and go through my handbag but find nothing.

Mrs. Arnemann had a charming apartment. Pictures of all her friends — artists, poets, musicians — enlivened her cozy living room, and she told a story about each one. Whenever she came to visit my sister, we would have a merry evening. She had attended the same school as my brother-in-law, and, even though she was older than he, those two could exchange many memories of their youth.

Upon this delightful winter followed an equally pleasant summer. I spent part of that summer with Louis Köster, Pastor Ritter's uncle who had once brought about my piano lessons with Brahms, and whose kind wife, a native of Rome, gave me lessons in Italian. They had a charming summer home in Düsternbrook, near Kiel, close to the water, and I have wonderful memories of the weeks I was allowed to stay with them. The "plattdeutsche" (Low-German) poet Claus Groth was a daily visitor in their house, and we became good friends.

He was a typical "Holsteiner": tall, slim, with brown hair, blue eyes, and ruddy cheeks. He was proud of his peasant ancestry and was very upset when he thought he had reason to assume that someone was looking down on farmers. He told many stories about the beautiful Holstein and Schleswig; particularly about a "Hallig" (small island) whose inhabitants were totally cut off from the mainland during the winter. Claus Groth possessed considerable physical strength. This was evident when he saved my poor aunt. She had fallen into the water from a plank bridge which led to a bathing machine, "Badekarren." With her soaked clothes she was very heavy, but he managed to pull her up and get her back on the bridge. He was none the worse for wear, but her scraped arms took a long time to heal. It is strange that he has a poem in his collection *Quickborn*, in which he praises not this lady whom he saved and who was such a close friend of his, but rather an aunt of mine, my mother's sister. She lived in Bernsdorf near Moritzburg, married to a village parson. Claus Groth visited her there, and describes his pleasant impressions in the Quickborn poem. The poet married a rich woman from Bremen who was a loving, intelligent wife. They had three sons. He later experienced unkindness from the so-called "world" here and there, which, in turn, caused him to utter occasional bitter remarks. When I later tried to encourage him to write again, he refused with a certain contempt for the world. According to Mrs. Arnemann, he created his most beautiful work before he got rich, when he still had a broken coffee pot on his breakfast table.

Besides the poet there were two university professors who were frequent visitors at the Köster's home: Professors Seelig and Dilthey. The latter gained prominence through his biography of Schleiermacher. We spent extremely stimulating afternoons with them on the veranda by the sea. Often Professor Forchhammer joined our circle. Small of stature, his large eyes gave him the appearance of an owl. He had erected part of a Cyclopean wall in Kiel which, to my knowledge, is still standing.

Professor Müllenhoff was another welcome guest. His son, a midshipman at sea, became my friend. He told me of a frightening experience. It happened when he had the watch up on the mast at five one morning. His sextant started to fall and in trying to grab the instrument, he himself fell into the sea. Fortunately, inspection was being held at this hour and his absence was noticed. He was in dreadful suspense while he was swimming in the rather rough sea. Finally, after several minutes he noticed that the ship was slowing down and stopping. The small boat which was launched rode right over the exhausted swimmer before the brave helmsman in it saved him. Unfortunately, while he was saved that time, he still lost his life at a young age.

The summer was followed by a congenial fall at my sister's in Hamburg. Then came a letter from Miss Preusser offering me a position with an English physician as governess for his daughters in Nice.

I accepted this offer at once and left for Nice, except that I made a stop in Eisenach where Mrs. Arnemann had a charming villa. Mrs. Arnemann was living periodically in Eisenach where she had founded a handicraft school with the fugitive Duchess of Orleans after the French revolution. The school was still flourishing. I spent several very interesting days in this Thuringian city. The imposing Wartburg made a deep impression on me. Its commandant, Baron Arnswald, was a friend of Mrs. Arnemann and invited us to a meal in his apartment with its Old-German furnishings. We viewed the paintings by Moritz von Schwind and the

Luther room, and then spent a pleasant time with the Baron. As we were leaving for home, he sat upstairs at the open window and played on the zither:

> *Und bis wir wieder uns begegnen,*
> *vergiss mein nicht, vergiss mein nicht.*
>
> *Until we see each other again,*
> *forget me not, forget me not.*

An example of perfect romanticism up there on the old Wartburg.

Mrs. Arnemann also knew Fritz Reuter. He lived in a newly built villa, now the Reuter museum, in a delightful location at the foot of the mountain. Unfortunately he was just then again "sick," so that I did not get to meet him. It is known that he began to drink heavily in prison, and since then he suffered from so-called "periodic drinking." But his charming wife received us and walked with us through her garden. She was beautiful, with her white hair — his Luise in *Ut mine Stromtid* — still graceful, and admirable in her loyal and loving care of her husband which she yielded to no one during his "illness."

Mrs. Arnemann was a genuine "Hamburger." She would use some of the amusing idioms of Hamburg, such as "mein alte Deern" (my old girl) and "mein alte Seele" (my old soul), or adding "hätt' ich bald gesagt" (I almost said), after giving an opinion. In the days when she still had her riches, she was a generous hostess. Jenny Lind and many other stars of art and science stayed with her. Her villa in Flottbeck was later occupied by the Duke of Augustenburg. His daughter, Princess Auguste Victoria of Schleswig Holstein-Augustenburg, who was born there, became the wife of Emperor Wilhelm II. Now Mrs. Arnemann had to live according to her more modest means, but her relationships remained the same, for whoever had once known her did not let her go; she was stimulating and charitable from head to toe.

We visited the Baron Arnswald several more times, and one afternoon, when I was looking out the window, I saw the Grand Duchess Sophie von Sachsen-Weimar walking alone but talking loudly. The Baron explained that she memorized long poems in order to sharpen her memory, and recited them aloud. She was knowledgeable in science and was in every way a highly cultivated lady who gave her daughters an excellent education. Her daughters married Prince Reuss (the former ambassador) and the Prince of Mecklenburg-Schwerin.

After this poetic time in Eisenach, I accompanied Mrs. Arnemann to Munich where we lived in the "Vier Jahreszeiten." We were immediately invited by the painter Piloty, first to his studio and then for dinner. He was just painting the "Triumphal March of Germanicus," and his wife was the model for Thusnelda. She was a lovely blonde who had been raised in the educational establishment of the famous Marie Hillebrand in Soden by Frankfurt a.M. She was a loyal, clever, observant wife, thus preventing the trouble which her husband's passionate temperament could have caused.

In answer to my question, Piloty explained that the idea for a painting is a sudden inspiration. "It comes like a spark, gains form, and then the picture stands clearly before my mind's eye." The couple was charming in their hospitality, and the adorable children contributed their part to make guests feel thoroughly at home.

Still another friend of Mrs. Arnemann's whom we visited was Moritz von Schwind. He had "The Story of the Seven Ravens" in his studio. He went into great detail in describing the cyclical development of his "Melusine," which he started grey on grey, then at a time of greatest happiness he painted in bright colors, and at the end he finished again grey on grey.

Mrs. Arnemann always tried to exert an educational influence on her surroundings. Since I had told her that I dreaded the sight of corpses, she resolved to cure me of this fear, and she took me to a well known convent where a young nun had just died of consumption. With a smile on her lips she was lying there, and the priest who stood next to her commented, "She is laughing at us."

Then she took me to the mortuary in the city where you saw the departed through a window. What I saw was not at all horrible: old gentlemen in tuxedos and women with white hair. I was told that at the request of relatives, some of the dead had an electric detector by their teeth which would ring a bell at the slightest breath. Mrs. Arnemann succeeded completely in her intent. From then on the sight of a corpse no longer filled me with dread.

After our stay in Munich we moved south. Slowly the vegetation changed. While in the north the trees were already losing their leaves, in the south everything was green and blooming. We spent a lovely day in Bolzano before I had to bid farewell to my travel companion. At that moment the bells were ringing so beautifully that I broke out in tears, and to Mrs. Arnemann's puzzled question, why I was crying, I could only answer, "The bells, the bells."

I travelled through Verona and went to see the amphitheater there. I stood by one of the seats high up and was deeply moved as I was thinking of the ghastly dramas which once took place here. I also visited the house of "Juliet," but then my time had run out and I had to proceed to Genoa. I arrived late in the evening and felt rather helpless when a gentleman, who may have been watching me, asked me for the name of my hotel. When I gave the name, he said, "I am just coming from there, and since I am now continuing my trip, you may use my carriage." Delighted, I accepted his offer. The thought that I was exposing myself to potential danger never occurred to me at that time. Only later did good friends make me aware of that. I spent the night in a pleasant room, and continued my journey the next morning by coach along the picturesque Riviera. It was a cloudy day. The sky and the Mediterranean Sea were quite grey. Even the much praised olive groves had a grey-green color.

Once again I was overcome by that feeling of infinite loneliness which gained the upper hand so often in my life. However, the sight of beautiful Nice among lemon and orange groves gradually dissolved this mood.

The coach stopped in front of the house of Dr. Gurney, the English physician whose children I was to educate and whose patients were primarily of his nationality. The large family consisted of four girls and four boys. I did not have anything to do with the boys. The mother was a delicate creature who gave the impression that a puff of air could extinguish her life. I did not see much of her while I was there, and I heard that she died soon after my departure. There also was an aunt in the house, one of those unfortunate women who feel superfluous as the fifth wheel on the cart, and do not even get any pity because they go through life embittered. The desire to escape such a fate drove me to that stubborn struggle against the advice of my brother and brothers-in-law after my father's death, which I finally won.

The children were all attractive and I became very fond of them. The boys were unruly, as is often the case in English families. One day their Swedish governess came to me in total desperation because the four-year-old Martin had jumped out of the bath and run into the street, the way he was. I was amused by the numerous paper dolls hanging on threads from the ceiling of the otherwise very elegant salon. The rising heat caused movement of these figures. I laughed at the poor taste, but the doctor rejected my remarks with the words, "My sons will be exposed to the heavy artillery of life early enough, we want to let them have the freedom now to do what they enjoy."

The lessons were very cheerful and not very numerous because the doctor demanded a lot of fresh air for his daughters. Going to the ocean beach was delightful. In Nice, even in those days, it was perfectly acceptable to greet one's friends — male and female — in the water, dressed in a bathing costume. Since all four girls, Marion, Lily, Amy, and Nora, knew how to swim, I wanted to learn too; but what a disaster! After I had learned the movements, I was to take a swim test on the third day. For this purpose the swimming teacher had a huge board with a handle on each of the four sides. The teacher took the front handle and we three ladies the others. Then he gave the signal to swim. He swam in front pulling the raft out to sea, while we were supposed to swim with our legs. When I saw only water and felt no ground under my feet, I was gripped by panic; like lead I hung onto the float and beseeched the teacher to turn around. I gave up swimming forever and only floated on the water with a swimming belt, which was very pleasant in the heat.

The walks were wonderful. There was a spot where three kinds of violets were blooming, and we always came home with fragrant flowers. A few times we saw the old King Ludwig I of Bavaria on the promenade. Then we heard that he was sick and later that he was near death. The King died on February 28, 1868, and was embalmed and displayed for public viewing. It was not a lovely sight but a touching experience. Two monks were kneeling by the bier reading psalms, which gave the whole affair a solemn character.

I thoroughly enjoyed the attractions of Nice. We explored the area in all directions. Our life was peaceful and pleasant except for one shadow which fell on this sunny existence: Every morning we had to kneel around the table for lengthy prayers and long discourses by Dr. Gurney with hostile remarks about those of different beliefs. To submit to this finally became impossible for me. I felt in danger of becoming a hypocrite. Since I represented the rational, religious principles of my father, I had to consider myself one of those attacked and could not join in these prayers. Therefore, I believed it to be my duty to give the doctor my opinions and, at the same time, give him notice that I would return home in the fall.

The family felt a deep sadness at my decision, and I too parted from them with a heavy heart. When they moved to northern Switzerland in late summer to escape the great heat, I accompanied them to Marseilles and then continued by myself to Geneva where I met my good friends from Scotland, the Mackintoshes. We took many excursions into the surrounding area including a visit to the castle Chillon, which Byron made famous with his "The Prisoner of Chillon." The dungeon, by the way, was not a dark prison but rather a large room with a stone floor, illuminated by a window high in the wall. However, the chain which was supposed to have fettered the prisoner was still hanging on a post.

I spent eight days in Geneva, then I headed for home. I saw three of my dear pupils again in Nice at a much later time. Lilly Gurney had been dead for some time, Amy was a widow. Marion and Nora were unchanged, devoted to me in loyalty and friendship. Two of the sons unfortunately did not prove themselves in the "heavy artillery of life" but went astray.

⟡

I interrupted my trip home with a week's stay at Mrs. Arnemann's in Karlsbad. The weather was favorable for our walks and longer hikes. My favorites were the health walks (Kurspaziergänge) in the morning. I accompanied Mrs. Arnemann to the spring. The orchestra was playing and we saw many interesting persons among the "Kur" guests. Mrs. Arnemann was the center of a circle in which Berthold Auerbach shone particularly because of his witty remarks. Mrs. Arnemann always had a clever response. Later, when she celebrated her fiftieth birthday in Karlsbad, she had become an exceptionally popular personality. She wanted to make the baths in Karlsbad available to needy, educated persons (deserving poor) and for this purpose she founded the "Elisabeth-Rosen." Annually she took a collection from the guests during her stay in Karlsbad, and in memory of the miracle ascribed to Saint Elisabeth of Thuringia she wanted to turn the money collected into "roses." I was privileged to assist her in this collection, and we achieved such good results that I extended my visit for several weeks. Mrs. Arnemann appointed the Mayor of Karlsbad the executor of the already rather large sum. He was to keep the identity of the applicants secret so that neither the host nor the other guests had any knowledge of it. This endowment became a great blessing and, as far as I know, still exists today, even though Mrs. Arnemann died many years ago at the age of eighty.

In Karlsbad Mrs. Arnemann introduced me to a gentleman from Hungary who was looking for a governess for his sister's daughter. His sister was married to the son of the old Princess Obrenovich. He described his sister's home in glowing terms. In her name he offered me such an enormous salary that Mrs. Arnemann, in her bubbling enthusiasm, persuaded me to accept the excellent offer.

Before returning to Hamburg, I paid a short visit to my sister, Klara Hoffmann, whose husband had been transferred from Leipzig to Dresden as "Konsistorialrat" (member of the regional church council). Mrs. Arnemann wanted to have a photograph of me and had recommended Hanfstaengl in Dresden. He turned out to be a most amusing person, a character. Hardly had I arrived when he ordered me to stand behind an armchair, my arms leaning on it. I made a "photograph face." Half laughing, half annoyed, he said; "It won't start for a long time, tell me something." I began a description of Hungary. He was pulling my gloves and handkerchief out of my pocket while admonishing me not to change my position. I told him about Mrs. Arnemann, when he suddenly shouted, "Now!" A good picture resulted which was to play its part in my future.

My brother-in-law, Pastor Ritter, in Hamburg was quite upset about my obligation to Hungary, and he told Mrs. Arnemann of his dismay that she had persuaded his sister-in-law to go to the "Hungarian swineherd." (The first Prince Obrenovich had in fact been a swineherd.) However, I had made a firm commitment, and after a short stay in Hamburg I set off for Hungary in October 1868.

⁂

IN HUNGARY

The estate of the family Obrenovich was in the vicinity of Temesvar. I had to spend the night in Budapest and according to the letter from the proprietor I was to find a sum of money there for the continuation of my trip. Up to that point I had covered the travel expenses myself. I found no money, only a letter notifying me that a car would be waiting for me in Oravitsa the next day. Since I did not have enough money, I had to leave my watch as pawn with the owner of the hotel. He knew the family Obrenovich well and had no doubt that he would receive his money. The trip along the Danube, past the "Iron Gate," was beautiful, but only on my return trip did I get to see much of Hungary and Budapest. Now I was hurrying to start my new position as soon as possible. The car was ready in Oravitsa and our drive began. I was amused to see that the upholstery of the seats had some holes and the ropes were worn, but the ride was very comfortable and the coachman in his blue jacket and hat drove the horses at a good speed. The scenery was not particularly attractive, quite flat, only here and there a hill planted with plum trees. This is the area where plum brandy was produced. The estate was at the Serbian border, and the few farm women I met wore Serbian costumes. A part of the population was Romanian, and one often heard three languages mixed together, Hungarian, Serbian, and Romanian.

At four in the afternoon the carriage stopped in front of a long one-story building. In front of the house was a pretty but small garden. The farm buildings, primarily intended for raising pigs and chickens, were behind the house.

The family was gathered for the coffee hour and received me warmly. The family consisted of the old Princess Obrenovich, her son, his wife (a Serb), her mother who was visiting the estate for an extended period, the brother of the young wife (also visiting), and finally the three children: a ten-year-old daughter, Lyubitsa, a seven-year-old boy, Ivan, and a little three-year-old girl, Maritsa.

Princess Obrenovich had transferred the business to her son after the death of her husband, a Hungarian landowner, but she was still the owner of the rich land holdings.

The furniture was curiously luxurious, the sofa of green velvet embroidered in gold. On all the chairs lay identical pillows. The food was extremely rich. Somehow the whole life here, although comfortable, seemed terribly alien to me, and I felt from the first day that my stay would not be very lengthy.

The old Princess spoke to me in broken German about her earlier life. As daughter of the above-mentioned swineherd, she was born in a cave. Often she sat down next to me and talked. Once, when I had returned from Oravitsa and was adding up the various expenses in my notebook, she said; "My dear Miss, I not can read, not write, but everything have in my head. But you everything must write when you go to town, I never do that, but always much buy and bring and never forget." In the village she had the reputation of being a "poison mixer" but I saw no evidence of such things. She had a collection of herbs in the attic, especially the yellow marigolds, called "death flower" there, from which she prepared medicine. She was always very friendly to me.

I rarely saw the son, because he had so much to do in managing the farm. The young woman was always courteous. Especially enjoyable was her mother, the Serb, who surprised me with her perceptiveness and understanding. With her and her son, who was unhappily married and therefore present without his wife, I had many pleasant conversations. His intelligent and interesting remarks enlivened the evening discussions considerably.

My older little pupil, Lyubitsa, made good progress in German but not in music. In my opinion, she was not musical, and since music is my life, this lack was an obstacle to my teaching. I did not have any responsibilities for Ivan since he had a male teacher, but he became very attached to me and asked my advice whenever he was in a quandary. Thus he came to me one day when his grandmother was on a trip. "I must write a letter, but I don't know what to say. How should I start?" I answered him, "Begin with, Dear Grandmama, and then tell her what you have seen and what you have enjoyed." — "And how should I close?" — "Your Ivan, nothing else." After some time he had managed to compose the following letter; "Dear Grandmama! Chair. Your Ivan." I laughed and asked him what it meant. "I was supposed to write what I had seen. I saw a chair." Of course, I dictated a new letter to him. The first one was really too laconic.

The little Maritsa was adorable. In her Serbian costume, a floor-length blue velvet dress with gold embroidery, she looked like a fairy. She spent much time with me. Already early in the morning she called from her room, which was next to mine, "Good morning, Susin."

Since I had decided not to stay long with the family Obrenovich, I wanted to learn as much as possible about the customs of the local people. At funerals they still had the tradition of the wailing women. We lived near the church where the dead were blessed, and the procession would pass our garden, so that I never missed watching it. The deceased was carried in an open casket and behind it walked the paid mourners. Their horrible wailing was truly ear shattering, but the family of the deceased was satisfied. I also attended a few baptisms. According to the Greek rites, the completely naked child was dunked into cold water three times. The poor creature was blue and out of breath after this procedure, and not all survived the baptism. I have been told that they now put warm water in the baptismal font. I was also able to attend a peasant wedding. The bride wore a gold crown, fastened to the head with a ribbon, and her Serbian costume. The wedding meal was served in the open at a long table, and consisted mainly of "Pilav," mutton cooked with rice, a very tasty dish. However, since everyone ate from the same bowl, I only pretended to participate in the meal, but secretly let the food slip into my handbag. Today civilization is supposed to have claimed its place there too.

The local people were of handsome stock, but my interest in them had unfortunate consequences. The morning after the wedding I awoke with a painful itch on my head and found that it had become inhabited by countless little creatures. Appalled, I immediately rode to the hair dresser in Oravitsa and had my hair cut very short and my head thoroughly disinfected. Relieved I returned home, and I was cured of my interest in Hungarian folk festivals. To my regret, I had one more unpleasant experience, for shortly afterwards my sleep was being disturbed by little insects. Upon my request, an exterminator was called to rid me of these bugs.

We had a visit from the boy, Milan, who later became the Prince and King of Serbia. He was extremely lively and uninhibited, and he and his cousin, Ivan's older brother, would bombard each other with pillows in the morning. The terrible fate of his only son, King Alexander, and Queen Draga later filled me with deepest sympathy. As is well known, the young royal couple was forced out of their hiding place, murdered, and thrown from the palace window on June 11, 1903.

At a festivity in Temesvar I made the acquaintance of a Baron Nikolich, a highly cultured person who, as far as I know, later became a minister in the Serbian government. I also met his brother whom I saw again on my return trip through Budapest.

The winter passed rather pleasantly, but my heart longed for home. Since I did feel sorry for the children of the Obrenovich family, I wrote to a friend in Norway who had gone through a very difficult time, and offered her my position in Hungary. I knew that she needed something to do and would give loving care to the children. The Obrenoviches were naturally delighted that they had a replacement. I arranged a meeting with my Norwegian friend in Budapest where we planned to stay at the same hotel. I was touched to see that the Obrenovich family was really sad at my departure.

In Temesvar I was met by the already mentioned brother of Baron Nikolich, who accompanied me for a short distance. The weather was cloudy and cold. Suddenly heavy snow began to fall. It snowed for several hours. To my horror, the train went slower and slower until it stopped, stuck in the snow. A new locomotive had to come from the next station and we had to wait. Meanwhile the heating ducts froze, and I sat in the ice-cold compartment and was freezing. Not till evening did the other locomotive arrive which took our train to the next station. I spent the night at the apartment of the station master who gave me his room. The bed was cold and the water in the pitcher was frozen, but once a fire was started in the stove the crackling of the wood calmed me and I slept well. The next morning I met my friend in Budapest.

We spent several stimulating days together. Through Baron Nikolich we gained entrance to the sessions of the Chamber, where we watched the Hungarian magnates arrive. This procession was quite entertaining and interesting. They all wore their dolman, and when they sat down they thrust their large swords down in front of them with considerable noise.

On our last evening we attended a concert conducted by Liszt. When he stepped on the podium a storm of applause broke forth and "bravo" calls were repeated over and over again. He was conducting a Beethoven symphony. Later in the program a singer appeared whose name I have forgotten. She was beautiful, but what most impressed me was her unusual outfit. She wore a low-cut dress that had branches with big, red cherries hanging down from its short sleeves, a peculiar appearance. Liszt himself did not make as deep an impression on me then as later in Weimar. He had already joined the Franciscan order and conducted in his clerical gown. His face was as noble as his character which he demonstrated in his championship of Richard Wagner.

The next day we parted. My friend headed towards my former field of activity, and I hurried to Vienna where I had reserved a room in the "Erzherzog Karl." Here I was to spend two wonderful days which I had been looking forward to all winter. Already at ten o'clock the next morning Johannes Brahms came to me. What a joyful reunion! He had become a famous composer. Outwardly there was little change. His blue eyes seemed deeper. The blond hair was still combed back from the beautiful forehead. His clear, quiet way of speaking had remained the same. I have never heard Brahms utter a single word which would hint at vanity. He remained the same modest, and yet so great person, for great he was and remained beyond the grave. That morning he spoke at length about his *German Requiem* and related that he had received complimentary letters from many clergymen.

Then we planned our meeting for the afternoon at the music hall where he had his grand piano. There he told me about the Hungarian gypsies and his interest in them and their music. He talked about his "Hungarian Dances," which were about to appear in print. Then he lit a cigarette and started to play a series of Strauss waltzes which he liked very much. It was pure joy to be together with him, totally relaxed, to listen, then to exchange a few words, then another waltz. — — — Finally we parted with the agreement to spend the whole next day together, since my journey was to proceed to Karlsbad the day after that. The thought to be so completely free and able to walk with the great artist in any direction, enraptured me already when I woke up in the morning. Brahms came at the appointed hour. We went to the Belvedere and enjoyed viewing the masterpieces there. When we felt hungry we sought out a small restaurant where we both could satisfy our appetite for asparagus to our hearts' content, accompanied by champagne. In the loveliest weather we went on to Schönbrunn. I was delighted with the beautiful garden. Up on the hill reigned the "Glorietta." We wanted to go up there, but the strange thing was that we kept returning to the same spot, even though the "Glorietta" was very close. After this had happened three times, Brahms turned to another gentleman and asked him to show us the way. The path was indeed very short and we reached our goal quickly. The view from the top was magnificent. After we had delighted in it for a long time, evening had come and we returned to Vienna where we settled in a well known restaurant for the remaining hours. Our supper consisted again mainly of asparagus and a little champagne, since we both loved it so much.

Now it became very "gemütlich" (cozy). On this occasion, Brahms told me the following amusing experience. He was teaching in Vienna, but sometimes, as he said, in his distraction and total immersion in his compositions, he would forget to teach for a few weeks. One day he remembered one of his students and thought, I have some time today, I will go to her. He arrived at the house and found the family at the coffee table. They were overjoyed, treated him to all kinds of delicacies, and the time went by in animated conversation. Suddenly Brahms remembered the lesson and asked; "But where is Miss Anna?" — "Miss Anna?" asked the mother, "Who is she?" — "Well, Miss Anna so-and-so, my student." — "You are not in the home of that family," said the mother laughing, and reminded him of their name. Everyone broke out in hearty laughter. Now they understood how it had happened that the great Johannes Brahms had come for coffee that day.

Brahms told me this story in his quiet but highly humorous fashion. We spent the remainder of the evening in merry discussions, during which we recalled our hometown, Hamburg, vividly. I remained in touch with the artist through letters.

In Karlsbad I helped Mrs. Arnemann again with the "Elisabeth Rosen." She told me that the Grand Duchess Helene of Russia had spent several weeks in this Bohemian spa, and that the highly intelligent and important Baroness Editha von Rahden, the maid of honor of the Grand Duchess, had visited her. In looking through some photographs on Mrs. Arnemann's desk, she had noticed the one of me taken by Hanfstaengl in Dresden, and had asked about me. Mrs. Arnemann must have given her a glowing report.

I spent the lovely late summer days in Hamburg with my sister. My three English friends, whose oldest sister had by now married the brother of Claus Groth, invited me again to spend several weeks with them, and I accepted for October.

During my days in Hamburg I happened to read in the paper that the Grand Duchess Helene of Russia with her entourage was staying in Salzburg. Something came over me like a sudden inspiration. I wrote to Baroness von Rahden that I had heard so much about her and that I was begging her to kindly let me know if she should hear of a position for a governess. I did not get an immediate reply, so I prepared for my trip to England. In the middle of these preparations I received a very nice letter from the Baroness, sent from Mecklenburg, which she closed with the words, "I have long wished to make your acquaintance, and I implore you in the name of Her Imperial Highness to come to the castle Remplin near Malchin on Tuesday, since we are returning to Russia in a few days."

I did not hesitate for a moment; already on Monday I arrived in a small hotel in Malchin. I asked if one could send a messenger to Remplin the next morning and was told that only the night watchman could take a message. That is what happened, and I promptly received an invitation to luncheon at two o'clock.

I arrived at the appointed hour and a footman announced me at once to the Baroness Rahden. An imposing, for me incredibly attractive, personality greeted me. She had blond hair and blue-grey eyes, which sometimes assumed a violet color, giving her face a special charm. She gave me a warm reception, and from the first moment I felt at ease with her. The bell for luncheon sounded soon, and we moved towards the hall where the court was already assembled. Before I could be introduced the door opened and a lady in her middle years in a white hat with a feather walked quickly through the hall. Everyone bowed to her. I did not know who she was, but it was obvious that she could not be the Grand Duchess Helene. It was her daughter, Grand Duchess Katharina. The castle Remplin was hers, because she was married to the non-reigning Duke Georg of Mecklenburg-Strelitz. In St. Petersburg she lived in a wing of the "Palais Michel" which belonged to the Grand Duchess Helene. She had three children, a daughter and two sons, who were not yet grown. Her maid of honor made an unpleasant impression on me, and this feeling was later completely confirmed.

Again the door opened. Everyone turned, and there appeared a very beautiful, majestic lady of about sixty years. This must be the Grand Duchess Helene, I told myself. She stepped towards me and asked if I had had a good trip. Then we took our places. At first I was uncomfortable being seated directly across from the Grand Duchess and feeling watched, but since I was sitting between the Prince and his governor I soon relaxed, engrossed in conversation with both of them.

After the meal I accompanied Baroness von Rahden back to her room but was immediately called to the Grand Duchess Helene. This rare woman, in spite of her high rank, had the gift to identify with the person she was interested in, so that one soon felt comfortable and revealed one's innermost thoughts.[1] With warm interest she asked about my family, and in a short time she was familiar with my life and its chief episodes. Suddenly she said, "I need a reader and would like to take you with me. Would you accept a position with me?"

I was amazed, surprised, and delighted, and yet I gave the incredible answer, "I am afraid that life at court would be too superficial; actually I have a burning desire to educate young girls." With a happy smile she said; "Good, I can also give you a position in the institute for young girls which is under my direction, or in a family whose sixteen year old daughter needs a governess. If you want to come with me, you have to be back here the day after tomorrow at two o'clock."

Already I felt the magic of this prominent woman and accepted at once. She bade me farewell, and I rushed to Miss von Rahden who was delighted at my decision. I said, "I imagine, I will run around the Palais Michel like a lost sheep." — "Where I am, you shall never feel lost," she said, and she truly kept her word.

I hurried back to Hamburg and told my family that I had met both the prototype of a lady-in-waiting, the maid of honor of the Grand Duchess Katharina, and the ideal of a maid of honor, Editha von Rahden, who from then on was to have a great influence on me and my life.

ENDNOTES

[1] Anton Rubinstein described her similarly in his *Autobiography*: "She knew how to put herself in sympathy with every one who entered her presence; were he a savant, a soldier, an artist, a writer, a statesman, a poet, — she could converse with all, and leave a pleasant impression on every listener." Ref.9 p. 59

AT THE RUSSIAN COURT

In Hamburg I quickly packed and said my "good byes," so that I arrived punctually at two o'clock in Malchin where everyone was ready to depart. I was taken to a compartment in which the Baroness von Rahden and the Princess Lvov were already seated.

The journey passed rather quickly. In Berlin the German ambassador, Prince Reuss, came to greet us. He had an audience with the Grand Duchess Helene and then joined us in our compartment and rode along for a few stops. He was an intelligent and charming man whom the Grand Duchess valued. The next morning breakfast was served in the compartment. In the afternoon we arrived in Wirballen where we spent the night. At the evening meal I again met the Grand Duchess Helene who was very gracious to me and told me much about Russian customs. As did everyone else, I acted quite uninhibited in her presence, yet there was not the slightest temptation to violate the respect one owed her. The next morning her own railway carriage stood ready, and from here on I seemed to be living a real fairy tale.

At every stop carpets were laid out and the larger stations were decorated with flowers; bands were playing, and everywhere crowds were shouting, "hail!" Occasionally, the highest official of the town or a high military officer would come to greet the Grand Duchess because she was very popular in Russia.

The landscape had become rather stark, a flat plain with a few forests, but with its peculiar charm, which has inspired many Russian painters to create beautiful pictures. Towards seven in the evening we arrived at the magnificent Palais Michel (Mikhailovsky Palace — now the Russian Museum).

The large staircase in the front vestibule is supposed to be one of the most beautiful in all of Europe. Halfway up is a landing from which a right and a left flight lead to opposite sides of a rectangular columned gallery, lined with statues. The foot of the stairs was always guarded by two sentries who saluted whenever the Grand Duchess ascended the stairs. When we entered, a priest was waiting on the stairs to receive the Grand Duchess with a crucifix. After she had kissed it, her whole entourage had its turn.

She proceeded to her rooms and I was led to mine which were in a different wing, close to the apartment of Baroness von Rahden. I had my dinner at the Baroness' together with the Grand Duchess' pianist, Joseph Rubinstein, who, by the way, was no relation to Anton Rubinstein.

The next morning I was summoned by the Grand Duchess. She had me read something to her as a demonstration, and then conversed with me for quite a long time. The next afternoon she invited me to tea, and I was amazed how graciously she did me the honors. When I expressed my surprise to Baroness Rahden that the Grand Duchess poured the tea first for me, she said, "That just proves that she is a 'grande dame.'" With these words Baroness Rahden, who always hit the nail on the head, described the nobility of the Grand Duchess.

Eight days passed this way for me in total uncertainty as to my future. Then, one morning, the Grand Duchess summoned me to the garden. In her red velvet coat and her tight hat over which she had tied an Orenburg scarf, she reminded me of a picture of Empress Catherine the Great. We walked slowly back and forth in the huge park which was adjacent to the Field of Mars where the annual parade took place. After a few words of greeting the Grand Duchess said, "You have told me that you have a great love for educating the young. Therefore, I offer you a position as teacher in the Mary's School which is under my protectorate. You would have your own apartment and always work two days and then be free for one and a half days. Everything would be provided, including your own servants, in addition to a salary. Alternatively, I offer you a position as governess in the home of Mrs. Leontyev where you would have a pleasant situation. I myself would like to keep you here in the Palais with me, but," she added with a gentle smile, "you prefer the young." I had long since been inspired by her great intelligence and charm and so I exclaimed, "Oh no, if Your Imperial Highness wishes to have me, I shall stay here!" "Good, agreed," she said, stretching out her hand, and dismissed me affectionately. Later that day a secretary appeared who settled all the remaining details, and I started my function the same evening.

The Grand Duchess Helene of Russia was the daughter of Prince Paul of Württemberg, an intelligent man, who, after the

View of Palais Michel (Mikhailovsky Palace) in St. Petersburg

Palais Michel — The Grand Staircase (1985)

The Grand Duchess Helene

Baroness Editha von Rhaden

death of his wife, still enjoyed life, and therefore sent his two daughters to a recommended boarding school in Paris for their upbringing. The two sisters had a very hard life there. The Grand Duchess Helene told me that often they ate the bread which they received in their painting class for wiping up the paint. Her lot was eased through her acquaintance with the sister of the renowned philosopher Cuvier. Baron Georges Cuvier took a great liking to her. In the home of the Cuviers the Princess spent enjoyable hours. The conversation always dealt with philosophy, natural science, and generally lofty subjects, and this had a beneficial effect on the mind and spirit of the Princess.

At age fourteen she came to St. Petersburg to her great-aunt, the Empress Maria Feodorovna, born Princess of Württemberg, widow of the murdered Emperor Paul I, and mother of Emperor Alexander I. The Empress decided immediately that her grand-niece would be married to her youngest son, Grand Duke Michael, the favorite brother of Grand Duke Nicholas, later to become Emperor Nicholas I. During that time the young Prince of Prussia, who later became the German Kaiser Wilhelm I, visited at the Russian court. He fell in love with the charming Princess and would have liked to marry her, but the great-aunt insisted on the marriage to the Grand Duke Michael.

The Princess Charlotte Marie von Württemberg had to convert to the Greek-Russian Orthodox religion, and at her baptism she assumed the name Helene Paulovna. All Russians have to use the Baptismal name of their father as second name, hence, Paulovna, daughter of Prince Paul; Grand Duke Michael Paulovich, son of Tsar Paul. In this way it is easy for Russian children to learn the succession of their rulers, since each name also contains the name of the father. There exists a bust of the Grand Duchess Helene from that period, a young Hebe. She must have been enchantingly beautiful in her youth. She demonstrated a great interest in everything that could advance her knowledge, and immediately took lessons in national economics so that she would understand the organization and institutions of the country where she was to live.

In the year 1824, the marriage to the Grand Duke Michael took place. He and his brother, Nicholas, had been educated by a very strict governor. Corporal punishment was not lacking, and a small incident, which a gentleman in a high position at the Russian court related to me, is very touching.

The two brothers had committed some forbidden act, and in their fear of the governor, they ran to the old nurse and asked, "Will you beat us, and then tell our governor that we have already been punished?" Unfortunately this did not have the desired outcome. The strict governor still punished each one with severe chastisement.

The marriage of Grand Duke Michael and Grand Duchess Helene could not be considered a happy one because he already loved another. But he held his young wife in high esteem, as she deserved.

The marriage produced three daughters: Grand Duchess Maria who died of consumption at a young age in Vienna, Grand Duchess Elizabeth who married the Duke of Nassau, and the Grand Duchess Katharina whom I had seen in Remplin. Sadly, the marriage of the Grand Duchess Elizabeth was cut short by her early death. Her resting place in the Russian chapel in Wiesbaden is lovely. In contrast to the monuments on the graves of the nobility in Russia, which do not represent likenesses of the deceased, she is represented in marble. Her peaceful, sleeping features appear sunny and joyous in the light that falls through the yellow window. She died at the birth of her first child.

The Grand Duchess Helene devoted much of her attention to the education of the young. She made frequent visits to Mary's School where young girls were prepared for their entrance into the world, and always thought of additional improvements. She became a protectress of art and science, and pursued her interest in medicine and therapeutics. She founded the "Polyclinic," where her personal physician, Professor von Eichwald, and his assistants worked daily. She always said, "I have no talents," but she achieved the most favorable results in every field through her great intellect and her high aspirations.

In 1853, at the beginning of the Crimean war, she, together with the famous surgeon Pirogoff and Editha von Rahden, founded the "Sisterhood for the Elevation of the Cross." Up to that time, there were no nurses in Russia. To remedy this situation, Miss von Rahden was sent to Berlin to study nursing thoroughly and then teach it to the Sisters in Russia. She worked for several weeks in

Bethanien and also with the "Grey Sisters" (Sisters of Charity). Together with the Grand Duchess she designed the uniform for the Sisters, a cheerful-looking outfit in bright colors with a light blue ribbon on which a gold cross was hanging.

It would be difficult to imagine a more ideal relationship than the one between the Grand Duchess Helene and her maid of honor, Editha von Rahden. Often, the Grand Duchess thought of a new project and the Baroness carried it out. The Palais Michel was the center of all intellectual and spiritual endeavors in St. Petersburg. Everyone who was interested in the welfare and advancement of mankind in any way gathered here.[1]

After Emperor Nicholas I had ascended the throne, it became his habit to ask advice on important issues from his already widowed sister-in-law, Grand Duchess Helene. Grand Duke Michael had died in 1849. For a long time the Grand Duchess had thought about freeing the people from the yoke of serfdom. She considered this seriously with Tsar Nicholas and he concurred completely with her plans. However, when Russia was defeated in the Crimean was, it broke his heart and he died in 1855.

His successor, Alexander II, also had the desire to abolish serfdom. Many meetings took place in the Palais Michel to discuss this issue. One evening the Grand Duchess Helene, full of enthusiasm, pointed to a big round table in a corner of a spacious room. "Here," she called out, "here we sat and discussed how best to carry out the plan!"[2] This noble Duchess went ahead of everyone else and freed all the peasants on her estates at once. Soon afterwards, in 1862, came the official declaration of the abolition of serfdom. Peter Petrovich Semenov, then a young man and all fired up for the cause, was the secretary at all these sessions. Several of the most prominent men in Russia took part in these deliberations, which were led by the Grand Duchess and Editha von Rahden. The Baroness had taken on the plan with glowing enthusiasm and helped to bring about its realization.

Editha von Rahden was born on the estate Funkenhof in Courland. Her solid and noble character revealed itself early on. When she was only twelve years old, she stayed with her father when he had to undergo an eye operation so that she could help him. She always lived for others, and was devoted in word and deed to the welfare of her fellowman. She was willing to make any sacrifice if it served to support the Grand Duchess. She was one of those rare people who achieve results through the power of their personality without saying anything. "The Baroness instructs already by her silence," a wise Russian once said to me. She became known to the musical world through her efforts on behalf of Richard Wagner as recorded in his autobiography, *My Life*.

A small circle of stimulating and, I would like to say, noble people, was always gathering in her salon in the evening, demonstrating the truth of Goethe's words; "A noble person attracts noble people." (*Torquato Tasso* I,1) Any baseness she detested, so that she could hardly associate with people who had committed a vile or devious act. If it was a case of human weakness, if there was a good reason — no deceit or lies — she could be very understanding, and her wonderful sense of humor would help her overcome her disapproval.

This reminds me of a small episode in my life. The Grand Duchess was staying in her lovely palace Oranienbaum on the sea. It was summer when the whole household of the court was together in the dining hall for the luncheon, while in winter everyone ate his meal in his own room. The conversation turned to the advantages of Moscow and St. Petersburg. A gentleman who was also a reader for the Grand Duchess set St. Petersburg above Moscow while I preferred Moscow. We got into a heated discussion and I, still rather young, may have expressed my preference quite dogmatically. As we rose from the table I heard a voice behind me quoting Mephistopheles' words; "Know'st thou, my friend, how rude thou art to me?" (*Faust* II, act 2, sc 1)

I thought, I have had enough of people, I will go to the animals. The Grand Duchess had a model farm with cows, and a Finnish cow, Adelma, was my favorite. I went there and got a glass of milk from my favorite cow, when suddenly a figure appeared next to her saying, "Well, my clever Miss?"

It was my opponent in the battle of words. Partly angry, partly amused I returned home, somewhat worried that there could be trouble if he complained to the Grand Duchess about me. The next morning I rushed to the Baroness von Rahden. She stood in front of me, her room bathed in sunshine, flowers surrounding her, flowers on the terrace, and beyond the terrace the view over the Gulf of Finland. With trepidation I told her the sequence of events. Her face assumed a very serious expression and she said, "It is terrible, whenever I'm not around, something happens." Suddenly, like the sun, her delicious humor broke forth and she laughed, laughed so heartily that I, though still subdued, joined in. In the afternoon she called for me and told me, "I have described the incident to the Grand Duchess in as humorous a fashion as possible, and I don't think there will be any unpleasant repercussions." So it was. In the evening, when I saw the Grand Duchess, who had already had a prior report of the encounter, she just said, "I hear you treated your poor colleague badly." She smiled and we went right into our reading material.

The Grand Duchess was still very beautiful. In her white hair, simply parted, she always wore a flower surrounded by white lace. These flowers were especially made for her. She dressed primarily in crepe de Chine, usually a white underdress and over it a gown of colorful silk. I see her before me as she stood at a reception for the poet Alexei Tolstoi, cousin of the Count Leo Tolstoi, writer of several historical dramas and beautiful poems. The Grand Duchess wore a white crepe de Chine dress, in her hair a pink azalea with a few scattered dew drops of diamonds. She looked so enchanting that Alexei Tolstoi later expressed his delight at her appearance, her great intelligence and her equally great goodness.

I had started my position with the Grand Duchess in early November, 1869. My work consisted of always having several days "du jour," which meant I had to be ready to be called to her at any time. Then followed two days when a colleague, Baroness Kleist, was on duty; in addition there were two gentlemen engaged as readers for Russian and scientific works. To reach the Grand Duchess, I first had to go down a stairway, pass through three large halls, ascend the large, red carpeted staircase in the vestibule, and then turn to the right where her rooms were situated. Here was first a lovely anteroom, then the so-called white room, with walls covered with white silk and a white carpet strewed with roses. Several paintings by famous artists were hanging on the wall, among them "The Martyr" by Paul Delaroche, the picture of a beautiful blond girl lying dead in the water, a copy commissioned for the Grand Duchess. The original is, as far as I know, in the Luxembourg in Paris. From there you entered the red room, with red silk damask wall coverings and furniture upholstered in the same material. A mirror door led to a room with light blue silk walls and a carpet in the same color. Here the Grand Duchess used to receive her more intimate friends. The next room was the actual boudoir. It was kept in grey silk because, at that time, this color was considered to be favorable for the eyes.

This was my work place. After the day's duties and often upon the return from a drive, the Grand Duchess would take a rest here, and then I would be called. At first she talked very little. She followed the material I read with great interest; slowly she began to interject a perceptive comment here and there, and sometimes this led to memories from her rich life. I remember that these interruptions occurred with special frequency during the reading of the biography of Christian von Bunsen, the eminent diplomat. I told myself often, "I have the best position. Others see the Grand Duchess at big receptions and admire the tact and understanding revealed in her conversations, while I can admire her here where she feels free from social pressures and informally demonstrates her rich perceptive gift."

The Grand Duchess often had small, intimate dinners in the red room, occasionally for only four persons. Here again, Baroness von Rahden exhibited her unfailing tact. As soon as she noticed that the Grand Duchess was absorbed in a serious discussion with one guest, she would draw the other guest into a conversation to enable the Grand Duchess to pursue a more intimate exchange. The Grand Duchess in her delicate approach knew how to draw out everything great and noble that lies within the human breast. I believe she was one of the most important women of the last century. Her superior intellect was coupled with sincerity and spontaneity.

The contrast in the handling of two similar incidents, told me by Peter Petrovich Semenov, illustrates her tactful, natural response. At a small dinner held by the Empress Maria Alexandrovna, wife of Alexander II, it happened to a gentleman that, while cutting his grouse, it slipped off his plate and landed in the Empress' lap. The gentleman felt terrible, but the Empress appeared to take no notice and continued her conversation in spite of the hen in her lap. The poor gentleman felt a quiet accusation throughout the meal. A similar incident happened at a dinner given by the Grand Duchess. Her neighbor let his cutlet slip from his plate onto her dress. She jumped up, shook the corpus delicti off with joyous laughter, and had her servant wipe the spots off her dress. Everyone took his seat again in good humor, and the unfortunate one was rid of his embarrassment.

Since the Grand Duchess had an extraordinary love for music, she always employed a pianist and a singer who would then live in the Palais. She did much to further the career of Anton Rubinstein and continued to follow it with great interest. In 1862 she established the conservatory in St. Petersburg and appointed Anton Rubinstein as its director. In 1859 he had already been appointed director of the Music Society through her influence. She immediately drew prominent teachers from Russia and Germany to the conservatory, for example the singer, Mrs. Nissen-Salomon, who trained great artists. At some of the Grand Duchess' musical evenings we were enchanted by the beautiful alto voice of the famous singer Lavroska, who later married the Duke Tserselev. The Grand Duchess always had several protégés who attended the conservatory at her expense. All the large opera houses in St. Petersburg, Moscow, Kiev, etc. had leading singers who had been trained at the conservatory in St. Petersburg.[3]

Among the artists who had been invited to the Palais Michel was Richard Wagner. He had directed six concerts and had amazed the audience by conducting Beethoven's symphonies without scores. He wrote more about this in his memoirs, *My Life.* Clara Schumann had also been invited, but both came before my time. When I started my position with the Grand Duchess, Joseph Rubinstein was living in the Palais. He was an ardent admirer of Richard Wagner and was working on the piano transcription of *Die Meistersinger.* He often came and played it for me, sometimes the whole piano extract.

Basically, we ladies at the court led a strange, almost lonesome life, since each of us had her own, closed off apartment where we even had all our meals by ourselves. However, through the kindness of Baroness von Rahden I hardly felt this loneliness. From the very beginning she took care that I would not get homesick. On December 24th (the 12th on the Russian calendar) I was sitting with Miss von Rahden, happy to be able to talk with her, when the chambermaid came and asked me to go to my apartment down the corridor. I was angry at having been disturbed, but I went. What a surprise was waiting for me! My room shone bright in the light of a lovely Christmas tree with many candles. On the table were numerous presents, all decorated with red ribbons because that was my favorite color. Among them was a collection of the poems of the Russian poet Chomyakov. They are so beautiful that they inspired me to learn the Russian language. All this had been prepared by Baroness Rahden. She now came herself, accompanied by Princess Lvov who also brought gifts for me.

December 27th was the birthday of Grand Duchess Helene. The Baroness explained the customs of the court to me in advance. Among other things, she told me that one had to attend the church service and kiss the Grand Duchess' hand as congratulation. "How dreadful!" I objected, "I have never yet kissed anyone's hand and I don't want to." The Baroness answered with a smile, "You will do it, and there will be a time, when you will consider yourself lucky to be allowed to kiss her hand." And so it was. My love and admiration for the noble, intelligent, kind Duchess grew from day to day. The Grand Duchess held "Cercle" on her birthday and had a kind, understanding word for each person.

Reading to her was my greatest pleasure. I now had permission to select books at the book dealer, which were sent to the Grand Duchess on approval. In this manner I had selected an interesting biography and had begun to read it to the Grand Duchess. I was astonished when my colleague, Baroness Kleist, told me that she was reading to her from that book when she had her turn. Sadly I hurried to the Baroness and told her of my disappointment. She admonished me very sternly, "You should be glad that the book provided an enjoyable hour for the Grand Duchess; who read it to her is immaterial. The main thing is that she got some relaxation." Rather ashamed, I withdrew and resolved to practice self-denial. Editha von Rahden was for all of us the best example in that respect.

Now came the Lenten period, which in Russia is ushered in by the preceding "butter week." Every day one eats blinis with caviar, a kind of egg pancake prepared differently each day. During this period, the Finns come to St. Petersburg with their low sleds pulled by small horses, and even members of the aristocracy do not disdain being driven around in these vehicles.

The fun of sledding down icy hills also begins at this time. The gentleman sits in front, and the lady kneels behind him, her arms around his neck. I tried it once in the garden of the Palais Michel with the grandson of the Grand Duchess, Prince George of Mecklenburg-Strelitz.. However, I am too timid and I did not like it. In the evenings one rode in troikas: big sleds pulled by two horses firmly harnessed and a third one in a loose harness but which still has to pull very hard. A coachman is in control. Our goal was the islands in the Neva where there was dancing in the restaurants. The court danced in the Palais on Yelaghin.

It was interesting to see the grand parade of the pupils of the Imperial educational institutions. It happened only once a year, during the "butter week." The girls, naturally, looked forward to it all year long. They all wore brown dresses with white collars and sleeves; coachmen and footmen were in the court livery: red and gold. There was the Katherine Institute, founded by Empress Katharina, where the nobles were educated free of charge, the Mary Institute, under the patronage of Grand Duchess Helene, also Smolny, and many others, all of them administered under the name "Institutes of the Empress." Usually a gentleman and a lady were chief administrators. Miss von Rahden had recently been elected as administrator.

After the "butter week" came six weeks of strict fasting. During this time dried mushrooms would hang in the stalls in long chains and be sold. From the homes spread an unpleasant odor of fried oil. Milk was also forbidden for those who held strict observance. It was replaced with almond milk in the elegant mansions. Delicious fish from the Black Sea was sold frozen.

The theaters were closed until Easter, but concerts took place. The Grand Duchess had invited Ferdinand Hiller, director of the Guerzenich-Concerts in Cologne, to St. Petersburg where he was a guest in the Palais Michel. He conducted several concerts and also played during the evening get-togethers at the Grand Duchess Helene's. Hiller improvised beautifully at the piano, and often improvised an accompaniment to Friedrich Devrient's recitations. I have never forgotten the superb performance by them of the Uhland ballad: "Das Glück von Edenhall." Devrient looked like his mother, the great actress Wilhelmine Schröder-Devrient. He was also very gifted, but he did not live up to his promise.

Hiller was a pleasant companion and I had been loaned to him, so to speak, as "Cicerone." A carriage and a sled were at his disposal so that we could reach the attractions of St. Petersburg easily.

He was particularly excited by the Hermitage. The Spanish hall with the magnificent Murillos, the Rembrandt hall, the Russian hall with Ayvasovski's "Ninth Wave," the gallery of Peter the Great — everything delighted Hiller. He also liked the furnishings of the halls. The comfortable sofas invited you to take a rest. I suggested that he take a ride in the reindeer sled of the Samoyedes on the frozen Neva. I had done this at one time and described it to him in great detail, but other duties prevented me from accompanying him on this excursion. In the afternoon he returned to me appalled. "My dearest," he said, "this was terrible. I am amazed that I stand here in front of you all in one piece. The sled was only a kind of table top laid on barrels. On this I had to sit sideways with my legs hanging down and the Samoyede sat in front with a long pole guiding six reindeer who raced away at full gallop. There was nothing to hold on to, and I clutched the table top as best I could, terribly afraid that I would be thrown onto the ice. Oh, my dearest, it was dreadful! The guide even offered to go around a second time, but I declined with thanks." After he had recovered from the initial shock, we both had a good laugh, and the Grand Duchess, too, was amused when she listened to the tale of this adventure in the evening.

Hiller left, deeply impressed by the spirit of the Grand Duchess, and returned to Cologne with a picture of her, which he had long desired, and a valuable ring with a big sapphire. He later wrote an article published in the *Deutsche Rundschau* — "Palais Michel" — in which he mentioned all of us. After several years he sent a book to Baroness von Rahden with the following dedication: "Take this book from me from afar, we'll meet again, perhaps on another star." He died in 1885, only a short time before Miss von Rahden.

Easter is the most important and holiest festival in Russia. The whole court assembled in the chapel of the Palais Michel. We ladies were all dressed in white; many had flowers in their hair. The Grand Duchess made her entrance at eleven o'clock in the evening and the Mass began. At midnight the resurrection was proclaimed with shots from a cannon and the ringing of the bells of St. Isaac, followed by a procession through the gallery of the Palais and back to the chapel. I, thinking that one was supposed to join the procession, followed along and did not notice that I was the only one walking behind the choir boys until we were in the gallery. It was too late to turn around, so I valiantly kept on going and returned to the chapel in the same way. A short service with beautiful singing once again celebrated the resurrection. At the end of the service one exchanged the threefold kisses during which one person says, "Christ is risen," and the other answers, "Verily, he is risen."

After the solemn festivity and the long standing, one was quite tired and happy to participate in the consecrated meal. It consisted of eggs, blessed by the priest, ham, and "pass-cha," a mixture of sour cream, eggs, sugar and spices served in the shape of a pyramid. Many other dishes followed and I did not get back to my room until four in the morning. During that night the clergy processed with burning candles around the churches throughout the city, and the people waited on the church steps with baskets of eggs, ham, and pass-cha to have them blessed. On Easter Sunday people in the streets would exchange kisses, and this custom made no distinction of rank — it held whether you met the Tsar or a beggar. One of my highly esteemed friends happened to meet the Tsar and, somewhat embarrassed, had to adhere to this custom.

Easter was late that year, and therefore the move to Kamenny-Ostrov followed soon afterwards. Kamenny-Ostrov (Stone Island) was one of the three palaces which the Grand Duchess had received as widow's residences after her husband's death. It was not customary to give the widow of a Duke more than one palace, but at the death of Michael, the young Grand Duchess had already earned such high esteem and love by her diligent study of Russian culture and her generous contributions to the welfare of the people, that the Tsar provided her not only with Palais Michel but also with Oranienbaum and Kamenny-Ostrov. The latter is an island in the river Neva. A short but lovely promenade leads to the beautifully situated palace. The living and reception rooms are on the first floor, the bedrooms upstairs. One part of the palace was not used but kept as a historical shrine. Here were the rooms which Alexander I occupied before his trip to Taganrog. Everything in them was kept just as he had left it. In addition, there was the room of the historic meeting with Caulincourt in 1812. Behind the building was a park with delightful paths along the shore of the river. The park formed a peninsula and its prettiest spot was at the tip. The Grand Duchess often selected this place to sit and relax.

It was a beautiful spring. The nightingales sang every evening. The Russian nightingale is not the same species as the German one. It is called "sprosser" and has a particularly strong voice. I could listen to the bird for hours. The white nights of Russia have a very special charm. I often felt as if a veil had been spread over us; the trees and flowers were sleeping and dreaming, and when the first ray of sun appeared they raised themselves up and joyfully looked to the new day. Then the nightingale fell silent but all the other birds began a concert. There was music and exultation without end. Whenever I stayed up until this hour, I was so elated that I could not sleep, my heart overflowing with grateful joy over the wonders I had experienced.

On days when I was not on duty, Editha von Rahden often invited me to join her and the other ladies for rides into the countryside and refreshments in the garden of a small restaurant, Prostoquash. We usually ate sour milk which seemed particularly delicious in Russia. Even the smallest dacha had an ice cellar, and tasty cold soups and the popular sour milk were served.

The brother of the Grand Duchess Helene, Prince August von Württemberg, who had a commission in the Prussian military service, paid a visit that spring. With him came two officers, von Lindquist and von Arnim. An entertaining life began; there were excursions, dramatic presentations in the small theater of the palace, singing, and dancing. Each morning I would see the brother and sister from my window as they walked with quick steps up and down the promenade in animated conversation . In spite of the great geographical distance, they had remained closely attached to each other.

Two more visitors came to Kamenny-Ostrov that year: Count Alexander Keyserling and his daughter, Helene, the godchild of the Grand Duchess. In the country the whole court takes the noon meal together which gave us opportunities to hear Count Keyserling talk. I almost want to say, he was a universal genius: scholar, researcher, extremely musical, with a gift for adding spice to the conversation with his wonderful sense of humor. He had been curator at the Dorpat University. He told us about a French writer, author of a book, *Sur l'art de diriger nos rêves* (The Art of Influencing Our Dreams). This gentleman had tried to stimulate the various senses of the sleeper. A friend had told him much about a certain lady with whom he enjoyed dancing to a particular waltz. The writer had a music box manufactured which played this waltz and secretly put it into his friend's bedroom, set to play at three o'clock. The next morning the friend said, "Imagine, I dreamt last night about that lady and again we danced the same waltz." Another experiment with the sense of taste did not succeed.

Count Keyserling had been a fellow student and roommate of Otto von Bismarck. He would relate many of Bismarck's pranks. One morning Keyserling was getting ready to get a piece of clothing from his wardrobe when Bismarck jumped out of it — in which state of dress one can imagine.

A delightful deception originated with him, which just recently, in March 1925, appeared in the newspaper under the heading, "Bismarck remembrances." Count Keyserling was not mentioned even though he was the unwitting cause of this prank. Keyserling had gone away on a trip for a few days when a card came for him announcing the visit of relatives from Courland who had not met him previously. When they arrived, Bismarck received them warmly and kept them in the belief that he was Keyserling. He asked about uncles, aunts, and cousins whom he had never known, and answered their questions about relatives so skillfully that no one became suspicious. He entertained the guests most generously and after a few days they left happily and wrote their cousin, Count Keyserling, a sincere thank-you letter. Only when Keyserling read the letter was the adventure revealed. He was greatly amused by the trick.

It was a pleasure to listen to Keyserling and to watch his animated features as he recounted some of his experiences. Consequently, there usually was a large group of listeners gathered around him. Once the conversation happened on Friederike Gossmann and I mentioned that she had the Turkish proverb, "this too shall pass," on her wall. Count Keyserling expressed his pleasure at these words and added that they are suitable for good times as well as for bad; in the former they are a warning, in the latter a consolation.

When summer came, the whole court moved to Oranienbaum. This splendid palace on the Gulf of Finland was once occupied by Peter III and Catherine II. Peter III had a small fortress built for himself which still existed when I was there, and there were many other reminders of him. The palace offered a view of the sea and was situated on a large terrace planted with beautiful flowers. Not far from it stood the so-called Chinese Palais where the Grand Duchess Katharina lived with her family. Down by the sea were the bath houses. Each of us ladies was assigned a certain hour for her bath and picked up and returned by a carriage.

Many visitors from St. Petersburg came to Oranienbaum, and here I became acquainted with His Excellency Peter Petrovich Semenov and his wife. At that time he was President of the Geographical Society. Semenov had studied in Berlin with Karl Ritter, the famous geographer, and had been his favorite student. His first wife died young, and he undertook a research excursion to Asia. A 15,350 ft. mountain in Turkestan bears his name. He had to spend the winter in a Siberian town where he met Dostoevski. He and the Russian writer became close friends. Dostoevski had just been released from the horrible "House of the Dead" which he describes in his book by that title, and was about to be married and return to St. Petersburg. Since Dostoevski was penniless, Semenov assisted him in realizing his plans. Semenov himself continued his travels through Asia before returning to St. Petersburg. There he met Elizabeth Andreyevna, daughter of the prominent statesman Zablotsky, married her, and became a very happy husband and father of one daughter and several sons. All his children inherited his intellectual gifts. His wife became my intimate friend and we remained true friends until her death in 1916.

Mrs. Semenov had enjoyed an excellent education and spoke, like all cultured Russians, flawless French, English and German. In addition, she had acquired a knowledge of Italian. Her extreme shyness and modesty prevented her from presenting her true self in a large group. Most people had no idea what treasure was hidden inside her little body. Her shyness also kept her from feeling comfortable at court, and however much she esteemed Grand Duchess Helene and admired Miss von Rahden, she usually persuaded her husband to go to the palace without her. He, on the other hand, felt perfectly at home there, and all members of the court were delighted when he came to spend a little time at Oranienbaum.

Mr. Semenov allowed his children complete freedom. It was his opinion that this was the only way their individual characters would develop. They were in the habit of getting up and going to bed as they pleased. As a result, one of their many servants, Marina — a favorite of mine — had the sole occupation to stand all day by the samovar in the dining room and serve tea to the family members as they came and went.

Other guests at Oranienbaum were Prince Meshcherski and his friend Mikluko-Maclay. The latter, though still young, had already made a name for himself as explorer. He had spent a time in New Guinea and had succeeded in making friends with the cannibals there, the Papuas. He had won their trust by landing at the coast at night. In the morning the superstitious Papuas believed he had fallen from heaven and worshipped him like a god. He was intending to return to New Guinea. Prince Meshcherski was one of those idealists you often meet in Russia. He wanted to free his people and make them happy, but in the end he did not possess the necessary energy to carry out his intentions.

Discontent was beginning to seethe among the people at that time. Nihilism had taken root. Its followers usually were distinguishing themselves by cutting their hair short. This was probably the reason why the Grand Duchess asked me, shortly after my arrival, to let my hair grow long. I was still keeping it short since the unhappy experience in Hungary. Her wish was naturally my command.

During the coming months I had occasion to watch the nihilists closely. The Grand Duchess had set up student kitchens, where students could obtain a good meal for very little money. She had selected a committee of ladies and determined that every day one of them had to serve in these kitchens and supervise the proceedings. All days were covered except Sunday when no one wanted to give up her freedom. As usual, Miss von Rahden stood ready to take the unpopular day and serve in one of the kitchens. I also served on Sundays. In St. Petersburg, every faculty had its own building. The medical school was on the island Vassili Ostrov as were the Academies of the Arts and Sciences. I worked Sundays in the medical kitchen where a great number of nihilists ate. I admit that the ladies did not make an agreeable impression on me, but among the male students were several interesting personalities. Later on I occasionally met young physicians who had taken their meals in my kitchen. Miss von Rahden, who took a great interest in these kitchens, once experienced a kind of revolution in the medical dining hall and was forced to climb on a chair to calm the excited students with a speech, which she finally accomplished.

The stay in Oranienbaum is among my most cherished memories. On the same high elevation as the palace was a wonderful spot from which one could look over the Gulf of Finland to the island Kronstadt, then the seat of the Russian admiralty. I sat here often pondering the miraculous turns of my life. After a winter in the barely civilized environment of Hungary I was, in the same year, led to the far north and welcomed into a highly cultured circle.

After spending the day exploring nature in all directions and picking strawberries or mushrooms, one gathered in the evening for animated conversation. The Grand Duchess did not always participate in the social evenings, and I loved those times best, because I could devote myself entirely to her. After the day's work — and there was always plenty of this for her — she was perhaps a little tired and sought recreation in literature. Sometimes she would retire early. Then I would read a lighter book, for instance *Wilhelm Wolfschild* by Panthenius, an amusing description of life in Courland. After the Grand Duchess had fallen asleep, I quietly left the room to notify the chambermaids and retire myself.

Whenever Anton Rubinstein was staying in St. Petersburg, he would make frequent visits to Oranienbaum. It was wonderful to listen to him play; there was a poetic feeling in his playing which I experienced with no other pianist. On one occasion, Joseph Rubinstein, the great admirer of Wagner, conducted a performance of the spinning song and the ballad from T*he Flying Dutchman.*

Into this joyful existence dropped France's declaration of war on Germany in the year 1870, and our "Prussians," as Prince August of Württemberg and his military escorts were called, left the same day. We missed them very much but could not allow ourselves to dwell on this loss because the suspense and anxiety about the progress of the war took hold of everyone.

The Grand Duchess Helene was infectious in her youthful enthusiasm when the erroneous news of the fall of Weissenburg was retracted. She was interested in every detail, even the nourishment of the soldiers. For instance, she had a sample of a new product, pea sausage, sent to her, and I had the pleasure of sharing with her the first pot of soup made from it.

The time had come for my vacation trip to Hamburg. When she engaged me, the Grand Duchess had promised, "You love your country, and that is good. You must see it every year, and I will give you the means to do so." She kept this promise. Strangely, my trip went quite smoothly. I travelled via Königsberg and Berlin, and experienced no obstacles. On my travels I have always encountered friendly people who showed concern for me and assisted me at customs inspections, etc.

I spent an interesting but sorrowful time at my sister's. Her three sons were at the front, and if there was no news from one of them, we tiptoed around the house avoiding one another, because nobody wanted to express his fears to the others. Our fears were groundless at that time; however, three months after the victory at Sedan my youngest nephew was killed in an attack. This was a great sorrow for all of us.

The four weeks of my vacation passed quickly. When I left, my sister presented me with photographs of our great military commanders. Knowing of my great admiration for Baroness von Rahden, she also gave me a beautiful cyclamen plant for her. This became an annual custom since it was the Baroness' favorite flower.

By the time I returned, the Grand Duchess had moved back to the Palais Michel. She listened with great sympathy to my report. She was particularly interested in the photographs of the commanders, and it gave me pleasure to present these pictures to her. Her brother, Prince August, was naturally one of them.

The Grand Duchess always saw to it that those around her got involved in a broad spectrum of concerns. Therefore, she found an activity for me. One of the many institutions she had founded was a boarding school for young ladies connected with a large day school. The top teachers came here and lectured in German, French, English and Russian. One of the ladies had to take notes, and those notes were then hectographed and given to all the auditors. These young ladies came from the aristocracy of Russia, and the Grand

Duchess had appointed the former governess of her daughter, Mademoiselle Troubat, head mistress.

At the wishes of the Grand Duchess, I participated in the lectures of this institute and assumed the note-taking for the lectures in literature, which covered German literature from its very beginning. In addition, I gave German lessons to the advanced students on days when I was not on duty in the palace. I had them write compositions and similar assignments and was often amazed how gifted my Russian pupils were. Through this activity I met many lovely, interesting girls and frequently attended their dancing lessons which were led by the famous ballet master Felix Kshesinsky. I was particularly fascinated by the graceful mazurka.

The ballet played a large role in St. Petersburg at that time. Of course, Russia has always produced the greatest dancers. Every Thursday a full ballet was performed at the opera house. One evening I saw the opera *A Life for the Tsar* by Glinka. I loved Glinka's music. In the second act at a Polish ball the mazurka was danced so gracefully in magnificent costumes that I decided the mazurka was the most beautiful dance I knew. The opera has a historical subject. It tells the story of a Polish invasion of Russia. The Poles hire a Russian peasant, Susanin, to lead them to the Tsar. He, however, leads them astray and most of them lose their lives and he himself gets murdered. The last act closes with the people rejoicing, bells ringing, and the national anthem being played. The custom of "swinging" is also represented on stage. If the people want to honor someone, they carry him on their shoulders, put him on a huge sheet which has to be held by a large crowd, and then throw him in the air by pulling the sheet. This type of veneration sometimes caused ill effects for the celebrant, and some are even supposed to have died as a result of it.

I was no longer living in the side wing of the Palais Michel but in an apartment directly above the rooms of the Grand Duchess. After reading late in the evening I no longer had to go down the stairs and through the large number of dark halls which were illuminated by only two candles. The appearance of these halls was then so spooky that two young ladies-in-waiting once returned and asked to be accompanied after I had told them a scary but true story. The story was one which Mrs. Mackintosh had told me in England about a young girl in York.

The young lady was returning from a visit to a friend who lived across from the York cathedral. To shorten the way, she cut through the cathedral. The service had ended and before she could walk all the way through the cathedral she found herself locked in. She knew that nobody would worry about her since she often spent the night at her girlfriend's. Being a brave young person, she made herself a place to sleep with the available pillows and was ready to calmly await the next morning. The moon shone bright and illumined the graves of the crusaders, the knights whose likenesses were etched on their tombs, representing them sleeping and with crossed feet, to signify their return from a crusade. All was quiet except for the rustling of a few mice and the "prisoner" finally became tired and fell asleep. Suddenly she was awakened by a strange song from the altar. She saw a white figure who, half screaming, half singing, uttered indistinguishable words. She crouched down so as not to be seen, but to her dismay, the figure came down the stairs and closer and closer towards her. She recalled a rumor that a madman sometimes took the white priest's gown from the sacristy and imitated the religious ceremonies, but she had always taken this for a legend.

Unfortunately she now had to believe this story. She had also heard that the man could be subdued by singing. Softly, with trembling voice, she began to sing a hymn. He quietly stepped towards her, knelt down, laid his head in her lap and fell asleep. Occasionally he would awake and she would sing again until he slept. In this way the night passed. The next morning, when someone came to clean, she was released from her dreadful situation. Since she had strong nerves, there were no lasting effects — no illness or white hair. It is understandable that those two ladies-in-waiting became apprehensive after hearing this tale.

After the war ended we had a lovely visitor in St. Petersburg who brought much life into the Palais Michel. She was the daughter of Count Keyserling: intelligent, lively, musical, and with a great sense of humor, like her father. When we were reading the scene between Mephistopheles and the student from Goethe's *Faust*, she commented, "Mephistopheles is really a delightful person, much more interesting than the others." A long discussion followed about the common observation that the so-called "good persons" are often quite boring while the bad ones can be the life of the party. I now think otherwise and believe in the power of the good, yet, I have always pondered over Goethe's poem, "Wanderers Gemüthsruhe" (Wayfarer's Composure) in the collection, *West-Östlicher Divan*:

> *About that which is base*
> *No one should complain;*
> *For it has power*
> *whatever one may say.*
>
> *In evil it bestirs*
> *itself to highest gain,*
> *with righteousness it deals*
> *according to its whim.*
> *Wanderer! — Against such odds*
> *do you dare resist?*
> *Whirlwind and dry manure,*
> *let them raise the dust.*

Throughout my life it has been my observation that the "dry manure" did not have any lasting effect. It raises some dust, but with courage and trust in God, evil will be overcome. "Never submit — summon the arms of the gods!" (Goethe's poem: "Beherzigung" — Reflection.)

ఈ

The following spring, we stayed at Kamenny-Ostrov for only a short time. When we moved again to Oranienbaum I was housed in a different wing in a much larger apartment. I had a young singer in my care, who was being trained at the conservatory by Mrs. Nissen-Salomon as protégé of the Grand Duchess Helene. She was later engaged at the opera house and had great success. Our rooms were on the ground floor looking out on the garden, and it was especially delightful when the Grand Duchess rode by in her little carriage and called us to the window. In this manner she once brought me a charming Berzelius lamp which enabled me to make hot water for tea at any time.

In late summer I travelled to Germany for my annual visit while the Grand Duchess took a vacation in Italy, accompanied by the Countess Keyserling. Upon my return I found the Grand Duchess not as healthy as before. She had hurt her arm while climbing into the carriage, and the wound took a very long time to heal. While I was reading to her one day, her face suddenly became so red that she immediately called for the doctor. He diagnosed erysipelas. Since I had already seen her in this condition, the Grand Duchess was less self-conscious with me than with others, and she called me every day to spend some time with her. She had to wear a mask of linen which was to relieve the unbearable itching on her cheeks. She suffered everything with great patience; only once she cried out quite pitifully; "What a poor dog I am!" She maintained her lively interest in literature, but listening for a long time was strenuous, therefore, she asked me to read a page silently and then tell her the contents.

In the summer of 1872 the Grand Duchess tried to recuperate at Oranienbaum. Everything was done to cheer her up, but she did not gain back her strength completely. The doctor ordered a second trip to Italy. When she returned, she often talked about her aunt, Princess Catherine of Württemberg, who had been the wife of King Jerome of Westphalia, the brother of Napoleon I. Grand Duchess Helene was especially amused by the extravagance of her aunt's wardrobe. She described, for instance, the innumerable pairs of shoes which were lined up in her aunt's bedroom, and she laughed so heartily that any thought that we could lose her was far from my mind.

In early January, 1873, she returned from an outing and said to me, "Imagine, I threw up during the drive." The natural ways of the Grand Duchess, her sometimes frank, outspoken manner, gave her personality a special charm. She could joke with the chamber maids, and the head maid, Miss Klein, once came to me in utter delight, "Her Imperial Highness called me 'Hans Bock' today." This particular chamber maid was usually very stiff and dignified. When I was called to the Grand Duchess and ran, skipping a couple of steps, she would throw her head back and admonish me indignantly, "Please, more measured pace!"

The evening after that same outing, which was to be her last, the sickness took a serious turn. The next day, the Grand Duchess asked me to get the silhouettes of *A Midsummer Night's Dream* by Paul Konevka from the library. After receiving them, she asked for the second set which did not exist. When she kept asking for it over and over again, we realized that her fever had reached its climax. I sat by her in the evening. Suddenly she said, "I wish I could eat those good beans now. We called them sow beans." Then she slept a little more. Her personal physician was in the next room, and on the other side was the chamber maid who was on duty. Nevertheless, I did not want to leave her and stayed for a long time in the dimly lit room. A storm was howling, and I saw shadows which took the shape of a coffin for me. Finally I had to go to my room, but I did so with a heavy heart.

The next day a telegram was sent to Professor Bamberger in Vienna, for her condition was now critical. All the family gathered in the bedroom. Baroness von Rahden remained by the bed and passed her all that the doctor had ordered. Everything imaginable was done to give her some relief, but on the same day — the 9th of January by the old and the 21st by the new calendar — this noble woman closed her eyes forever. We all knelt down in reverent silence.

What I did those next days, I cannot say. I had lost infinitely much, and walked around as in a dream. I heard that Professor Bamberger had come to take care of the embalmment. I saw the deceased taken to another room, saw the painter who had come to draw her features one more time. She lay on the bed beautiful, serious, as if asleep. After Bamberger had completed his work the next day, she was laid out in the chapel, and the public was permitted to view her for several hours each day. She had been so popular with the people that they all came, all to see the beloved Grand Duchess one more time. Two ladies-in-waiting were always standing at the head and foot of the coffin. They were relieved after one hour, except for Editha von Rahden who always stayed close to her mistress for two hours. The chapel was brightly illumined, lights everywhere. When the chapel was closed to the public, a Requiem Mass was celebrated. For the lovely hymn "Zum ewigen Gedächtnis" (Eternal memory, blessed repose, to her, eternal memory) we knelt down, holding candles in our hands. The words and melody of this hymn are truly moving. The Requiem Mass was also celebrated at night, at which time this service made such a sublime impression, that one really felt removed from this earth.

The viewing continued for several more days. Some of the former ladies-in-waiting came to take their place as servants by their beloved mistress once more. Then the deceased was taken to her final resting place in the church of the Peter and Paul Fortress. All Russian rulers since Peter the Great and their relatives are buried here.

The church was open day and night, and two soldiers were always standing guard. I often went there during that winter on ice cold, moonlit nights, across the frozen Neva, to gather courage and strength in this holy place. At midnight, the carillon in the tower of the fortress church would play, "Ich bete an die Macht der Liebe" (O pow'r of love, all else transcending). The hours in that wonderful, solemn space are forever etched in my memory.

As the Grand Duchess had done all she could for Russia during her life, so she provided for the Russian people at her death. She determined in her will that her wealth was to be used to establish a large hospital for internal diseases with her personal physician as director. Thus this magnanimous, noble woman will never be forgotten.

The daughter, Grand Duchess Katharina, invited Baroness von Rahden to continue to stay in her apartment in the Palais Michel, and Editha von Rahden made it her business to carry on in the spirit of the deceased. I myself received my salary for another year as well as everything required for the time of mourning.

The Baroness showed concern for each one who suffered from the great void. I met her in the library the evening after the burial. She was outwardly quite composed, and her first question was, "What can I do for you?" I had not given it a thought. In my grief over the passing of the esteemed and loved one, everything around me seemed dark. Her question aroused me and I declared I would like to stay in St. Petersburg. I wished to be near Miss von Rahden.

"The wife of the Minister of Justice, Countess Pahlen, is looking for someone to continue music and language studies with her oldest, sixteen-year-old daughter. A French governess is in the house for the younger children. Would this position be acceptable to you?" asked the Baroness.

She had once said to me, "Often, when people are in uncertain situations, God presents them an opportunity on a silver platter. If they grasp it, all is well; if not, they must suffer the consequences and cannot complain." So I grasped it, and accepted without hesitation.

ENDNOTES

[1] "A new era for art was dawning within the palace of the Grand Duchess Helen...A truly remarkable woman! I never in my life met her equal...It must also be remarked that her entourage was remarkable; the Baroness Raden...was accounted among the cleverest women of the times, and the Grand Duchess owed much to her...After his death (Grand Duke Michael's) the palace of the Grand Duchess became the centre toward which flowed the current of all intellectual life of the capital."
Ref. 9 pp. 58-60

[2] "The wife of Grand Duke Michael, Elena Pavlovna, played an important part in Russian public life,... actively helping the work of emancipation of the serfs."[Ref. 1 p.171n] "Alexander was subject to liberal influence in his closest circle. His brother Constantine had become an ardent supporter of emancipation. Possibly even more effective was his aunt, the Grand Duchess Elena Pavlovna...Her palace was a centre of liberal ideas...The experts prepared the legislation, but it was largely due to the advice of Constantine and Elena that the Tsar was induced to force it through."[Ref. 1 p.335]

[3] I have already spoken of the enthusiasm kindled in the hearts of those who, under the patronage of the Grand Duchess Helen, had labored on behalf of the Russian Musical Society and its early classes in her palace....The best musical talent in St. Petersburg was offered almost free of charge....Zaremba, Leschetizki, Nissen-Salomon, Wieniawski, and others asked but a ruble a lesson in the classes at the Michael Palace. And these classes were soon crowded with pupils of different ages and degrees of social standing....An orchestra and choruses were organized....The Grand Duchess took a deep interest in this enterprise; she frequented the classes, contributed to their support, and bestowed her patronage not only by smiles and gracious demeanor, but by substantial pecuniary aid."[Ref. 9 pp.95-96]

RUSSIAN ENCOUNTERS

The very next week I started my new occupation, for idleness was unbearable. The Countess Pahlen was still a beautiful woman, the mother of four daughters and three sons. My employment was most enjoyable. The oldest daughter, Marussia, (pet name for Marie) was musically gifted and we both loved to play four-hand piano pieces together. The next two daughters were very beautiful. I had them only for German and English lessons. The youngest children had their nanny, Mademoiselle Guinand. She was very pleasant and always helpful and we became friends. We took all our meals with the family. Only in the evening were we by ourselves in our little salon. Then we read Pasquale's *Palais Royal*.

The Russian houses are very spacious and elegantly decorated and furnished; every room and hall is heated, so that they are comfortable even in winter.

I had already formed several friendships in St. Petersburg and received frequent invitations for the evening. Even the Grand Duchess Katharina was kind enough to occasionally ask me for dinner. Her children had grown up. Baroness Rahden tried to ease the year of mourning for her by inviting a small group every Wednesday for programs such as lectures by prominent persons. One of these was a pastor of the Herrenhut Brothers, named Hans, a gracious, intelligent man who spoke about the relationship between the Old and New Testament.

Then followed lectures by Mr. Semenov, President of the Geographical Society, and a connoisseur of art. He himself owned a gallery of paintings by Dutch masters which went to the Hermitage after his death. He also had a collection of photographs of paintings found in European museums, and he brought the appropriate copies to each lecture. One after the other, we covered the German, Italian, Spanish, and Russian schools. These were memorable evenings. Another entertainment for these Wednesday evenings was play reading. We read dramas and comedies with distributed roles. Needless to say, I did not miss any of these gatherings.

At Easter, Grand Duchess Katharina again invited me to participate in the Mass and the subsequent breakfast. For this occasion she used the large halls of the Palais; otherwise she occupied only a wing of the Palais in her simple, unpretentious way.

To my regret, my stay in St. Petersburg was interrupted when the Pahlen family moved to their estate in Courland. Their lovely manor house stood at the shores of a small lake. Life was simple but very comfortable. In the afternoons we would take excursions into the nearby woods in three carriages, to our great amusement.

For a family celebration I wanted to contribute a small surprise. I picked the Singspiel *"Der arme Heinrich"* (Poor Henry) composed for children by Karl Reinecke. I played the accompaniment on the piano. Scheduling the rehearsals presented some difficulty since the plan should remain a surprise and the parents were usually at home. I had no choice but to take the children into the woods and conduct the rehearsals there.

This provided great amusement for the little troop. Mademoiselle Guinand and the tutor also had their parts in the play. Mademoiselle's German with a French accent, and the little disturbances, unavoidable out in nature, gave plenty of cause for laughter. Our project did not interfere with the regular, scheduled lessons, or with visits to neighbors.

Courland, like Russia itself, is very hospitable. Marussia and I spent a few days with her aunt, the elder Duchess Pahlen. The Duchess was unusually gracious. Her youngest daughter, who became the Countess Lieven, had some outrageous ideas which kept life from getting dull. One time she brought her horse up the stairs into the salon, to the amazement and horror of the guests. Later she became a follower of Lord Radstock who had come to St. Petersburg to win converts to his sect. I got to know him too. He was a good person, but in my opinion somewhat narrow in his piety. The aristocrats admired him very much, and he gave weekly Bible classes in different homes. I preferred visits to the various parish houses, which were there the true centers of culture. We sometimes spent whole days with the old Prior Raison. He expressed to me his displeasure with the anti-semitism which he saw in his diocese. He was especially upset by the way the Jews were mocked.

</33

Refreshed, we returned to St. Petersburg. Baroness von Rahden resumed her interesting evenings which provided welcome stimulation to all participants.

I now met Mrs. Abaza, the wife of the Minister of Finance. Earlier she had been a singer at the court of the Grand Duchess Helene who had called her to St. Petersburg from Berlin. If her marriage was troubled, she did not reveal it to the public, but she compensated herself for her husband's frequent absences through interesting musical evenings which she arranged in her home. We repeated that Singspiel by Reinecke on one occasion, except that the parts played by Mademoiselle Guinand and the tutor were taken by other children.

My life was greatly enriched by my contacts with the daughter of Count Keyserling who had become engaged to Baron Taube and was in St. Petersburg to make some purchases. I met her frequently at Baroness von Rahden's, and we developed a friendship which has lasted to this day.

Countess Pahlen and I had agreed that I would leave in the spring, but I did not know yet where I would go. My sister begged me to return to Germany. But, as dear as she was to me, I could not imagine being apart from Editha von Rahden. Again, as happened so often in my life, an opportunity presented itself "on a silver platter." The sister of Mr. Semenov, Mrs. von Grot, passing through on the way to her country estate in the Ryazan Province, was looking for a lady for her two daughters. She set a day and time for a meeting at her house and engaged me on the spot for three months. Once more I celebrated the wonderful Easter festival in the Palais Michel and the day after Easter with the Pahlen family, and then, in May, 1874, we set out on the journey to the estate of the family von Grot.

We started by train. The first rest stop was in Moscow. Unfortunately, we stayed only twenty-four hours. I had hoped to enjoy the city and its innumerable churches. I did see the Kremlin with its magnificent old-Russian rooms and visited the mountains from which Napolean watched Moscow burning.

The next day we rode only a short distance by train, then we continued in the family's own "tarantass". This is a closed carriage with no springs whatsoever. Since the roads are often terrible I was actually in pain during this bumpy ride and was happy when we stopped and ate the lunch we had brought along. We ate at an open spot, surrounded by woods. The inevitable samovar insured that we could refresh ourselves with tea. To my surprise, the old servant Sergei took a big box out of the carriage, which contained a croquet set. He put the wickets in the sand and right away we played two games. Our trip continued on the horrible, rough roads. We were now in the area of the famous Russian "black earth," which is particularly rich. Left and right we saw nothing but green fields, plantings of watermelon. This lovely Russian watermelon with its delicate pink meat, decorated, one might say, with a sprinkling of black seeds, is deliciously refreshing for the people of this region during the extremely hot summer. They even sell slices of it in the cities.

We arrived at the single story but spacious manor house just in time for the evening meal. We had supper on the veranda which offered a wide view over the golden grain fields and the adjacent woods. Those who had their back to the view could see the beautiful scene reflected in a huge mirror.

I now got to know the Russian country life. The old cook of the family, who had once been a serf, provided us with delicious dishes: little pastries baked in carefully folded paper containers, an excellent cold soup prepared from kvass (the favorite drink of the Russian people), herbs, and cold salmon, and the "accoshke" which consists of sour milk, cold pieces of meat, and cucumbers among other ingredients.

The garden bordered on woods where the wild iris were in full bloom. They are exactly like our purple garden iris. The white pirola which blends into the ground, spread its orange scent. Many different kinds of berry bushes were in bloom too, among them the "klukva" (cranberry) which is used for jelly, sauce, dessert, and as juice to relieve fever. In the afternoons we went for rides in a peculiar carriage called "linyeka." It consists of two softly upholstered sofas on wheels, with the backs lengthwise down the center, so that the passengers on the two sides have their backs to each other. This vehicle is very nice and comfortable, but on the bumpy roads I was always in fear of slipping off, even though my companions who were used to this kind of travel held on to me.

We sometimes rode to a place where flax was blooming in great profusion, not blue like ours but yellow, and just as beautiful. We also visited the farmers. We ourselves had only one farm woman for milking the cows, and we loved to watch her. First she would pet the cow and call her by all the well known national names of endearment: my soul, my little dove, my golden one. Should the cow kick her, she would shout, "Do you belong to the court?" which is expressed with the one word, "dvoryanka" in Russian. Our neighbor, Peter Petrovich Semenov, the brother of Mrs. von Grot, told me with his prophetic intuition that this term contained the basic feeling underlying the approaching revolution. It was wonderful for me that the Semenov family lived on the neighboring estate. We had become well acquainted in Oranienbaum and St. Petersburg and I now spent my Sundays with them. They treated me as one of the family and I always felt thoroughly at home there.

The Russian garden often consists of intersecting paths which provide refreshing shade. The sunny areas between them are planted with beautiful flowers. Since the versatile Mr. Semenov was among other things a botanist, I gradually learned the Latin names of the garden flowers and the wild flora. He was also the President of the Entomological Society, and had all of us carry a bottle of cyanide so that we could catch any interesting beetles and kill them painlessly. In St. Petersburg, Semenov had numerous cabinets filled with samples of almost every existing species of beetle and our finds were to be added to this collection.

Mrs. Semenov was well versed in the scientific and artistic endeavors of her husband. In addition, she was an excellent homemaker and even did the canning of the fruit herself, as was common for Russian ladies. This procedure fascinated me. It was done outside in one of the shady paths where the whole cooking apparatus with a brazier and copper tongs was set up. The different berries, especially the white field-strawberry called "Glubnika," would spread a delicious aroma while being cooked.

❧

After my summer in the Ryazan Province with the von Grot family, I stayed a few days in St. Petersburg to spend some time with Miss von Rahden, and then I travelled to Hamburg. While there I was struck by a terribly painful attack of sciatica. My sister made every effort to relieve my pain, but nothing helped. On my return trip to St. Petersburg I had to smile when my fellow travellers thought me totally paralyzed. I was hoping for relief from the personal physician of the Grand Duchess, Professor von Eichwald, and, indeed, he effected a total cure with Spanish Fly — cantharidin. To show my gratitude, I embroidered a light blue silk material with all the medicinal plants which he had used on me over the years: the red foxglove, digitalis, the black berries of the henbane, the red opium poppy, and finally the white orange blossom which he mixed with all his medicines. My friends laughed at this piece of work, but he asked me to have it made into a pen wiper. I had this done in the shape of a pair of bellows with ivory handle and tip. It was always on his desk, and he had only to lift the top handle to wipe the pen. He used this wiper until his death.

✧

My friend, Baroness Taube, née Keyserling, and her husband were living at Yervacant and asked me to visit them in their simple palace during the winter. I was happy to accept and took the night train to Reval (now called Tallinn, the capital of Estonia) where I arrived the next morning and climbed into the waiting sled to travel the seventy verst to Yervacant. (1 verst = 3500ft). After about forty verst, the horses were changed, and I took advantage of the opportunity to take off my heavy fur coat and drink some hot tea. The trip continued with one more stop, albeit unscheduled. Up to that time, the road had passed through thick forests of pines and firs which in their white gowns offered a beautiful sight. But then the sled, pulled by three horses, went along a narrow dike in the deep snow, and suddenly the vehicle tipped to one side and I rolled down the side of the dike. The coachman helped me to climb up. At that moment an Estonian farmer came along the road with a lower, smaller sled. Since I preferred to ride in this, I asked the coachman from the palace to ride ahead and announce my coming. As it was getting dark, I began to feel embarrassed about the ride on the small sled, and when I finally saw the light from the windows of the palace, I breathed a sigh of relief. The inhabitants of the palace were, naturally, quite surprised to see me arriving in a peasant sled. I was delighted to have arrived after the hardship of the ride. Fur coat and boots came off and I entered the warm, bright rooms where all kinds of delicious refreshments were waiting for me.

I stayed for several weeks and lived in a large room with four windows. The room had six beds, each one with a screen, intended for six hunting guests. Since the whole palace was heated, my room, with views over snow covered meadows, fields, and woods, was very comfortable. At night I sometimes heard strange noises and imagined that bandits were hiding behind the screens. However, I relaxed when it was explained to me that the noise was the cracking of the old wood furniture.

In the mornings the Baron rode in a sled to his various farms. We ladies were literally snowed in. The house itself was extremely large, but the living room of the Baroness, covered with flowered cretonne, was cozy and inviting. Here we sat and there was no end to our talking and reminiscing. When the Baron returned, a very rich dinner was served. Neighbors occasionally visited in the afternoon for coffee and were treated to quickly prepared whipped cream cake. Coffee was served in a huge hall. It contained no furniture other than the grand piano and the coffee table with chairs, but the plants — blooming mock orange and even laburnum in tubs — created a feeling of spring. After two weeks came the most wonderful part of my stay: a visit from Count Alexander Keyserling, the father of my friend, who had come for a week from his nearby estate Raykuell.

This wonderful, interesting man enlivened everything. He was an honorary member of the most diverse scientific associations; he was a mineralogist, entomologist, geologist, and above all a philosopher. He studied Kant with us. His gifted daughter had already grasped the Kantian system, but I had to work myself into it. These discussions were fascinating, and the time flew by. In the evenings we made music.

∽

The few weeks had gone by only too quickly, and I had to return to St. Petersburg. I rented a room in the Sherbin house, across from Palais Michel. From my room I could see the windows of the apartment of Baroness Rahden. She often invited me in the evening to come and read to her. Once, I told her I wanted to "make good" for a small mistake I had committed. She replied, "One cannot make good for anything, but one can do better. So, do better." Another time she advised me, "Help everyone to his advantage, but let no one take advantage of you."

The delightful evenings of reading at Miss von Rahden's continued through the winter. I kept my evenings free and scheduled all the lessons with the von Grot family in the morning. It was a lovely winter.

The Grand Duchess Katharina and her family had moved to Kamenny-Ostrov. In spite of the beauty of the place, I always became very melancholy there, remembering the deceased, no matter how often I had been invited. A sudden illness of the husband of the Grand Duchess, Duke Georg von Mecklenburg-Strelitz, caused us great concern. The illness took a serious course. A nurse, Baroness Budberg, took care of him. But once he got up unnoticed, which brought on a hemorrhage causing his death. Early in the morning they called me to Kamenny-Ostrov and took me to the room where the Duke was lying. The Protestant minister held a funeral service just for the family and closest relatives. Duke Georg, the son of the deceased, asked me to play a chorale on the harmonium. Although I have made music all my life, I had never played the harmonium. I began the chorale, but not a note was heard. Duke Georg pulled the registers and I continued to play. "The sound is trembling," he whispered to me. I pulled myself together, and now Bach's chorale from the *St. Matthew Passion,* "Wenn ich einmal soll scheiden" sounded full and expressive. Before the Duke was transferred to the Protestant Church of Anna, the church which the Duke had attended, there was a final service of mourning in the large hall of Kamenny-Ostrov.

The Empress Maria Alexandrovna, wife of Tsar Alexander II, her daughter, Maria Alexandrovna, (who later became the wife of the Duke of Edinburgh), and the whole imperial court attended this service. I had been asked to continue playing chorales quietly at the end of the service while the deceased began his final trip to the church. I was deeply moved as one person after the other joined the procession until I was left all alone in the hall. After the last note had sounded I too walked behind the coffin. The Duke was interred in the family crypt in his home town, Strelitz.

∽

That summer I stayed in St. Petersburg. I gave several English classes at the Helene School in the mornings and gave German lessons to a young girl in Kamenny-Ostrov. Since Baroness Rahden was also in town, we often got together and went for carriage rides.

The Russian country estates have always interested me very much. The life there is quite different from that in other countries and one gets to know another side of the Russian people. For this reason, I was delighted when I received an invitation the following spring to come to the estate, in Chernigov, of the Countess Tolstoi , widow of the poet Alexei Tolstoi. His dramas are still being performed in Russia. I had met him earlier in Karlsbad and had seen him again at the Grand Duchess Helene's.

On the estate of the Countess Tolstoi was an abundance of everything. The Countess was never without guests and each person lived according to his desire. She was an unusual and interesting individual who was fond of contemplating philosophical questions. Her first husband was a Mr. von Müller. Alexei Tolstoi was a frequent guest in his house. The poet fell so desperately in love with Mrs. von Müller that he declared he could not live without her. As was the custom in Russia during that period, and with her permission, he bought her from her husband.

The widow was still in deep mourning for her husband (he had died on October 10, 1875) and wore a black gown with a very long veil, which, however, did not seem to get in her way. I remember a particular incident which is typical of the Russian trait not to permit an obstacle to get more attention than absolutely necessary.

We were taking a long walk which led us to a wide but quite shallow stream. To my surprise, the Countess said; "We have to go across here." She walked through the water and her long train formed a black trail behind her. I had no choice but to follow her through the water. Naturally, I had to change my clothes as soon as we got home. — In the evening we regularly made music and the Countess would read us poems by her husband. Then she might

throw out some statement or question which would be discussed
for a long time. I particularly remember one of those statements,
"An abstract husband is actually better than a concrete one." We
discussed this for a long time without arriving at any conclusion
on the somewhat difficult subject.

&

After these few, but highly stimulating days, I took my annual
trip to Hamburg. I had hardly arrived when I received a telegram
from the Baroness von Rahden. She was on the way to France,
and invited me for a short stay in Berlin. It was lovely to spend
two peaceful days with her at the Kaisershof. After this short in-
terlude, I accompanied her to Kreiensen where we parted. I
remember the little tug at my heart as I watched her yellow coach
disappear. The Baroness was travelling to Arcachon where the
Grand Duchess Katharina was undergoing treatment, while I was
riding to Gmunden to my dear friend Countess Prokesch-Osten,
née Gossmann. She, her husband, and their three daughters received me warmly.

Their villa was in a beautiful location. From my balcony I
overlooked the whole lake and on the other side the mountain with
the "Sleeping Greek Woman." The rock formation presents this
shape. I could see the residence of the former royal family of
Hannover whom Count and Countess Prokesch saw often. The
Wesendonk family was also in town. Friederike Gossmann had
not changed; it was as if we had seen each other only yesterday.

I enjoyed the delightful dramatic improvisations by the little
girls. All three were very gifted and vivacious. The fourth child, a
cute little boy, had died of measles while in military school in
Vienna. "Tiffi" showed me her son's little garden, where she had
left all his tools the way he had used them. I saw the three daughters again much later when they all were married to Austrian
aristocrats. Tiffi herself and her husband still visited me a few
years ago. However, she was already suffering from a torturous
nerve disease which killed her a short time later.

&

The physician in St. Petersburg had ordered me to get treatment for catarrh in Soden near Frankfurt, and I followed his advice. The Baroness Rahden had told me about an interesting woman who had established a boarding school for young girls in Soden, and she had asked me to give her regards to this lady. After I had settled in my hotel room I climbed up the mountain and visited the director of the school. The moment we met, my heart was drawn to Marie Hillebrand.

She was small in stature, but what energy emanated from her expression and her movements! Her face was illuminated by her big soulful eyes which revealed such genuine goodness, that one had to love her. Her hair presented an unusual look. It was beginning to get gray and was parted in the middle with two little braids on each side. She simply wrapped these braids around her ears, and if, as happened often in a conversation, one of them fell down, Miss Hillebrand, quite unperturbed, would again wrap it around the ear. She was the daughter of a Catholic priest who had converted to the Lutheran faith. Her mother had died early, and her father married a second time soon after the death of his first wife. A hard life began for the little girl. The stepmother insisted on teaching the child herself, but she was so impatient that Marie became intimidated and her life was made miserable by the many beatings she received from her stepmother.

The girl herself, however, did not become bitter. She showed loving concern for her step-siblings. The most prominent of them was Karl Hillebrand, the well known literary historian. He had participated in the revolution of 1848 and was awaiting his sentence in the Rastatt fortress in Baden. Marie Hillebrand borrowed four thousand marks from friends and went to the prison kitchen in simple clothes. There she made friends with the cook by darning her socks and such things, and in this way she saw her brother on his walks in the prison yard. Finally his death sentence was pronounced. In her droll dialect she told me how she engineered the escape of her brother: "The cook brought me into the yard. There comes my brother accompanied on his walk by two soldiers. I shake his hand and secretly slip him a piece of paper. On it was written: "Pretend you're sick." He followed these instructions and the attendant of the sick, who had been bribed with a huge sum, enabled him to flee. Brother and sister met on the bridge of

Kehl, rode together to Paris and took an apartment on a fifth floor. The sister managed the household without any help.

Karl Hillebrand became secretary to Heinrich Heine. For some reason he refused to introduce his sister to Heine. However, she met George Sand and spent wonderful hours with her, even though Miss Hillebrand did not approve of the way in which George Sand ended her relationship with Chopin. She had deep sympathy for the great artist. Slowly the situation in Paris improved for brother and sister. Karl Hillebrand moved to Italy where he settled permanently.

"Now I had to return the four-thousand marks," said Miss Hillebrand, "and that is how my institute was established." "But didn't your brother refund you the money?" I asked. "No," she answered, "he steeped himself in his literary work. I established my boarding school in Rödelheim near Frankfurt and spent happy years with my children, until a cholera epidemic broke out, and sadly, one of my young girls became its victim. After that, nothing could hold me in Rödelheim and I settled here on the mountain in Neuenhain near Soden."

Life at Miss Hillebrand's was so interesting that I visited her from now on every summer. In her school the children did not go home for vacation but had to stay a full year. For many this time was extended to several years. Miss Hillebrand was an excellent pedagogue. Each one of the older girls had a younger one to look after and be responsible for. In other words, she became a substitute mother. Joys and sorrows were shared by "mother" and child. On one occasion when we were all going on an excursion to the Feldberg in several carriages, I saw an older girl with her little one having an afternoon snack in the pergola. Asking Miss Hillebrand about it I was informed, "The little one has been naughty and cannot go; naturally, the mother must stay with her. One must never leave a child alone with his or her angry thoughts." The young mother did not seem to see the situation as a sacrifice but rather as a matter of course, and she listened without the slightest regret to the joyous reports after the outing.

Miss Hillebrand gave most of the classes herself, but mathematics and languages were taught by specialized teachers, even though she was fluent in English and French. In her religion lessons she combined all denominations and made the love which

Jesus preached the center from which the spiritual threads move in all directions. Love of God became the incentive to follow Christ, but not to imitate him. The imitation of Christ is a misunderstanding of Christianity which has sometimes brought death to those who were misled by it. Particularly attractive were the history lessons. Once a week they had a so-called "war." The two opposing teams were lined up face to face, and asked each other questions about the material learned that week. The team which answered all questions well was the winner, and the losers left ashamed.

A birthday party for Miss Hillebrand was very entertaining because one of the girls had obtained permission to dress up in Miss Hillebrand's clothes and did a marvellous imitation of her. The little braid around the ear was prominent in the parody. Miss Hillebrand laughed heartily as she watched her double present a scene with another girl in which she viewed her reflection in a window while the other stood behind her and secretly imitated all her movements. The girls also sang and danced beautifully and presented dramas during the vacation. I watched a performance of Schiller's *Wilhelm Tell* where they brought in some grass they had just mowed to represent a meadow. Every pupil contributed a piece of clothing and other objects to the theater wardrobe when she left the school, so that there were always plenty of costumes and stage props. Self-sacrifice and a sunny disposition acquired when young will stay with a person through life. I found this confirmed in all the graduates of this school whom I met later in their lives.

℃

I spent some time in Hamburg before returning to St. Petersburg. The winter was quiet but offered much that was interesting. Princess Helene, the daughter of Grand Duchess Katharina, had blossomed into a youthful beauty, was very musical, and had fully developed her lovely soprano voice through excellent lessons and diligent practice. Everything the Princess undertook she did thoroughly, and never succumbed to the danger of believing that her high position entitled her to do something superficially. Anton Rubinstein spent some time in St. Petersburg that winter and frequently conducted women's choruses from his operas. The Princess would then sing the solo part.

Grand Duchess Katharina always strove to emulate the example of her mother. She arranged wonderful musical evenings at the Palais where the aristocracy and the intelligentsia gathered. These gatherings were by no means stiff and formal; on the contrary, I remember them as very relaxed. At first we sat at round tables and a small supper was served, interspersed with some musical numbers. After the meal the tables were removed, and one could be entranced by the compositions of the great masters without any interruption. Anton Rubinstein often played Chopin with all the poetic feeling of his performance style.

I remember Christmas Eve of that year as a particularly delightful celebration. Everyone had his own Christmas tree. Under mine was a set of precious Russian china. The cups as well as the creamer and sugar bowl were light blue on the inside. The outside was white with blackberry vines and berries in relief. Unfortunately, this gift was among my precious possessions stored in a trunk which was stolen from the house of my friends, during their absence.

The harmonious winter was interrupted by the news of the declaration of the Russo-Turkish war on April 24, 1877. A busy life began for all of us.

The Empress appointed Baroness Rahden President of the Red Cross, which came to play a large role during this war. Now the extraordinary organizational talent of the Baroness became evident. On the day of her appointment, she took me with her to inspect the still totally empty rooms of the marine depot which were to be her headquarters.

The different departments of the Red Cross were to be set up here. The rooms were huge and quite bare. Within two days everything was changed as if by magic. Editha Feodorovna von Rahden, as the Russians called her, had arranged a large, beautiful hall for Princess Helene and her friends. Here bandages were cut and readied, and we often heard happy laughter from this area. I was engaged in cutting out underwear; others were busy collecting and packaging goods for entertainment and refreshment of the soldiers. Since the Russians love games like checkers, "muehle", and backgammon, I made it my business to send these games to the army. We worked cheerfully from morning till seven in the evening. Sundays I still worked in the student kitchens. With this heavy schedule it was always a welcome relaxation for me to read to the Baroness in the evenings. Every morning we looked for the newspapers with great anticipation to find out if Plevna had finally been conquered. It was a long wait before General von Todleben took the city on December 10, 1877. I was standing by the desk with a large pair of scissors, but they fell from my hand when the beautiful, fiery Princess Volkonsky stormed into the hall and lifted the Baroness high up in the air: "Plevna is fallen!" What joy! We all ran to the two ladies and pressed their hands. Their hands must have been quite sore afterwards, for our demonstration of joy was rather forceful.

However, this did not mean that the war was over, and the Grand Duchess Katharina put on a welfare bazaar at the Palais Michel. The beautiful halls were transformed into sales rooms of all kinds where beautiful society ladies and charming young girls displayed products from all the Russian provinces. Princess Helene worked particularly hard. She was in charge of pricing the items. Many lovely items had been imported from France for the bazaar, and it was no small task to convert the prices so that a considerable profit could be reaped. She often asked for my assistance in this effort, usually late in the evening and deep into the night. I was primarily selling toys; among them were amazing monkeys which could do all kinds of tricks and won the admiration of the public.

When the war was over, the Baroness von Rahden assembled all the volunteers who had worked in the Red Cross offices for a final gathering. She introduced us to the Empress who kissed us and gave each of us a gold medal with blue enamel which was inscribed in Russian with the following words by Editha von Rahden: "Power does not lie in strength but in love."

එ

Once again I was completely free. Therefore, I accepted a position for three months in the home of a senator and travelled with the family to its estate near Novgorod. Here we lived totally isolated, but surrounded by magnificent forests. Wolves and bears lived not far from us, and I could not stroll through the woods by myself. However, accompanied by the master of the house, I was able to forge into the thickets. Now and then shots were fired into the air to scare away any bears who might be nearby.

My young, sixteen-year-old student was an adorable girl and very gifted. We really did not study very much. Since the Russian winter is so long, one spends as much time as possible outdoors during the summer. Every house has one or more porches where all the meals are served, even when it rains, and these meals are so generous and frequent, one hardly does anything but eat. The beautiful white nights tempted me to stay up late, and when I finally went to bed, I was kept awake by the sweet, sobbing song of the nightingale.

The woods had such an abundance of mushrooms as I have never found anywhere else. The edible agaricus are called "white mushrooms" and are named for the trees under which they are found. When there is such a profusion, it is a real joy to pick them.

&

As always, I spent four weeks at my sister's in Hamburg. On this visit I had a memorable encounter. Ernst Haeckel had met my brother-in-law in Bergen and had been welcomed into his home. Now he was in Hamburg at my sister's — bringing greetings from the relatives in Norway. He impressed me as typically German: tall and blond. He was very eloquent during the meal and told us many interesting things. Then he began to philosophize and claimed we did not have a free will.

My sister and brother-in-law had been called away from the table, and I continued the discussion with him. When I contradicted him with firm conviction, he picked up a knife and said; "Now see, if I had my free will, I could stab you with this knife. But since I do not have a free will, I cannot do it, it is impossible for me." — I glanced at the open window and thought, it is a high ground floor, I could jump out if I had to. He must have watched me, for he began to laugh. Later I heard much about his idiosyncrasies; for instance, he is supposed to have baptized one of his children with wine.

After my return to St. Petersburg I frequently went to the home of Mrs. Abaza where there was much music making. At her home

I also met the Russian poet Turgenyev whose acquaintance I had previously made at Madame Viardot-Garcia's in Paris. I had just read *A Nest of Gentlefolk*. In this work one of his characters is a noble young Russian woman, the type I often met. So I had several points of contact for conversation with the poet. Mrs. Abaza herself had fascinating experiences to relate. She had been in Bayreuth during the summer and had experienced the *Ring of the Nibelungen*. She was an enthusiastic admirer of Richard Wagner and decided to present a performance of the song of the Rhein maidens from the first act of the *Rheingold*. She asked me to be one of the singers. Naturally, I accepted with pleasure. Since the text may offend the ear of a strict moralist, I asked the Baroness Nicolay, "Did you understand everything?" — "Yes," she answered, horrified, "You all sang with such frighteningly good diction."

During my work for the Red Cross I had met a Russian woman who now took voice lessons from me. She lived in Pavlovsk. In this town was also the Palais of the Grand Duchess Constantine, born Princess of Sachsen-Altenburg, whom I got to know later and who was friendly inclined towards me. I came for whole days to Pavlovsk where I was richly fed and paid. Frequently I strolled through the woods alone to my heart's content. To my delight, the pirola, which smells like orange blossoms, was blooming there, as was another white flower of the same family. In the fields I found cornflowers and the pink corn-cockle which forms the family crest of Baroness Rahden. At the pond I picked yellow iris. Back in town, I made bouquets from all the flowers I had picked and brought them to Baroness Rahden. Her Russian maid looked with disdain upon my flowers and called them hay, but her mistress accepted these wild but beautiful children of Mother Nature with love, and they made her room look like a garden.

As winter approached, the director of the Botanic Garden, Dr. Regel, gave me some bulbs of the genus colchicum. According to his instructions, the Baroness left them on the table. One evening she was sitting there, crocheting some woolen children's clothes when, to her delight, the bulbs — without earth or water — brought forth beautiful, bright purple, crocuslike flowers. They are very poisonous, and Medea, who came from Colchis, is supposed to have used them for her magic potions.

I welcomed an invitation to attend the lectures by the academician von Schrenck in his home. Here we learned about the processes on the earth which we see daily without giving them any thought. This intelligent, knowledgeable man knew how to captivate our interest from beginning to end. His fascinating wife became my friend. Three delightful daughters and two younger sons completed the Schrenck family. After the conclusion of the series of lectures, the house continued to be a gathering place for prominent and learned persons, and for everyone who was interested in matters of the mind and spirit. Here I met the marshal of the nobility in Livonia, Baron von Bock, whom Wilhelmine Schröder-Devrient had selected as husband for her third marriage. However, country life in Courland was not to her liking, and she had deliberately challenged the Livonian aristocracy with her nonchalant remarks, to her own great amusement. She had long since passed away. Her husband was kind and very musical, and I had many pleasant conversations with him. He was particularly fond of folksongs. Since I had acquired a large repertoire during my travels, he asked me to sing a true Norwegian folksong. I had once heard a song when I was standing on the balcony of my sister's house in Bergen. A blond fisherman with a red cap was sitting in his boat singing the simple, mournful melody. I held it in my memory and played it right away on the piano, and had someone give me the words — a poem in a regional dialect. I now sang this song, accompanying myself on the piano, and asked the ladies and gentlemen to guess the meaning. Everyone had a different interpretation, except that all agreed it had to be about an unhappy love. Everyone was wrong. Here is a free translation of the curious text:

> *I went out to the Seidagrunde,*
> *and that was early one morning;*
> *when likewise Olaf von Karamunde*
> *anchored his boat without warning.*
> *I hit him hard with my fishing pole,*
> *He hit the boat, his eyes did roll;*
> *I was so glad and sang with joy;*
> *I now have the depths to myself.*

Schrenck's home was of historic interest in so far as the furniture had belonged to the Bismarck family, and the Schrencks took it over when the Bismarcks left. Herbert Bismarck visited the Schrencks during a short stay in St. Petersburg and I sat next to him at tea. He was an interesting person in his way. While he seemed absorbed in quiet conversation he watched his surroundings keenly. We talked a great deal about Eugen Richter who had made Otto von Bismarck the object of his attacks. He agreed with me when I said he seemed like a hunter trying to chase a noble stag to death, but fortunately without success. "But," he added, "he does give my father a lot of trouble at times."

To this select circle belonged the botanist, von Maximovich, whose daughter was a friend of mine. He was an important and sociable man. In the spring he delighted me with a shipment of the most beautiful Alpine flowers from the greenhouses of the Botanic Garden. I was especially elated over the soldanella (bindweed) which grows high in the Alps at the edge of the glaciers. I found one later on the Julier in Engadine at the edge of the snow.

The Botanic Garden in St. Petersburg was really a treasure. A number of huge greenhouses led you through the five continents. First Europe's fruits of nature, combining beauty and usefulness. Here the wild flora of the Alps was prominent. Then it becomes gradually warmer: Asia with sago, rice, indigo, etc.; North and South America; then Africa. Here, in the tropical heat, our coats and furs were unbearable, while outside people were cold at -15 degrees Centigrade. By way of Australia we returned to normal temperatures. In the spring the director of the Botanic Gardens, Dr. Regel, provided me with Alpine plants , which I sent to Count Alexander Keyserling on Raykuell in Estonia, for whom I had enormous admiration.

He had invited me to his palace Raykuell. In his garden he had erected an artificial hill and planted it with Alpine flora which did exceedingly well here. My shipments of new Alpine plants from Director Regel were always a welcome addition for this hill.

My time at the Count's home flew by, as did my later visits with him in his winter residence in Reval. At that time his wife was still living. Her maiden name was Countess Kankrin. She always welcomed me with generous hospitality. Her specialty was her method of preparing coffee, like no one else, and she always stuck a tin of this specially roasted coffee in my suitcase, where I found it to my delight upon my arrival in St. Petersburg. In Raykuell I was always given the same room which Baroness Rahden occupied on her visits, which pleased me. The Countess unfortunately suffered an early death from a short, serious illness, and after her passing I did not return to Raykuell for a long time.

Count Alexander Keyserling

Peter Petrovich Semenov

I now had quite a number of acquaintances and also friends in St. Petersburg. My relationship with the Semenov family became very close, and this friendship grew ever warmer. Still, I desired to take employment during the summer. Since Russian families almost always take a lady or gentleman along to their country estates for the further education of the children, a position was easily found. I went along to the estate of a ministerial official to teach and supervise his two sons. I loved the location to the north of St. Petersburg on the Neva. The magnificent river, originating in Lake Ladoga, rushed past us towards St. Petersburg, so that on one occasion I engaged a boatsman to row me there in one hour. I visited St. Petersburg almost every weekend from Saturday till Monday morning, but I usually made the trip by train. Thanks to the generous nature of the Russians, I was allowed to stay in my employer's town house which was always attended by several servants. On these weekends it was a great pleasure for me to visit Baroness Rahden and read to her. Because most of her friends were away during the summer, she had much time for me. I told her that I spent my free time sitting in a swing reading the *Theological Ethics* by Richard Rothe, which gave me much food for thought. The volume on duty contained among others the admonition, "One should not make too much fuss with one's own person," which I thought well worth taking to heart. Another place he wrote, "If life gets too humdrum, and little annoyances bother you, then your life is like somewhat cloudy coffee. Drop everything and take a trip, however brief. One returns purified, the coffee grounds have settled." These, and many other thoughts from the book I related to her. "And that is now your crutch," she said with a smile. "Yes," I answered, "that's how one limps through life. But even limping, one moves forward."

Later that summer, the Empress put all educational institutions under the direction of Baroness Rahden. "Protectress" was her title. (The Russian word has no other equivalent.) I was in Hamburg when the appointment happened. Prior to that, there was a chance that she would move permanently to Kostroma where her sister was caring for her sick husband, General von Thimroth. The Empress, however, did not want to lose such a valuable person to a provincial town. When I received a request to bring her hyacinth bulbs, I knew it meant she was staying.

While in Hamburg I received a letter from Adelheid von Asten, née Kinkel, begging me to visit her in the clinic for nervous diseases of Dr. Wiederhold in Wilhelmshöhe near Kassel. When I arrived there, I found my friend severely ill. She had lived in an unhappy marriage and finally pressed for a divorce. The day before the decree was to be final, by coincidence her wedding anniversary, her husband shot himself in front of the door to her apartment. This terrible shock caused her nervous breakdown. Slowly she improved, and after a while I was able to spend some pleasant hours with Adelheid. I heard from her that her father was living in Switzerland, her brother Gottfried studying in Zurich, and her oldest brother Hermann already employed. We enjoyed recalling memories from our youth. These pleasant hours, the pure air, the lovely surroundings, and the excellent medical treatment all contributed to effect a gradual recovery.

I now felt the need to see two women who had influenced my life significantly: Mrs. Mathilde Arnemann and Miss Marie Hillebrand. The former lived in Weimar at that particular time, where her granddaughter was painting in the studio of Professor Struys. She invited me to come for a few weeks. From there it was easy to arrange a visit to Miss Hillebrand. Reassured about the condition of my friend Adelheid von Asten, I began my trip to Weimar where I was received with open arms. Professor Struys was a rather interesting Dutchman. He asked me to do a few sittings for his eight students. I agreed and initially found it amusing, but after a while it got tedious. Mrs. Arnemann took me to Eduard Lassen whom I had already learned to like through some of his compositions. He was an intimate friend of Mrs. Arnemann and welcomed me as her protégé.

We also called on the conductor Müller-Hartung whose two gifted daughters I had met at Miss Hillebrand's school. He immediately urged me to sing with the choir in a church concert which Liszt would conduct. We were to perform Liszt's *Seven Last Words of Christ* in the Herder church in the presence of the court. At the first rehearsal Müller-Hartung said, "I must ask you to pay close attention on the evening of the performance to what I will explain to you now. Our great man, whom we all revere so highly, is totally consumed by his creation. It may happen that he will be so overcome while he is conducting, that he will lay down his baton.

If that happens, I beg you to immediately look slightly to the right where I will be standing by a pillar behind Liszt and continue the conducting."

The rehearsals were very interesting. Since I sang first soprano I stood very close to Liszt and could examine his fine features which revealed the kind soul of a great man. He called us his children, and never let the rehearsals drag on to tedious lengths. — On the evening of the performance every last place in the church was taken. We sang full of devotion and were deeply moved when suddenly Müller-Hartung's prediction came true. Liszt put down the baton and looked up in what I can only describe as a holy act. The faithful Müller-Hartung was ready and the concert proceeded without the least interruption.

The next time I saw Mrs. Arnemann was at the funeral of my sister, Therese, when we both accompanied her to her final resting place. Mrs. Arnemann herself joined her in the eternal rest soon afterwards.

While visiting Miss Hillebrand in Soden I was again impressed by her gentle, persuasive methods. It was delightful to observe how she could transform people who were stiff and unapproachable so that they became cheerful and almost jolly. She had become famous, and people came from far and near to inspect her establishment. One day a very reserved English family with two daughters came, looked at everything and stayed for supper, but never said a word. This got to be too much for Miss Hillebrand and she called, "Oh, it would be much nicer to eat outside on the veranda! Please, everybody help, we want to carry everything outside." Nolens volens, the strangers had to carry dishes, tablecloth, napkins, etc. outside and set the table. The ice was broken; there was much laughter and talk and we parted as good friends. Yes, Miss Hillebrand was a magnificent woman and deserved to be mentioned in the encyclopedia with as much praise as her brother who owed everything to her initiative and sacrifice.

From Soden I returned to Hamburg and enjoyed the remainder of my vacation, even though I was concerned for my brother-in-law whose health was failing.

છ૭

My duties in St. Petersburg were keeping me very busy, tutoring for several families and continuing my service in the student kitchens. I noticed a certain unrest among the medical students, a ferment, which gave cause for concern. Rumors of a plot to kill the Tsar were going around. One day at dinner time we were suddenly shocked by an explosion at the winter palace. Dinner at the palace happened to have been postponed because the arrival of a guest, Prince von Battenberg, was delayed when his train ran late. This postponement saved the family of the Tsar, but a large number of loyal soldiers became victims of this attempt on the Tsar's life because the anarchists had dynamited the barracks and the dining hall above them. We lived in an incredibly tense atmosphere.

At the same time I suffered a heavy personal loss with the death of my brother-in-law, Gotthard Ritter. He still wrote in his journal, "Thank God, the Tsar was saved. May God protect him!" He was still available for all who needed his help and was lovingly preparing five hundred young people for their confirmation, when he was struck with a serious liver ailment of such intensity that he had to give up the confirmation classes. He did this, by writing a touching farewell to his students. Then he wrote the tenth verse of the eight-fourth psalm in his journal: "For a day in thy courts is better than a thousand." (Denn ein Tag in deinen Vorhöfen ist besser denn sonst tausend.)

Even though I had been deeply troubled by his condition for a long time, I was stunned when I received the news of his death by telegram. It was difficult to obtain a passport in those days, but through the kindness of Baroness Rahden, I obtained one immediately and hurried to Hamburg. Still, I arrived too late. All Hamburg had participated in the funeral; even the strict orthodox clergy paid him homage with the words, "He was a Christian." I still see him before me at our last parting; he was standing at the open door, wearing his gown because he was about to officiate at some function, following me with his thoughtful, kind eyes, calling, "Auf Wiedersehen".

Whatever I have been able to accomplish in my life with God's help, I owe to him. His innumerable admirers established the Gotthard Ritter Foundation which quietly helps the deserving poor. My sister was appointed president of the foundation. She was devastated by her loss, yet, characteristically, even in her deep sorrow she remembered to give me a cyclamen plant for Miss von Rahden when I parted.

The Baroness received me with such genuine sympathy and warm-hearted friendship that my sadness gradually lessened. I decided to spend the whole next summer with my sister, but until then I had to devote myself to my duties in St. Petersburg. I found a great unrest as a result of the explosion in the winter palace. I had made many acquaintances during my work for the Red Cross and could have led a sociable life, but I preferred to limit myself to association with a few friends, and to read to Miss von Rahden when her time permitted.

❧

Miss von Rahden had two nephews in the Navy who usually spent their Sundays with their aunt. When she had other duties, I substituted for her in her domestic role. Once I dined alone with the two young midshipmen, and afterwards we talked in the small salon. Among other things we discussed hypnosis. The older one suggested that we try self-hypnosis by staring into a metal ball. There were several objects in the room suitable for this purpose. I found the bronze foot of a lamp on the table particularly appropriate for our experiment. I stared steadily, silently, without moving, at the shining metal. There I saw a red-gold coffin very clearly. I became frightened and closed my eyes. A terrible headache hit me. When Editha von Rahden came home she was quite upset over our experiment. It did not have any effect on the young men, though.

The following Sunday, March 13, 1881, I was watering my flowers when I saw the Tsar drive by in a closed coach. On each side rode several Cossacks for his protection. He was taking his usual Sunday ride to the Grand Duchess Katharina where he would drink a cup of chocolate. I got busy at my desk, and then I saw his coach drive out heading for the Catharine canal. Suddenly I heard a terrible explosion. I grabbed my coat and fur hat and ran down the stairs. Now I heard an even louder bang and saw a battalion of Navy men running at a distance. In front of the Palais I met the Baroness, also in great fear, running towards the canal. There we ran into the castellan, Mr. von Samson-Himmelstjerna. He shouted,

"It was an assassination attempt. The Tsar was saved. Grand Duke Nicholas rode with him to the winter palace!" The Baroness hurried there in a small sled, while we waited apprehensively in her apartment for her return. After about an hour she returned. We rushed towards her on the stairs. "The Tsar is dead. He bled to death," she whispered. Tsar Alexander was riding along the Catharine canal when a man threw a bomb into the coach. This bomb, however, did not wound him. Humanitarian that he was, he climbed out to ask one of the Cossacks if he was hurt. At that moment, a second bomb exploded, hitting the Tsar in the hip and shattering the coach. Grand Duke Nicholas then took his brother to the winter palace in the small sled of an imperial courier. The attending physician who had been summoned was unable to stop the flow of blood and, in the presence of his court, the Tsar passed away.

The Tsar had married the Duchess Dolgoruky after his first wife's death, and his family was so loyal that they gave her the place at the head of his bed. The conspirators were immediately arrested, among them was the Countess Sophie Perovskaya, who had been standing on the Michael Square in front of the house Sherbin, where I lived, and had watched and signalled with her handkerchief which way the Tsar was coming. I had watched the Countess waving her handkerchief without knowing its significance. All the conspirators were hanged.

There followed a time of dreadful agitation. My family in Hamburg was greatly concerned for my safety and asked me to leave St. Petersburg immediately. Of course, I stayed, even after a sequel which involved me. A few days after the assassination the young Baron Rahden stormed into my room with the words, "Don't be alarmed!" Naturally, I was terribly alarmed. "This part of the street including your house, has been mined." He told me briefly about a newly opened cheese and butter store. A certain general with a few policemen had previously been asked to inspect the store. When he came to an opening covered with straw, he asked what was behind it. He was told that cheese was stored there, and this satisfied him. Now, after the assassination of the Tsar, stricter measures were taken and houses everywhere were searched under supervision. A mine was discovered behind the straw, and the owners of the store were unmasked as anarchists.

The Tsar was laid out in the church of the Peter and Paul fortress. The pedestal and the coffin were trimmed in red and gold. The Russians generally believe that the deceased is in the light, therefore, the resting place must not be dressed in black. Only those who remain behind wrap themselves in dark colors. There followed many prayers and Masses. One service which I attended was held at the spot where the assassination had taken place. During the marvellous hymn "Eternal memory, blessed repose to him" we all fell on our knees and hardly an eye remained dry.

That was the end of the "Liberator Tsar" who, for the benefit of his people, had emancipated the serfs. This was their gratitude. After the entombment, which proceeded with great reverence, work began immediately to erect a church by the Catharine Canal. In the center were the cobblestones where the bomb had exploded, enclosed by a golden fence. Those were terrible times. The ferment continued and finally developed into the big revolution of 1905.

I spent much time in Raykuell with my friend Keyserling who led a lonesome life after the death of his wife. After breakfast, which he enlivened with fascinating tales, we would go to the sheep barn where now, in the springtime, we could observe many little lambs with their mothers. Then we would ride in a small, low wagon pulled by two spotted horses through beautiful forests and over large fields to various Estonian farmers. Count Keyserling was very popular with them. I was particularly intrigued by the women, many with lovely red-golden hair, which, however, was hidden under a kerchief in church on Sundays. Count Keyserling experimentally applied a variety of fertilizers on small fields of oats. Dates of blooming etc. were later recorded in the log books. If we returned by one o'clock, we would look through the microscope at the insects we had collected, check them against the reference texts, and arrange them according to their species. This activity was so interesting that we often forgot about hunger and thirst, and the three o'clock dinner hour came before we knew it.

Of these meals I remember especially the delicious toast with reindeer marrow which was served with consommé. We had mocca in small cups in the salon, where we sat in the so-called gondola, an S-shaped sofa ideal for conversation as one sits face to face. After an hour of following one's own pursuits, we would meet in the large salon and make music together. We often played Mendelssohn's "Songs without Words" arranged for piano and harmonium. The upper voice was on the harmonium, expertly played by Count Keyserling while the piano accompaniment fell to me. At eight o'clock we had tea with a delicate Courland pastry, a caraway cake, and a side dish such as asparagus.

Mail came only three times a week with letters and newspapers. The *Augsburger Allgemeine* always contained much that was interesting in its scientific supplement; at that time it featured Hebbel's journals which I read to the Count.

A stay in Raykuell was instructive and enjoyable at any time of the year. The garden always offered something new. The Count had planted a large variety of bulbs whose fast progress we observed. Late in the evening we often took our field chairs into the grove and heard the nightingales sing into the white nights.

I also paid a visit to Baroness Taube in Yervacant. Since a longing for Raykuell had always stayed awake in both of us, we asked one afternoon for horses to bring us to the Estate of Count Keyserling. When none were available, we started out on foot. We had walked for about an hour without meeting anyone when we heard a rooster crowing. "A Raykuell rooster, a Raykuell rooster!" shouted the Baroness and clapped her hands. She was right. We had arrived on the Raykuell property. A short while later we entered the palace. We asked the servant not to say anything and hurried quietly into the Count's study. We found him sitting at his desk, calculating how many sunflower seed cakes his oxen would need each day. He was pleasantly surprised to see us and at once ordered rich cake. We sat at the round coffee table in a corner and had an animated conversation. He told us about the earlier life at the court and talked about the attributes of mankind. He suggested that there is a big ledger for each person. On one side is a list of everything that people have done for you, on the opposite side that which you have done for others. This second list should be more numerous and is more valuable than the first, he said, and these deeds are preserved not only on paper but in the memory of people. We both felt somewhat defensive and tried to justify ourselves, but our excuses fell rather flat. At other times he gave free rein to his sense of humor. The saying, "Better loving not to be loved, than not loving to be loved," he jokingly paraphrased with the verb, to pinch, thus, "Better pinching not to be pinched, than not pinching to be pinched."

He was a noble heathen whose great soul strove for the highest and best. He did not talk about his feelings, but one day he took me upstairs to the attic of the palace. There was a large white marble cross which he had prepared for his grave. On it were written the following words: "Verily, the spirit of truth will show you the way." A lengthy path, with borders of roses which he had planted, led from his garden to an open area in the woods where his wife and one daughter had already been laid to rest.

On my visits to Raykuell I often saw his son, Count Leo, who had a marvellous gift of conversation. He had studied history in Berlin and had been a welcome guest at the home of Bismarck. After he finished his studies, he withdrew to his small estate. His wife was highly educated but also quite capable in domestic matters. They had three adorable children. Their son, Hermann, became the founder of the "Schule der Weisheit" (School of Wisdom) in Darmstadt. On the occasion of a Christmas celebration, I got to know the whole family. The Master of Raykuell, Count Alexander, was of the opinion that the Christmas celebration should be a short, poetic vision. When his children were small, he set up the tree only for Christmas Eve. It was like a fairytale which was dissolved by the next morning. He thought that the holiday would thus make a deeper impression on the children.

The relatives from Yervacant, Baron Taube with his wife and their three children, also joined the Christmas festivities. Baron Taube was a real country squire; refined, upright, charitable, and with a sense of justice that is hard to find. His wife, quite the daughter of her father, whose beauty and sparkling conversation had already attracted attention at the soirées of the Grand Duchess, entertained the assembled children. She would invent highly imaginative fairy tales in which the friends of the family appeared in various transformations. For instance, the family physician appeared as a talking umbrella. His Excellence Semenov was a big beetle who released all the friendly beetles who had been imprisoned by a bad beetle witch.

I celebrated the following Christmas at Yervacant. I had spent the preceding weeks with Count Keyserling, and we rode by sled to his daughter's. As we rode through the deep snow the sled sometimes leaned to the side and I would desperately clutch the sled. The Count commented, "These fears are sensations which cannot be rationalized away. All preaching does no good. It is the same with jealousy. You can say a hundred times, 'there is no reason, you are wrong, you make yourself nervous, your soul suffers needlessly.' All these words are spoken to the wind. Only forbearance brings relief." The Count demonstrated such forbearance during his wife's final illness. In order to be always near her and calm her, he had his desk brought into her sickroom and took care of all his business under her eyes.

ෆ

At about the same time, the sister of Baroness Rahden, the widow of General von Timroth, moved to St. Petersburg. Baroness von Timroth had nursed the General until his death. As already mentioned, it had been considered that Editha von Rahden should move to Kostroma. The Empress, however, appointed her president of the Russian educational institutions, thereby tying her to St. Petersburg. The Timroths had found a nice, comfortable apartment not far from the Palais Michel, and I too was always welcome to visit. The sons of Baroness von Timroth were extraordinarily ambitious and intent on pleasing their mother. During the strenuous preparation for an exam which he passed with high marks, the oldest son, Emanuel, had evidently overexerted himself, became very sick and suffered a hemorrhage. Upon the pleading of her sister, Editha von Rahden decided to travel to Germany with her nephew. Instantly, I decided to accompany her and overcame her initial objections. My company turned out to be helpful, as she admitted to me later on. We travelled with the sick young man to Berlin to consult Professor Gerhard. When I heard a quiet sobbing early one morning, I knew it was my beloved friend who had been informed of the sad prognosis for her nephew's condition. Professor Gerhard sent us to Davos. We travelled first to Graubünden and spent a night in Chur. Since there was no train to Davos at that time, we rode in an open carriage through the Prattigau via Klosters to Davos. In spite of our heavy premonitions, we enjoyed the ride through the beautiful country, and I gave voice to my delight by yodelling and singing some Norwegian and English songs. The farmhands who met us listened in silence. "It would be different in Italy," said the Baroness, "there they would shout: Bravo, bravissimo!"

In Davos we lived in the spa hotel. There were about ten people around the dinner table, among them a charming young American woman and the ambassador to China, Mr. von Brandt. Ten years later he and I were the only ones from that group still alive. The Lutheran minister in Davos, a very young man, was also suffering from that terrible disease. Another pastor captured our attention. We saw this gentleman with white hair and an interesting face leaving a bookstore. I was so captivated by his appearance that I entered after he left and asked who he was. "That is Pastor Ludwig from Frauenfeld, a very distinguished, educated, and humanitarian man," was the reply.

We decided to go to Frauenfeld on one of our excursions, and had dinner at the small hotel there. When we were sitting in the garden after our meal, we heard the ringing of the little village church bell and saw a long funeral procession winding down the steep mountain. The hotel owner told us that the deceased would be buried in Frauenfeld and that Pastor Ludwig would give the graveside sermon. We would have liked to stay and hear him, but, as so often, young Emanuel's fever shot up, and we had to hurry back. If we had stayed, we would have witnessed a deeply gripping occurrence. After Pastor Ludwig had concluded his moving remarks and was saying the blessing over the lowered departed, death seized him and he fell into the grave.

We were looking for a companion for our young friend and found an interesting, intelligent student from Courland who had overexerted himself studying history, and who would provide suitable companionship.

Emanuel was still feeling tolerably well and we were able to undertake shorter walks. On one such walk we found the low growing gentian in the most beautiful blue color I have ever encountered. The Baroness had given me a pretty container for the plants I was collecting since I had been in the habit of sticking the flowers I collected into my hat. This habit had caused an embarrassing experience. I had picked several beautiful, large thistles and stuck them into my hat. Suddenly two cows came towards me who, apparently, had an appetite for thistles, and nothing could dissuade them from their intent. In my fear, I fled onto the porch of a house, but one of the cows followed me even there. In desperation I grabbed a chair, held it in front of my face and called, "Please, please!" The cow paid no attention to my cries, the thistles were too tempting. Finally, a woman came and rescued me from this trap. Another incident on a different walk caused us to laugh just as hard in retrospect. On a narrow path on the side of a mountain we met a cretin with his cows. Remembering my former adventure with cows, I asked him if his cows were bad. He became so incensed, that he stormed towards me swinging his stick. Trembling, I shouted, "No, good cows, good cows!" and he finally let me pass.

Soon it was time to part from Emanuel. The Baroness had to get back to her hard but rewarding work, and several students were awaiting my return. Our young friend had found a companion with whom he could take walks and otherwise spend pleasant hours, and this was a small consolation for us.

∾

The coming winter in St. Petersburg was uneventful but enjoyable. As spring approached we received word from the doctor in Davos that Emanuel's condition had worsened and he had had to be transferred to a hospital in Baden-Baden. His mother travelled there while the Baroness moved into her sister's apartment to take care of the other son. I went there often and tried to entertain the young man with various activities such as acting out proverbs, to give the Baroness a few cherished hours of rest. I also had the great pleasure of giving German and literature lessons to Semenov's only daughter. She was extremely gifted, and I frequently learned more from her than she from me. She painted beautiful aquarelles, and had a special gift for representing the autumn mood in the country in wonderful colors. The oldest son also studied German with me. Since he had made contact with various scientific institutes, he was glad to be able to correspond with them in German.

The whole Semenov family was quite unusual; everyone did what he wanted, but I never heard them quarrel. The reason may be found in the fact that each member was involved in substantive matters and could not be bothered with trifles, much less with pettiness.

Then the news came that the young Baron Emanuel Timroth had passed away. He had succumbed to his severe illness in Baden-Baden and his mother brought him to Courland for the interment. After her return, her sister Editha could move back to her own apartment in the Palais Michel, and we resumed those pleasant evenings with interesting literature. Now and then I was beginning to have a feeling that all was not well with her. The Baroness often sat lost in thought, and I noticed a deep sadness in her beautiful eyes. Still, I was unprepared for the day when she quite abruptly said, "Tomorrow the physicians will come to me and sign my death sentence." Suddenly it became clear to me; she suffered from that terrible, incurable disease which claims so many victims.

At the same time I sustained the previously mentioned theft. During my absence, a trunk with all my silver and many other valuable objects was stolen. The Grand Duchess Katharina heard of my loss while she was in England, and out of the goodness of her heart, she sent a telegram inviting me to move back into the Palais Michel. I was given the rooms next to those of Baroness Rahden. This was a fortunate turn of events, since it allowed me to assist the Baroness during the hard and sad days which were to come.

The doctors decided to operate immediately. True to her character, the Baroness accepted her fate with heroic spirit, and bravely endured the intense pain which followed. The doctors guaranteed that the operation would allow her to live at least ten more years. At first it appeared that they would be right. I remember a particular evening when she rode to the Empress for dinner, wearing a light grey silk dress, white lilac (fastened with lace) in her hair and a small gold-brocade ribbon. She looked rosy and ethereal, her eyes shining once again, so that my heart beat with joy and hope. She was able to go out in the evenings again!

One time we went to a musical soirée at Mrs. Abaza's. Editha von Rahden was sitting to the left of the grand piano; I was sitting on the same side, at some distance, so that I could observe her. Everyone came to greet her and congratulate her on her recovery. Then the door opened, and Dostoevski entered. Even though the hall was quite large, he saw the Baroness at once, hurried towards her and kissed her hand. Such deep compassion spoke from his beautiful, expressive eyes in this greeting, that tears welled up in mine. Miss von Rahden was also deeply moved. Dostoevski sat down beside her and started an animated conversation with her. His sunken cheeks gave witness of the hardships he had suffered in the *House of Death* in Siberia. But all that seemed to be forgotten now. He as well as the Baroness were so excited, and engrossed in their lively discussion, that it was a great joy for me to be allowed to watch them.[1]

In the summer she said to me, "I would like to see the place once more where I spent such happy days with the Grand Duchess and her entourage. It was in Ragaz and we were joined by the great Field Marshall Moltke. He was a man of very few words, and we wanted to get him to talk, so we decided that at dinner everyone was to speak a different language. He selected Turkish. There was such a gibberish, we could hardly talk for laughing. German, French, English, Russian, Italian, Latin, Greek, and Turkish, all interwoven. The worst of it was, that we could neither understand nor answer Moltke."

I arranged to take a trip to Ragaz with the Baroness. We stayed in the same hotel where once the Grand Duchess Helene and her court had resided. In the garden was the same croquet game which had amused Anton Rubinstein, his brother Nikolay, and other gentlemen and ladies of the court. The Baroness related that Nikolay Rubinstein had complained that his nose was getting in his way, so that he could not see the balls on the other side. His nose was certainly strongly curved, but that gave his face, framed by thick blond hair, a most attractive appearance — so much so that later on a woman in Moscow was so enraptured by him that she shot herself on his grave.

My room in the hotel was one story higher than that of the Baroness, and so situated that I could see her on her balcony. It was delightful to watch her feed the birds at breakfast. She spread her love over her whole environment, people, animals, and even flowers. Unforgettable for me is an excursion to the charming Maienfeld, where the cyclamen were blooming, covering the floor of the woods like a carpet. The Baroness sat down on a high, moss-covered rock. "Pick as many as you can for me. I can no longer do so myself," she added sadly. She could no longer use her arm when she stooped over. The sun was just about to set, throwing its last rays over my beloved friend, so that she appeared transfigured. She was beginning to mention the pain in her arm quite often and one evening she said to me, "I know I am approaching a period of great suffering."

At this time another lady from St. Petersburg came to visit the Baroness, and I used this opportunity to see my old friend, Miss Hillebrand. This visit was a pleasure mixed with deep sorrow. She too was soon to leave this world. She had diabetes and her mind was not always what it used to be, but her generous soul which always thought of others and asked nothing for herself, was evident up to the end. I remember a moment when she was free of pain, and we were sitting on a bench in her garden with a splendid view of the Taunus, the children playing below.

"Look," said Miss Hillebrand in her dialect, "it won't be long before it is said, once upon a time an institute stood here, but she who founded it is dead, and now nobody knows anything about it anymore." I answered, and still stand by my words, "The seeds you scattered here, have taken root, have blossomed and have born fruit." Miss Hillebrand and her work shall not be forgotten.

The weather was nice and we made many excursions with the children. However, I was so worried about the condition of Miss von Rahden that I longed to be back with her and returned to Ragaz after a relatively short stay. She and I took one more extended excursion by carriage into the Engadin. We ate at the lovely Pontresina. After the meal I went with a guide to the Rosseg glacier. Upon my return, Editha von Rahden was almost fainting, the altitude at Pontresina was too much for her. The horses were hitched up and we rode to the much lower Samaden where she quickly recovered. The next day we rode on the romantic Via Mala to Thusis where we spent the night before returning to Ragaz. A short while later we began the return trip to St. Petersburg. My heart was heavy for I feared that this would be her final journey. A few days after our arrival in St. Petersburg, her doctor announced that another operation was necessary.

The day before the surgery, the Baroness wrote me a note asking me to make several preparations for the arrival of her sister. In spite of her deathly fear of this operation, she thought of everything, even small details, to give pleasure to others. The operation appeared to be successful and we even took frequent little walks together. On one such walk she mentioned to me that she had found an excellent position for a lady whom I knew. Amazed, I exclaimed, "but that is the family whose members have caused you so much trouble through their intrigues!"

"Oh," she replied with a spiritual expression in her beautiful eyes, "if you knew the joy of repaying evil with good."

Yes, she was ready for heaven. Unfortunately, a few weeks later the surgeon declared that a third operation was required. I immediately sent a telegram to her personal physician who was on a trip. His reply was, "I shall return at once. The knife shall not be used again."

She suffered great pain in the ensuing period, but she bore it courageously. She had some personal, final words for each person. Since she was bound to her bed, she often sent me off with messages — once a lengthy one to Mr. Semenov. After I handed it to him he rushed to his room and I heard him sobbing.

Before her first operation, Miss von Rahden had been served very poorly. Her old chambermaid had suffered a stroke, and the new one was not worthy of her. I succeeded in finding a kind, faithful soul who was very pious and was a great comfort to the Baroness, especially during this period of great suffering. She still received visitors. When the Grand Duchess Alexandra Josephovna came out of the sick room in tears, she said, "Yes, she is unique." The Abbess of the convent of Kostroma, a Countess Tolstoi, brought her a beautiful picture of Mary with the baby Jesus, knelt by her bed, and thanked her for everything she had been to her. As she left, she said to me, "Editha Feodorovna is a Paulus." The Duke of Mecklenburg-Strelitz, oldest son of Grand Duchess Katharina, knelt by her bed and thanked her for her help during his illness and even yet. Pastor Hesse came out of her room with the words, "I could give her nothing, she alone did the giving." The Grand Duchess Katharina and all her family stayed near in loyal concern, but all human love and caring could not slow her upward flight.

Her own family had also come, and her oldest niece, who resembled her in character and spirit, was constantly taking part in the care. This girl later devoted herself entirely to the care of the Baroness von Osten-Sacken who had become blind. She read to her for hours and generally tended to all her needs. She was now present very early one morning when Baroness von Rahden asked that her bed be brought to the window. The sun shone upon the sick woman. At that moment she must have had a wonderful vision for she looked up to heaven with a blissful expression. After a few more days of great suffering, her great, noble soul was called home, during the night of October 9 (new calendar October 21), 1886.

There followed an uninterrupted sequence of prayers. Every school and institute sent a delegation to hold a memorial service at her bed. The Empress, too, ordered a service at which she participated. From central Russia came the famous Mr. von Chicherin, a learned and prominent man. He wanted to know everything about her last months. When I told him about our excursion to Maienfeld, the sunset and the cyclamen, he said, "You saw the final glow of the Alps." —

He himself came to a tragic end. His wife was reading in bed when a fire started and the bed curtains burst into flames. Endangering his own life, he saved his wife but was burnt so extensively that he died after a short time. His wife, who had already buried two adorable children, was threatened with death in the Russian revolution in World War I. She only escaped because her cook fled with her, carrying her on his back.

The Baroness was buried in Peterhof where her parents' grave was. A special train was made available, and I rode in the car with the coffin. I took one leaf off the wreath and put it in my Bible, where it still is. Strangely, its green color has not faded. It was a great distance from the station to the cemetery. The landscape, covered with snow, looked cheerful and lovely. Mr. Semenov stayed at my side during the long walk. He and his family have remained my true friends. It was he who immediately invited me into his house which became my home for a long time.

The nature of the Russian is of exceptional kindness. He is generous and simple in his giving. One hand does not know what the other is doing. It happened to me several times that I came to the Semenovs and other Russians to ask for some help for the poor and thought I should apologize for asking again, when they replied with surprise, "What do you mean? We cannot remember having given before." It is instantly forgotten. Once, when I expressed my amazement at this trait to Countess Volkonsky, she smiled, "Well, we are so disorganized that we hardly know the state of our financial situation. So we give left and right, wherever help is needed." I, however, thought to myself: You have a deep compassion for your fellow man, which is and remains touching.

It is well known that when the prisoners in chains were marching by on the way to Siberia, the people hung sacks with bread and other food at the windows with a note, "For the unhappy ones." The Russians are also exceptionally fond of children. In the streets of St. Petersburg and in the villages one often sees men with children in their arms or sitting with them on the ground playing with marbles.

I led a quiet, active life in the Semenov house. Mrs. Semenov was very musical and we often played fourhand piano together. She was knowledgeable in diverse fields, and the life with her intelligent and prominent husband had broadened her interests even further. She was particularly interested in opera and subscribed to the opera season. In my mourning, I was not inclined to accompany her to these performances. Instead I enjoyed pleasant and instructive hours in the company of the master of the house. Peter Petrovich had, in addition to his scientific interests, a great devotion to art. As an art connoisseur, he was then writing a biography of Rembrandt, of course in Russian. He shared much from his book with me, while I often read to him from a book about the lives of various Dutch painters.

To illustrate how helpful my kind host was and how he never hesitated when he had the chance to relieve someone's burden, I want to relate an incident which happened about two years before the death of Miss von Rahden. I had received a terribly frightening letter with a drawing of a ball, a dagger, and an exploding bomb, and an invitation by the anarchists to come at one o'clock at night to number 180 of a certain street I knew well. Noncompliance with this order would be punishable by death. I was really upset. Such invitations usually meant that the nihilists or anarchists wanted to draw a person into their ranks. I hurried across the Neva bridge to Peter Petrovich and already envisioned myself floating in the river. My kind old friend was also frightened, drove with the letter to the Minister of the Interior, and returned with the assurance that two detectives would be sent for my protection.

In the evening I hurried with my letter to Baroness Rahden, who had been with the Empress in Tsarskoe Selo during the day. She tired easily in these days and was not receiving anyone, but I ignored everyone and rushed to her room. "Something terrible has happened. I shall be murdered tonight." She took the letter, read it, and looked at me in amazement. "That is quite impossible," she said, laughed, and added, "Today is the first of April." Strangely, this had not occurred to the rest of us. For the second time I had been made a complete April fool. Relieved, I rode to Semenovs who immediately notified the Minister. It was discovered later that a law student had allowed himself this rather dangerous practical joke.

Much as I enjoyed my stay at the Semenovs, I was equally happy to follow an invitation by Count Alexander Keyserling to spend several weeks with him in Raykuell and afterwards some time at his daughter's in Yervacant. He met me in his town apartment in Reval. At tea we naturally talked about little but the passing of our mutual, beloved friend.

The next morning after breakfast the covered sled stood ready at the door; we put on our fur coats and boots and rode through the woods towards Raykuell. Snow lay heavy on the branches of the trees and the landscape looked like a fairyland. Although we enjoyed the beautiful views, we were happy to reach our first stop after about thirty verst, where we could take off our furs and relax in a warm room. The samovar was brought out at once and delicious "kollach" and fresh butter was served. "Kollach" is a pastry in the form of a basket. For me the handle was a particular delicacy. The portly postmistress stopped by our table, and at the request of Count Keyserling told us the news from every estate in Estonia. When we had heard enough of engagements, marriages, and births and were sufficiently warmed, we put our wraps back on, climbed into the sled, and rode on.

"Now we have heard a bit of gossip," said Count Keyserling. I objected, "Oh no, there was nothing malicious! It was quite amusing, but really no gossip." "You are right," he said. "If one enjoys relating a mistake someone else has made, that is gossip, regardless whether the person involved is hurt by it or not. Certain attributes of men and women are revealed here, such as jealousy, envy, passion. Of course, I don't mean noble passions as exemplified in Martin Luther. Luther's heart was burning, and the smoke from his burning heart sometimes obscured his vision, but that did not diminish his greatness."

At the second station we did not rest very long and we reached Raykuell towards evening. As we approached the palace on the birch lined avenue, Count Keyserling quoted the lines from Goethe's poem *Mignon* "Kennst du das Haus, auf Säulen ruht sein Dach?" (Know'st thou the house, on columns rests its roof?) The quotation fit the house perfectly. The old servant and the house-keeper, formerly the maid of Baroness Taube, were standing by the columns to receive us. Through the open entrance door one saw the brightly illumined hall, a thoroughly comforting view after the long, wintery drive. The room in which Baroness Rahden had stayed when she was visiting Raykuell had been prepared for me, another sign of the sensitivity of these considerate people. The windows of my room looked out over the farm yard. Early in the morning I heard the doves cooing. I also heard the crackling of the wood in the hall as the starter kindled the fire in the stove, which was tended from outside. This immediately gave rise to a feeling of contentment. Then Adolfine, the housekeeper, brought me a glass of fresh milk, and I looked forward to the conversation with my host over breakfast which consisted of coffee steaming on a hot stone in a bronze pot and the delicious Estonian caraway cake with butter. The gardener always saw to it that that there were some harbingers of spring in the windows or flowerboxes, so that while outside the sun made the snow glisten like a thousand diamonds, the heated room with its snowdrops, blue scillas and auriculas was filled with a touch of spring.

Two days before Christmas the Count drove with me to Yervacant to celebrate the holidays there. It was a cold evening. Since there was no moon, it was quite dark, and only the stars shone brightly. Count Keyserling showed me Orion and named the stars which represent the belt. He even had made up a little verse about it, which I have forgotten. As we arrived in Yervacant the whole family Taube was there to greet us. The two little girls wore adorable pink dresses decorated with golden angel hair.

One morning the Count asked me, "Did you hear anything last night?" I confirmed this. I had heard steps and been quite afraid. The Count had also heard steps. To get to the bottom of this, I asked my friend, Baroness Taube, to show me all the rooms in the upper story of the extensive palace.

From my room we went through several furnished rooms until we finally came to a hall which was empty except for a large cupboard. We saw nothing unusual. I asked what was in the cupboard. At first I received evasive answers but they only increased my desire to see the contents. Finally it was opened, and we saw several large candelabra used for laying out a corpse and a black velvet cloth with a silver cross used for the same purpose. My fear became even greater through this discovery and a feeling of something sinister was added — the punishment for my curiosity. To calm me, a maid was asked to sleep outside my door, but she snored so terribly, that I could not sleep a wink.

I was moved to a very comfortable, small room on the first floor. To get there I had to pass through a small hall with historic pictures: Queen Elizabeth of England, Henry IV of France, and a Russian tsar whose evil black eyes stared at me threateningly when I passed. I really had jumped from the frying pan into the fire. The source for the noise during that night which had been the cause for all this upheaval was never determined. I, however, was haunted by all kinds of ghost stories.

In the meantime, New Year's Eve had arrived and we amused ourselves with "Bleigiessen," a game where you melt small amounts of lead, drop the liquid into cold water, and tell your fortune from the resulting shapes. I mention this trivial incident only because my shape looked like a primitive carriage with two figures, one of whom wore a kind of crown. Count Keyserling said; "You will be riding next to a crowned head through the coming years." This prophecy came true for me.

The lovely time in Yervacant passed and I returned with Count Keyserling to the quiet Raykuell. We talked a great deal about natural phenomena, and the Count expressed his surprise that so few people know the order of the colors of the rainbow: red, orange, yellow, green, blue, indigo, violet. He made the word "roygbiv" from the first letters. Since this sounds like "roastbeef," one will never forget it.

It happened that Count Keyserling told me of his acquaintance with the Princess Elisabeth von Wied who had spent a winter with her great-aunt, Grand Duchess Helene. A short time later she married Prince Karl von Hohenzollern, who assumed the throne of Romania, first as Prince and later as King. Count Keyserling described her charming simplicity and spontaneity. She has become known by the name "Carmen Sylva" because she published her poetry under this name. He described the sincere admiration the Princess had held for Baroness von Rahden, and by a sudden inspiration he added; "You should write to Queen Elisabeth and tell her about the last days of the departed."

And I wrote. It was good for me to recollect all the words the Baroness had given her friends during her final weeks, while she was in such great pain, and to share them with the Queen. At once I received an answer beginning, "If you only knew what great favor you did for me!" Unfortunately, this letter too was among my things lost in Russia. In it, the Queen described the amazing influence which Editha von Rahden exerted on everyone, and she added, "She did not want to rule, but she ruled. I would have followed her blindly, but she did not permit it." The Baroness could not suffer extreme enthusiasm. I remember her rebuke upon such an occasion: "You must not mistake the creation for the creator."

A brief exchange of letters between the Queen and myself ensued, and as a result I was asked to come to Romania as Director of Studies at an institute which was under the patronage of the Queen. This institute was a refuge for children of all classes, primarily orphans. It was a grand idea, but the outcome did not fulfill the noble intent.

Since my dear sister, Therese, had followed her dearly beloved husband into death after only four years, there was nothing drawing me to Germany at that time, and I followed the call.

ﮠ

ENDNOTE

[1] This musical soirée must have happened several years earlier. Dostoevski died in January 1881, and this is 1885. It seems understandable that Susanne Schmaltz, in her memory, connects this touching scene with her friend's final illness.

AT THE ROMANIAN COURT

I travelled to Romania by way of Vienna and Budapest, where I spent a night. From there, the train followed the Danube for quite a while. The Iron Gate seemed to me particularly romantic even if somewhat spooky, and I was happy when I finally arrived in Bucharest. A carriage was waiting for me and took me close to one of the smaller palaces of the King. Its name was Cotroceni. Immediately I was asked to introduce myself to the Queen.

She was one of those personalities who make you feel comfortable as soon as you meet them. She appeared so natural and unassuming that one forgot her high position and talked to her like a friend. I brought several little souvenirs which had belonged to the Baroness. She took a pen-wiper, in which you could still see the ink which the Baroness had wiped off, and said with a melancholy expression, "Look, such a little thing survives a person — and what a person!"

We had found each other in our love for the departed. In such soil loyalty will grow. I have seen cases where people became friends on account of their common antipathy for someone. Nothing noble will spring from that. But our love for the Baroness established a friendship which lasted until the Queen's death. A statement by Carmen Sylva, "I live in an Edelweiss atmosphere," in my opinion applied even better to Editha von Rahden. Lord Byron says something like this in one of his poems: "The man who stands on the highest mountain amidst ice and snow is lonesome there, but he is closer to the sun than those below" (*Childe Harold's Pilgrimage,* Canto Three, verse 45). This thought also fits Editha von Rahden. She often had to feel the cold of her environment but possessed warmth from her inner light. Queen Elisabeth did not feel this coldness as much because she was able to overcome it through her imagination. The dreamy look in her beautiful blue eyes revealed her fanciful inner life. When I met her, though, she already had to wear glasses, and later her eyesight became so weak that she had to resort to a typewriter.

Queen Elisabeth of Romania (Carmen Sylva)

She had lost her only little daughter to diphtheria. A very beautiful photograph depicted the little girl, on her mother's back, looking into the distance with those same beautiful, dreamy eyes.

One day the Queen read me one of her poems: She meets a simple woman at the beach. In response to her question how many children the woman had, she received the answer, "Nine, and you?" "I have one, in heaven above." The Queen read this poem with so much feeling that we remained silent for a long time afterwards. I was reminded of a comment by Marie Hillebrand: "Carmen Sylva dips her pen into the heart."

Now my work at the institute began. Most classes were taught by former students who had passed their exams. In my opinion, that was a mistake, because it brought no fresh air from outside. For this reason, I engaged two young teachers from the French part of Switzerland, but they were unable to establish a foothold. Dr. Gachassin, a Frenchman with a Romanian wife, told me at the very beginning, "Here exists a xenophobia, a hatred of strangers." As time went by, I myself experienced examples of this hatred from the children, but not nearly as much as my poor young French women. Nevertheless, I persevered for a couple of years, which the Queen appreciated. Minister Sturdza, who had studied in Germany, was a great help. He carried out my request to use a separate house in the garden for children who were sick, and to have them cared for by a nurse. Until then there were no special provisions for sick children. I also established the procedure that the Queen would be notified whenever a child got sick. By the way, I thought the Romanian children were beautiful.

When I was not otherwise occupied, I would spend my Sunday mornings with the Queen. She had a great variety of interests and talents. At that time she did much painting, primarily aquarelles. She had made beautiful illustrations for a Bible at the large monastery. She was also an excellent organist. Her conservatory was a curiosity. It was full of magnificent plants with colorful parrots flying around calling in Romanian; "Long live King Karl!"

The King was extremely friendly, and just as unpretentious as his wife. Whenever I sat next to him at the table, I had to entertain him with my tales about Count Keyserling, his life with Bismarck as a student and other funny little experiences.

In the summer the whole court moved to Castel Pelesch beautifully located near Sanaia in the Carpathian mountains. We, that is, the whole institute, also moved to the country where we were housed rather primitively in a very old building. The house had a big yard with an old church. This settlement was in a lovely area, also not far from Sinaia, so that I could easily visit the Queen when she invited me. "It must be rather primitive there?" the King asked me with a smile during one visit. "Quite so," I responded. "I have to sleep on a sack of straw, but at least it is something really different."

The church service on Sunday as well as all other religious functions took place in the old church. I witnessed several baptisms, always by immersion as required by the Greek-Orthodox church even for adults who convert to this faith. The old priest, in his white flannel robe with a slit on one side, did not disdain to join in the hora. This is a typical Romanian dance. The dancers hold hands in a closed circle which gets smaller when they step forward and raise their arms. The dancers move forward and then back again, all to music, very serious and ceremonial. I learned this dance easily and participated often.

Our hikes were quite an experience. The whole band of students, led by a few gypsies with violins, walked singing through the lovely country. If we happened to come to a broad but shallow creek, everyone took off shoes and stockings and marched through the water. When we arrived at a suitable spot — usually on top of a mountain — we settled down, made a fire, roasted meat, and corn porridge, the national dish. Everyone was very cheerful; there was singing and dancing, and we did not hike back until quite late. Occasionally we had some incidents caused by the students' hatred of foreigners, but we always returned home safely.

In the evening I often sat on the church steps with the old priest, who was still a handsome man. I had learned the Romanian language sufficiently to be able to understand and write it, and so I enjoyed listening to him. He told me in all seriousness that Adam and Eve now live on the moon.

I received frequent invitations to Sinaia. The charming, picturesque Castel Pelesch won my special admiration. By the stairs leading from the vestibule to the upper story were two gnomes holding rock-crystals which were providing electric illumination in the evening. Upstairs was a beautiful music room with frescoes by Dora Hitz. Musical instruments of all kinds, like harp and violin, were arranged in picturesque groupings revealing the Queen's artistic sense. She loved to walk up and down during conversation. Once I tore my dress on a chair as I walked with her. The Queen laughed and said, "See, that happened because you always keep such a respectful distance from me. If you had stayed closer to me that would not have happened." Among other things, she told me about the student balls in Heidelberg and demonstrated how people danced in those days. She held me and we waltzed with outstretched arms down the corridor.

When I was visiting the Queen, I did not live right in the castle but rather in the small hotel in Sinaia. The wife of the German ambassador, Dr. Busch, whose apartment was very close to the hotel, befriended me. Once we planned a hike with her oldest daughter to one of the peaks in the Carpathian Mountains. We started out at five o'clock in the morning and arrived at our destination after a long and strenuous climb. At the top we immediately made a fire and Miss Beata Busch got fresh water for tea from a spring. Before long we had a delicious breakfast and enjoyed the beautiful view. All of a sudden I realized that it was quite late and I had an appointment with the Queen at ten o'clock. I had to make my way down at top speed! Forgetting the proverb, "make haste slowly," I stumbled over a tree root. Consequently I had to go home and change and unfortunately arrived a little late for my appointment with the Queen who was punctuality herself. Although my excuse was received most kindly, I felt great remorse for my offense and did not let anything like it happen again.

എ

When the court had moved back to Bucharest and the institute too had again taken residence in town, various festivities took place at the court. Because of my position, I was frequently invited to these affairs, but I never took part since I did not want to incur the expense of the formal dress. However, I did want to see the ball, and so I went with Mita Kremnitz, the wife of a local physician, to the gallery of the ballroom. (She collaborated with Carmen Sylva on her books. The novel *From Two Worlds* was written by the two ladies. In the correspondence between the Princess and the professor, Carmen Sylva is of course the Princess.)

In order to reach this gallery which was rarely used, we had to pass through a storage hall filled with all kinds of objects, and then go up a steep stairway. We reached the top just as the music announced the entrance of the Queen. Everyone wore Romanian costumes, which looked very impressive. The Crown Prince, nephew of the King, had come on a visit and was in the procession. The dancing included the newest, popular dances. We spent considerable time viewing the delightful spectacle. On our way down my friend's high heel got caught on a step and she tumbled down the steep stairs. Fortunately, she was not hurt, but our light was extinguished. In total darkness we had to feel our way among chandeliers, picture frames, and other such objects, and were glad to get back to the brightly lit rooms.

At Christmas I took a vacation and travelled to Dresden where my oldest sister was living. She was seriously ill and I was thankful that I could see her once more. Before leaving for Dresden, I prepared a Christmas celebration for my pupils. At my request, the assistant directress decorated a huge Christmas tree. I found out later that this did not have the desired impact. Upon seeing the lighted tree, the children immediately threw it over and tore it apart. The intended introduction of a German Christmas tree was a failure.

The Queen too had to abandon many an idea. She had had the lovely thought to found a "City for the Blind." Romania seems to have an unusual number of blind people, and a proper institution for the blind did not exist at that time. They were sometimes housed with families, but not very often. Usually they whiled away their lives in misery. The Queen thought it would be beneficial to establish a small community where the blind could carry out their crafts in the streets. They would have an opportunity to make brooms, brushes, shoes, etc., while they were supposed to be always singing and happy. Collections were taken and pictures of the Queen sold to get the project off the ground. She continued to tell me about this in later letters, but in the end the project must have come to naught because I never heard any more about it. The Queen always sought to help her people, but she found little support and was often deceived. For better or worse, she had to resign herself and escape into the realm of poetry where her creative gift blossomed.

While I was very busy preparing the examinations there was increasing political unrest. The approaching change of the cabinet was of utmost significance for me. Minister Sturdza resigned. He had been well-disposed towards me and had always been ready to consider my requests for better equipment and methods in the institute. Without his support I did not care to remain in the Balkans.

My two year stay had given me much of beauty and value: my friendship with the Queen, the study of a people totally foreign to me, the hikes by myself with a bottle of cyanide in my pocket for collecting butterflies and beetles — all remain as happy memories. Two changes, which I introduced, have survived as far as I know: For children with infectious diseases I established an infirmary with a nurse always on duty. Further, when a child died, which certainly did happen occasionally among five hundred pupils, I had the body brought to the church for a Greek funeral rite.

Now I departed from Bucharest and on my trip I had the unpleasant adventure of having the train get stuck in the snow, so that I was almost frozen when I arrived in Russia. Immediately I found a refuge in Semenov's house. Mr. Semenov was delighted with the specimens I had collected for him. Among them he discovered a new species of the small, colorful, iridescent chrysomelidae. In honor of our old friend, he called it Chrysomelid keyserlingi.

I received an invitation to come to Estonia and spent several weeks with Count Keyserling. At first we stayed in his house in Reval, in the square around the cathedral where the aristocracy used to have its apartments. We had much company because everyone in Count Keyserling's large circle of acquaintances wanted to hear about Romania, which was quite unknown at that time. I, however, was anxious to see Count Keyserling's interesting daughter, Baroness Taube, who lived out in the country. Soon we started on our sled ride to Raykuell. As on our previous trip, the woods were covered by deep snow, the postmistress at the first station gave us the news of the neighbors, and the servant, Otto, and the housekeeper, Adolfine, were waiting by the open door between the columns of the palace.

Before we headed for Yervacant, we spent some time sorting the beetles. By having a chrysomelida named after him, the Count was given a small symbol of recognition among natural scientists, and this seemed to please him very much since he always strove for truth. He used to say; "In biological science alone is truth. If, after thorough investigation a flower or a beetle has been identified and categorized, that cannot be shaken, it is true, while in most other sciences something new is always being discovered which shows the old to have been incomplete." We stayed in Yervacant with Baroness Taube for an extended visit. During the morning hours we would classify the beetles we had brought along, which was at times a difficult but always an interesting occupation.

As spring and summer passed and winter approached, I wanted to get back to work and accepted a temporary position in St. Petersburg with a motherless girl of twelve years. Since her father was busy during the day, I thought it would be nice to give loving care to the child. The fall was beautiful that year, and the family remained in its country home longer than usual. In the garden of the estate was a large pond with all kinds of water bugs. I was extremely interested in these, and wanted to see their transformation. For this purpose I caught four larvae of dytiscus in a glass of water. How can I describe my surprise the next morning, when I found only one fat larva. This cannibal had eaten the other three. I lost interest in further observation and threw the monster back in the pond. Baron Osten-Sacken, a great nature lover who visited me often, laughed at my disgust. In the future we concentrated on botany which also intrigued me.

∽

My life in St. Petersburg had become serious and quiet when I had a sudden revelation through the great singer, Therese Malten. With her, a sun rose for me, which once again illuminated my life and whose rays are still my companions. Angelo Neumann had come to St. Petersburg with the artists he had engaged to perform the complete cycle of *Der Ring des Nibelungen*. In spite of the high cost of tickets, I treated myself to the complete cycle, although I sat in the fifth balcony. I had never been so high up, and at first I was so dizzy that I had to grab the seats for support until I became used to the view into the depth. I had studied the text of the four music dramas thoroughly, but the music was a new experience and touched me deeply. Even the first notes of *Das Rheingold* which wonderfully arise from the deep, touched my soul. And when the Rhein Maidens have their joke with Alberich which ends so seriously, I watched and listened breathlessly. I felt removed from reality, as this marvellous creation heightened its impact from act to act. In the second act of *Die Walküre* I was enraptured by the jubilant sound of Therese Malten's "Hojotoho." I was captivated by the description of Siegmund's love for Sieglinde, devastated by the announcement of death for the Walküre. These words, in her sacred, transfigured rendition, made me realize: Therese Malten, you understand Wagner and have made his creation your own. Our enthusiasm reached its climax during the third act, when Brünhilde is expelled from the realm of the gods and sinks into Wotan's arms, illumined by a prophetic premonition. Unforgettable!

Then I saw *Siegfried*, intently followed the boy's development, accompanied him up the rock and through the fire, and was enraptured at Brünhilde's awakening. Her movements and the expression in her face during this scene were unforgettable. "Heil dir, Sonne, leuchtender Tag," she sang with such a warm tone, almost solemn, that I myself sank into a solemn mood. Finally, under the impact of the final song of rejoicing, I left the theatre elated. With intense anticipation I looked forward to the conclusions of the cycle, *Die Götterdämmerung*.

Wagner's genius overwhelmed me when the funeral march began as the moon broke forth and Siegfried's body was carried up the mountain. "Schweigt eures Jammers jauchzenden Schwall" Brünhilde sings approaching Siegried's bier with slow, majestic steps. This scene, together with the final tableau touched me deeply.

Therese Malten was called out a countless number of times that evening. I rushed down to see her close up, but I went too far into a cellar and had trouble finding my way back to the main floor. Yet, I was not too late, stormy applause was continuing and Brünhilde reappeared on the stage and bowed to the audience.

After the performance I drove to the Princess Volkonsky's home where we revelled in our enthusiasm. The excitement was shared by all the guests who were assembled here, and this select group decided to present to the singer the horse which she had used in *Die Götterdämmerung*. However, the horse belonged to the imperial cavalry and the request by the aristocracy was denied. We remained together until three in the morning. At home, resting on my bed, I thought about the great nobility of Therese Malten's art. Her overpowering emotion which was particularly apparent in the passion of the final scene had moved me so intensely that I could not sleep, and I decided to visit the singer.

Early the next morning I rode to the flower mart and gathered roses and narcissi into a bouquet. It was March in Germany, but still February in Russia and it snowed continuously. My little sled stopped in front of the hotel where Therese Malten had taken a suite. I had myself announced, but to my regret it was her lady companion who received me. I had been told that the singer rarely admitted strangers. However, when I told her companion that I came from Dresden, she left and almost immediately Therese Malten entered.

When I saw her, I understood Lohengrin's words, "My eyes saw you, my heart understood you." Her simplicity and openness dispelled any shyness on my part. Since she had been invited to a soiree by the Grand Duchess Elizabeth, the wife of Grand Duke Sergei, she wanted some information which I was able to give her. I saw her again on the evening of the soirée. She wore a simple, white dress, adorned only with a bouquet of violets, her pretty blond hair tied in a bun. The next day St. Petersburg society revelled in praise of the refined simplicity of her beautiful appearance.

The directors begged her to remain for a second cycle, but she had prior commitments, including several concerts, and had to leave. Her recitals won as much acclaim as her operatic roles. I was privileged to hear her later in all kinds of concerts and to join in the cheers which greeted her renditions of Schumann's "Überm Garten durch die Lüfte" and Liszt's "Loreley" among many others.

After Therese Malten's departure, St. Petersburg seemed dreary and empty. Therefore, I was delighted to accept an offer by the wife of General Baumgarten to give music and foreign language lessons to her fourteen-year-old daughter during the summer. We spent the summer on their estate near Kamenets Podolskiy. I took

Therese Malten

Therese Malten as Brünhilde

along the piano and voice extract of Parsifal and studied the work eagerly.

Life on this estate was most interesting and the work with my student easy and pleasant. The city of Kamenets Podolskiy was inhabited almost exclusively by Jews. In earlier times they had been given new names — some of them most peculiar, but they had been allowed to maintain their customs. On each visit to town I learned something new. The estate was surrounded by imposing mountains. The son of the family, who was in the diplomatic service in Munich but home for his vacations, planned many excursions for us. I remember very clearly how we drove into the woods on a very rough road in order to hear the wolves howl. In the summer they find plenty of food and are not dangerous, but their howling was still horrible. I much preferred to sit on my balcony at night and listen to the song of the nightingale.

Finally it was time for me to get ready for the trip to Bayreuth to hear *Parsifal*. I took my leave from the family and my pupil and travelled by way of Breslau. On the way to the border, the carriage got stuck in the mud and had to be pulled out by some oxen. I had to spend the night in a small hostel where I was kept awake by a terrible grunting noise. "Yes," said the hostess in the morning, "those were our pigs running around in the hall." But the coffee was excellent. Refreshed, I continued my journey without any more adventures.

After a short rest in Dresden, I went on to Bayreuth, full of anticipation. I stayed at the "Gasthof zur Sonne." The name already made me happy. It matched my mood and reminded me of Brünhilde's awakening in *Siegfried*. In the afternoon an endless procession of carriages rode up the hill to the Festspielhaus. In front of the theater surged a multitude.

At last a fanfare sounded, the sign that the performance was to begin. We heard the wonderful prelude with the "Amen" of the Catholic Mass. I was entranced. When Therese Malten as Kundry rushed on stage, out of breath with dishevelled hair, to bring balsam for Amfortas' wound, I was in ecstasy. The artist's skill at expressing Kundry's new longing for atonement and her desire to free herself from the power of Klingsor enraptured the audience. After the first act I ran to the nearby woods and, in tears, fell into the arms of Princess Volkonsky. Again the fanfare called us. In the next act in the scene with Klingsor as well as with Parsifal, Therese Malten was so magnificent that my delight knew no bounds.

Her facial expressions revealed every emotion: repentance, admiration of Parsifal, yearning for forgiveness. I was so deeply moved, I could not speak with anyone but stayed by myself until the third fanfare sounded. The whole third act was like a revelation for me. Kundry's baptism, the Good Friday spell, Parsifal with the glowing grail chalice in his hands, and the death of Kundry — they were experiences of overwhelming majesty. After this performance I again felt that someone who was able to portray so convincingly the search for that which is great and noble must herself be great and noble.

Returned to Dresden, I was able to ponder all I had experienced. Therese Malten had entered my life, and everything, whether work or play, was imbued with poetry. I had the great joy to be allowed to visit the artist in her home. My association with her inspired me to new tasks.

At that time she still lived in her little house in Klein-Zschachwitz. The house sat in the middle of the garden at the edge of a beautiful pine forest. In one direction was the view of the Elbe, in the other, a large meadow and the eleven hundred year old church of Hosterwitz. In her garden she grew vegetables and lovely flowers.

Once I decided to ask her opinion when I was in a quandary. I thought of giving an acquaintance my honest opinion in an embarrassing situation, but leaving several points out. "No," advised Therese Malten, "nothing halfway. I have never approved of partial measures, and certainly not in this situation. Either all or nothing." I adopted these words as my guiding principle from then on.

WORKING IN GERMANY
AND ENGLAND

Although I was enjoying my life then very much, I thought it would be wrong to refuse an offer to substitute for two months at an excellent boarding school in Berlin. The lady who headed the music and literature studies of the older girls had taken ill and needed a three months leave. The working environment which awaited me in Berlin was interesting and enjoyable. I was employed for certain daytime hours and certain evenings, otherwise I was completely free.

I had met Mr. von Helmholtz and his wife previously through Baroness von Rahden. Our acquaintance was now renewed. Helmholtz was a fascinating person. Along with all his erudition, he was kind and friendly. Often he would not say a word, but one could feel an inner harmony which spread over all who were present. "I feel as if the high priest is entering the hall," I once said to Mrs. von Helmholtz. She smiled, but agreed with me.

Some time later, this world-famous physicist was called to America and his wife accompanied him. On his return he fell down some steep stairs on the ship in Bremen. Unfortunately, this fall caused serious injuries and the great man, who could have made many further contributions, left this world too soon. Mrs. von Helmhotz was a strong woman and bore this hard blow with courage and composure.

I met her alone one afternoon soon after her husband's death. "There will be just the two of us today," she said, "and we shall spend a few pleasant hours. What would you like to eat?" Then we had a most enjoyable evening. As our conversation progressed, she said, "I have started a crusade against all gossip. It is so sad to hear the harsh judgments people pass on each other, and to find out how much weight is given to insignificant comments and trifles."

Anna von Helmholtz, née von Mohl, was a remarkable woman, remarkable in the literal sense of the word, for her comments were always worthy of remark. She was considered harsh, and she was;

but inside her was a feeling of great benevolence and a true love of mankind. She made many a sacrifice without letting others notice.

While I was staying in Berlin, the Luisenstift needed a new directress. Someone had recommended me for the position and I was asked to see the Empress Frederick (Victoria). The Empress was most kind. I told her that I had to decline the position since I had never taken an examination. She kept me a while longer and I love to remember the hour with her. She spoke much about the illness of her departed husband.

I saw the Empress again a short time later. I was visiting her lady-in-waiting, Miss Fabre du Four, when we heard a heavy knock on the door. "That is the signal that the Empress is coming," she said, and I fled into her bedroom. Soon I was called back at the request of the Empress. Even though she had gained much weight, she did not look well. She ascribed it to a bad cold, but, in fact, she had already fallen prey to that insidious disease which she suffered with such great patience. She would sometimes bite her hand to keep from screaming in her terrible pains, and thus her death was truly a relief for her.

છ્ర

After this short stay in Berlin, I returned to Dresden. I was delighted when, after a few weeks, I received an invitation from Queen Elisabeth of Romania to come to Holland. The famous masseur, Dr. Johann Georg Metzger, spent his summers in a beautiful country house in the small resort town, Domburg, and many of his patients followed him there.

On the way to Holland, I spent a night in Middelburg on the island of Walcheren and was amazed by the beautiful old oil paintings in the hotel. Most of them were portraits, discovered somewhere at an antique dealer's. Such valuable pictures are occasionally found in Dutch hotels, a rather unique happenstance.

From Domburg I continued in an open carriage which eventually drove into a parklike garden and stopped in front of a lovely, small house. What a surprise! The Queen herself was standing there opening the door for me. This embarrassed me, but she called right away, "What, no grey hair yet? Look at mine." And, in fact, hers had turned silver-grey. After this greeting, I was taken to my rooms, which lay in an adorable little house in the middle of the garden. At tea in the afternoon I was introduced. The Queen's brother, Prince von Wied, and his wife, born Princess of the Netherlands, were present. The Princess was a charming lady, and in her unaffected way she called, "Elisabeth, look at the rascals (Bengel) down there!" Those were her sons.

The Queen's friend, Helena Vacarescu, was also here. The two ladies often got up at four in the morning to work together. After tea, Miss Vacarescu recited selections from her collection of poems, "Chants d'Aurore" which was crowned by the French Academy, and the Queen read from her short stories. We retired early, as is the custom in spas. The next morning it was refreshing to swim in the ocean, gentlemen to the right, ladies to the left. The Queen looked lovely in her bathing costume, and she called to her brother, "You are the ocean god, and there come the river gods!" She was referring to her sons. There was a casual and gay atmosphere which lasted right into the big breakfast which we all attended with our hair hanging loose, at the request of the Queen. The sight was so funny, I had to laugh at everyone, including myself. In the afternoon we all rode in an open carriage to the home of a Dutch aristocrat with a beautiful park. The deer were so tame, they ate from our hands. At tea, a bowl of mulberries was passed. The young lady-in-waiting of the Princess Wied whispered to me, "Oh, I am so glad, I have never eaten mulberries before." The Princess Wied, who had not heard this comment, exclaimed, "What childhood memories! How long has it been, since I last saw mulberries?" Of course, she was served the whole bowl.

On our way home, I rode for a while with the Queen. Suddenly I remembered that New Year's Eve in Yervacant when my lead formation was interpreted as a little coach with two ladies, one of whom wore a crown.

Doctor Metzger was a big, strong man. His consultation was sought at most of the royal houses in Europe, and he treated royalty with the same frankness and ease as all his other patients. He told me that he possessed a strong magnetism in his thumb and had been able to cure a man of a long-standing, painful knee problem with one application of pressure with this thumb. His treatments were also very beneficial for the Queen, and after several weeks she went home well satisfied. When my stay came to an end, I parted from the Queen with a grateful heart. We remained in touch by correspondence. Her last, beautiful letter contained the words, "Here, at the grave of my king, I am waiting." She did not have to wait long. Soon after writing that letter, she followed her husband.

ဢ

At home in Dresden, I found the "Grünen Blätter" of Dr. Johannes Müller to which I had subscribed. Since the opera season had not yet started, I used my free time to read these journals and they fueled my desire to meet Johannes Müller personally. I decided to go to Mainberg and sent word of my coming. The castle, built in the year 1000 AD, was most attractive and unusual. Every room had a special name, the "Pillbox," where I first stayed, the "Yellow Dream," the "Gypsy Camp," the "Rococo Room," the "Goethe Room," and the "Biedermeier Room." I always occupied the last one on subsequent visits. From the windows one overlooked the Main and magnificent meadows and woods.

Johannes Müller was a highly respected person. His sole aim was to help people understand themselves which, in turn, would help them understand their fellow men. At that time, there were only a few guests at Mainberg, which I found much more enjoyable than later stays when the number of visitors had grown considerably. There were no servants at Mainberg, only so-called "helpers," young girls, primarily from the upper classes, who took care of things. They received only a small allowance, but were there because of their admiration for Dr. Müller and they loved their work. Their reward was a dance every Thursday evening which Dr. Müller arranged himself. The helpers, some of whom were real beauties, wore flowers and garlands, and almost everyone danced, even a seventy-three-year-old lady participated.

Whoever wanted to discuss a personal problem could confide in Dr. Müller. The walks with him provided the best opportunity for such discussions. On Sunday and twice during the week he gave extremely interesting lectures in the afternoon. I remember one about carrying a grudge. He was of the opinion that a cultured person should never carry a grudge, and "embracing" this fault showed a lack of education. At the close of his lectures he would display his wonderful sense of humor. This gift of God he possessed in abundance. I met many young people here who were devoted to Johannes Müller and who distinguished themselves in various fields later on. The great freedom given to young people at Mainberg never led to excesses. Frequently, there were engagements — and many an unhappy marriage may have been prevented because the parties had a chance to get to know each other thoroughly ahead of time, and did not discover each other's faults after they were married.

Following my visit to Mainberg I made my second trip to Bayreuth. Again, I lived in a different world. As before, I stood in front of the house which held such magic, and heard the fanfare which called me inside where new impressions awaited me. The music touched me even deeper than the first time. Parsifal's

Therese Malten at Bayreuth

161

wanderings to the Gralsburg, the Good Friday spell, and Kundry's marvellous conversion — to be allowed to hear and see such art is a gift of grace from God. To my great joy I had the good fortune to see and talk with Therese Malten on the days between the two performances. Filled with these impressions I returned to Dresden.

I was living in the Hotel Bellevue. Soon after my return, an English lady, Mrs. Melville, came and asked me to recommend a governess for her only daughter who had had many different governesses and was not easy to guide.

"Please, show me a picture of your daughter," I asked her. She brought the picture and I studied it for a long time. The longer I looked at this face, the firmer I became in my desire to educate this girl myself. Her features expressed so much intelligence and spirituality that I told myself: This girl can become somebody. Mrs. Melville was delighted with my offer, and we decided that I would begin my position with her in October.

Before beginning my new position, I spent a pleasant time in Dresden. Among other things, I reaped something that my dear brother-in-law in Hamburg had sown. Some years earlier, a large marble relief of the burial of Jesus had been placed in the St. Petri church. The artist, Hermann Schubert, who had created this masterpiece, was bringing it from Rome to Hamburg. My sister and her husband immediately invited him to stay at their home. A warm friendship developed among the three. Hermann Schubert belonged to the circle of artists around King Ludwig I of Bavaria, which included, among others, Marees, Böcklin, Schwind, Lenbach, Feuerbach, and Liszt. After he returned to Rome, he met the woman who was to become his life's companion. Since 1873 they had lived in Dresden, where I now met him as a happy husband and father. The hospitality which the young artist had once enjoyed in my sister's house, was repaid to me many times over. Mrs. Schubert was a very talented woman whose actions were guided by highly idealistic goals. Already as a child she had learned to use her wealth not for outward show and pleasure but to deepen and expand her intellectual and spiritual pursuits. As homemaker, she knew how to create a relaxed atmosphere and how to make her guests comfortable. I spent many pleasant hours in their home. Professor Schubert was always engaged in new projects. Even in the winter of 1917, during the war, he had started another piece, but was unable to complete it, for he contracted pneumonia and succumbed after a few weeks. The children held on to the family values and were as genuine as their parents.

Their son, Professor Dr. Otto Schubert, not only gained high acclaim as an architect in his hometown and elsewhere, but he also won recognition far beyond Germany's borders with his comprehensive book, *The History of the Baroque in Spain*.

The time came to say my good-byes. I travelled to England by way of Ostende. When we started the voyage, it was very foggy. The ominous sound of the fog horn terrified me. I saw that the life boats were lowered and asked, "why?" The answer, "In case of a collision," caused me to be very apprehensive on the entire passage. But we landed safely in England, and I reached my destination by train on a branch line from London. There I got to know and, I must say, instantly love, my new student. My intuition had not misled me. The intelligence of this girl was of considerable help in her education. One could calmly explain to her why this or that in her thinking and acting was not right. In this way, our association was uninhibited and harmonious.

When the family moved to the townhouse in London, Violet had piano lessons from Dannreuther. He was an excellent teacher. I was particularly interested in him because he was a great admirer of Richard Wagner who had stayed with him in London. I loved to observe the piano lessons and then hear stories about Richard Wagner afterwards. Dannreuther showed us the beautiful writing of the composer in an original score which Wagner had given to him.

We had a lovely Christmas celebration. Violet and I decorated the splendid tree with silver stars and icicles which I had ordered from Dresden. Many guests had been invited for dinner and a very old silver goblet filled with beer was passed around. Everyone had to take a swallow and make a speech which was very amusing. On New Year's Eve the parents were away on a trip and I was alone with Violet. At midnight, when my pupil had already laid down to rest, I sat down on her bed, and we read Tennyson's wonderful New Year's poem. When we came to the line, "Ring out the false, ring in the true," we experienced such a solemn feeling that I remember it to this day.

The following year I did not spend New Year's Eve with Violet, but rather with friends in Wales. An acquaintance had introduced me to a Mrs. Schwabe. When she had given her secretary a few days off, Mrs. Schwabe had asked me to take her dictation of some letters. Now she invited me to her castle in Wales. It was beautifully situated, not far from the old castle of Carnarvon, where Edward II had been born in 1284 in a very small room, unfortunately not to a happy life! Because of his weakness for flattery, he suffered a horrible end.

Mrs. Schwabe was a highly educated woman. She was very wealthy and hence able to freely follow her inclination to support artists. Jenny Lind had once lived with her, and Richard Wagner was one of her acquaintances. Since she was also interested in politics she had become close friends with Cobden, the champion of free trade. His life-size portrait was hanging in her salon.

Mrs. Schwabe led an active social life, and just at the time of my visit she had invited the famous, later infamous, poet Oscar Wilde along with numerous relatives. Wilde was big and strong; his hair was parted in the middle and hanging straight down on both sides. At dinner he always had expensive orchids in his lapel. One morning I was busy with the translation of an article about our disability insurance which had been requested by Chamberlain. From my window I saw the water, the mountains, and the long railroad bridge which connects the mainland with Anglesey. In the midst of my work I was disturbed. The door opened and Oscar Wilde entered. He was interested in the translation. After discussing the social issues we touched on the religious. He was of the opinion that Christians were all low spirited, and that Jesus himself had been gloomy. I contradicted him and pointed out that he even changed water into wine at the wedding at Canaan. "Well," he laughed, "but he never did that again." I could not find an answer to that statement.

On New Year's Eve we all formed a circle, as was the custom, held hands and sang the old Scottish song, "Auld Lang Syne." After we had entered the new year, we still lingered over pleasant conversation and Oscar Wilde improvised a ghost story. He told about a family who had acquired a beautiful castle and were moving in. What a surprise, when they entered the dining hall and found that ghosts were sitting there having a joyous meal! Half scared and half nonplussed, the new lord of the castle stood and stared while the ghost at the head of the table remarked with indignation that it was their dinner time, and he and his friends thought it was strange that the new owner wanted to disturb them. Somewhat abashed, the new master said that his family wanted to eat too. "We won't allow it," said the first ghost; "we shall keep our dinner hour." Oscar Wilde was telling this sometimes with sarcasm, sometimes with irony, and then again in a totally serious manner. Initially we laughed, then we began to wonder about the point of the story and were all in suspense. However, our curiosity was not to be satisfied. It was getting too late and we had to retire, the tale unfinished. Oscar Wilde used the theme of this story later in his short story, "The Ghost of Canterville," but with drastic changes. In that story the courage of a young girl breaks the power of the ghosts and releases the house from their spell.

The next evening, the last one before my departure, Oscar Wilde sat next to me at dinner. The conversation drifted to a theft which a society lady had perpetrated upon her cousin. The latter had shown her a pearl necklace and the secret drawer in her desk, where she kept it. Soon afterwards, the precious necklace was gone, and automatically the suspicion fell upon the lady. She, apparently indignant, decided to sue her cousin, and a prominent attorney took her case. Suddenly, in the middle of his statement, he received a letter proving beyond doubt that the lady was a thief. Strangely enough, the matter seemed to rest with that. We were all appalled, and I said, "I hope her social status will not be taken into consideration, and she will be put in prison." "Have you ever experienced that someone got better in prison?" Oscar Wilde asked. Not long afterwards, he himself was in prison.

The next morning I met him again on the station platform. I was travelling modestly third class, he, wrapped in a beautiful fur, first class. What a dreadful contrast to the later incident when he was on the platform waiting for a branch line, displayed, so to speak, dressed in prison garb. Lord Grimthorpe, with whose family I was to live later on, said correctly that one should have given the poet writing material from the beginning, rather than forcing him to wind heavy rope which caused his delicate hands to bleed.

I had become friends with Mrs. Schwabe's secretary, Helene Klostermann. She was an outstanding person. Years later I saw her again in Berlin after she had become directress of a well-known school in Bonn. Her work for Mrs. Schwabe was pleasant but quite strenuous, and so she was given a four week vacation during which I substituted for her. This was an interesting occupation for me. It gave me the opportunity to get in contact by letter with many prominent persons. Mrs. Schwabe's devotion to writing could take on huge dimensions. Sometimes I could not help laughing, when she interrupted an interesting conversation, saying, "Come, let's write a little." This "little" could stretch out to three hours. She was very practical and had a folder made with twenty-five sections where she filed her letters alphabetically. She was also practical in everyday affairs. Once, when she saw me about to give one of her men a too generous tip for an outing in a rowboat, she said, "Never, 'plus paraitre qu'etre,' and your means are not in proportion to this gift." I enjoyed my four weeks with her very much. Then I returned to my professional position with the Melvilles.

Life with my pupil, Violet, was extremely stimulating. We were steeped in the study of history for which both of us had a particular interest. Macaulay and Taine offered the best material for it. We studied English and French history as well as the works of Georg Weber, Ranke, and Gregorovius. This was an excellent way of dispelling the boredom which we felt in the unpleasant country home which had been rented for us. Nature had nothing to offer, the land was flat and dreary. The minister's Sunday sermons caused us either to yawn or to laugh, which we were unable to suppress in spite of valiant efforts. One time he wanted to condemn the sins of the hunters. He leaned far over the pulpit and shouted, "There they ride to hell, raise the red lantern: danger, danger!" We could not control ourselves any longer. Such moments can be actually painful.

We were glad when our departure neared. We ran into the fields, threw our hats into the air and shouted, "Hurrah!"

Joyfully we returned to our nicely furnished study and "Gemütlichkeit." London gave us plenty of compensation for the past three months. Violet was still going to bed quite early and I had my evenings free. By chance, Sarah Bernhardt and Eleonora Duse were in London at the same time, and during one week I saw both of them as the Lady of the Camelias. It was most interesting to watch the difference in concept and in acting of these two great artists. When in the final act Bernhardt, already dying, gathered all her strength and called out, "I do not want to die," chills went down my spine. When Eleonora Duse whispered these same words from the depth of her soul, trembling, almost begging, I wept.

Princess Volkonsky wrote to me from St. Petersburg, "How I envy you that you can hear the Duse." With the letter in my pocket I went to a florist that same day to order some irises for the Duse, who was to appear as Cleopatra that evening. My way home led along Duke Street. Suddenly the Duse stood in front of me. I grasped the opportunity and addressed her in French, "How fortunate that I meet you, Signora Duse. I have a letter from Princess Volkonsky." — "And I a telegram," she said and pulled it out of her pocket and read it to me. Then I gave her my letter to read, which pleased her very much. We shook hands and I went on my way.

In the evening's performance, the slave girls in Cleopatra's entourage carried my irises. At the end of the drama, I wanted at least to see the Duse climb into her carriage, and I joined the crowd waiting for her. Finally she came, followed by a theater usher who carried a mass of flowers. She advised him to put the flowers in a waiting cab, because she could not stand the strong scent. However, he misunderstood her broken English and was about to put all the flowers in her hansom. I quickly explained things to him, and he then followed her wishes. I left and was just about to cross the street at a corner when the hansom came around the corner and stopped right in front of me. "Please, come in," said the Duse in her soft, gentle voice. She did not have to ask me twice. Instantly I was in the carriage. Soon we reached the hotel Savoy where the artist was staying, and we took the lift up to her room.

"Make yourself comfortable," she said, "I will be right back. I just want to change. Please, order something to eat." I did not do that but just waited for her to return. She appeared in a simple black silk gown, and partook of a Spartan meal. I stuck to lemonade, which was very refreshing in the heat of that summer. Eleonora Duse told me much about her life, and then she confessed that she was always in fear. The threat that her estranged husband might take their daughter was always hanging above her like a sword of Damocles. She told me that the daughter was in a boarding school in Dresden, but that I should not visit her, because she wanted her brought up without any fuss. I adhered to her wishes. This daughter is now happily married to a Professor of Aesthetics at Cambridge University. The hours with Eleonora Duse were wonderful and unique. I never saw her again. She left London that same week.

❧

The London season had ended and we moved back to the country home of Mrs. Melville. After several weeks I started on my vacation trip to Dresden. I stayed a few days in Berlin because Therese Malten was appearing there as guest artist in the role of Eva in *Die Meistersinger*. During the entr'acte the lady next to me dropped her opera glasses and they landed at my feet. Before I could pick them up, my neighbor on the right had bent over for the same purpose. However, she bumped into the first lady and her hair got caught on a button. It was up to me, sitting between them, to put an end to this comic situation. Through this incident I met my neighbor on the left, a charming English woman, Mrs. Napier Miles, who had come to Germany with her son, Napier, because they both adored Therese Malten. They had followed the artist from Dresden to Berlin.

Since her little house had been subject to frequent flooding, Miss Malten had built herself a larger country house in Dresden. She had literally acquired this house by singing for it. The house was of simple elegance with stairs leading from the garden to the veranda, bordered with blooming geraniums. As I could not find enough words to express my delight with this real artist's home, Therese Malten said thoughtfully, "Every place can be beautiful, but I like it best at home."

After a short pause, she continued, "I will tell you of an experience which demonstrates how much I love my home. It was the year 1881, and I was concluding my six week guest engagement in London with a final German performance as Elisabeth in *Tannhäuser*. After the conclusion I was invited to the box of the Prince of Wales, later King Edward VII, who after many kind words of appreciation asked me to give him and his wife the pleasure of spending an evening with them. The beautiful Princess also urged me. At first I was not sure how I should respond to this request, but then I said haltingly, 'Unfortunately I have to pass up this high honor, because I must be in Dresden on June 21.' The Princess thought one could send a telegram, the Prince suggested I delay my departure. I felt my face flush. I thanked them again for the honor, but insisted on my planned departure. The Prince said, 'You must have a reason which we do not know.'

'Yes, Your Royal Highness,' I answered firmly, 'June 21 is my birthday which I always celebrate at home, and I do not want to make an exception this year.' The Prince pressed my hand and shook it, saying, 'That is nice. I will be thinking of you on June 21.' He was not offended by my refusal but continued to be very kind to me."

One evening after a performance I went to the "Europäisher Hof" and saw Anton Rubinstein sitting alone at a table. He came at once and greeted me warmly, and we spent an hour together. He had come to Dresden to see the performance of his *Children of the Heath* with Therese Malten and was looking forward to it. Otherwise he made a very melancholy impression on me. He talked about his fear of becoming blind and of his sadness at the death of Baroness Rahden, whom he revered greatly and to whom he dedicated his *Paradise Lost*. He also included a portrait of Editha von Rahden in the piano pieces which he published under the title; "Portraits of Kamenny-Ostrov," a short, beautifully melodious composition. I told him of a dream which the Baroness had had in Ragaz. She had dreamed that she had met Anton Rubinstein and had been astonished to see him wearing pink bows with long ribbons on his shoulders. "Anton Grigorievich, why are you wearing these ribbons?" she had asked him. — "Because I am so happy," he had replied. We were both quiet, then he said with a deep sigh, "That was a dream." He looked so incredibly sad that my heart grew heavy. I never saw him again.

My friends, the Semenovs from Russia, were also in Dresden. They came every year to see Miss Malten. Naturally, they lived in the Hotel Bellevue. We saw Kretschmer's *Folkunger* together in which Therese Malten represented the Queen with grandeur. We also saw Goldmark's *Queen of Saba* with her in the title role. We three left the opera house enraptured and stayed together until late into the night.

On evenings when Therese was free, she often invited us for dinner, since the Semenovs had come to Dresden just for her. We were always charmed anew by her graceful way of playing the hostess. These were festive days for me. But they too came to an end. The Semenovs had to go home and I had to return to England.

At my arrival at the Melville's country home, I found Violet in the process of erecting the statue of Therese Malten as Brünhilde. That was a most suitable reception. After several delightful weeks we prepared for our departure. Mr. and Mrs. Melville were going to Italy, Violet and I to the south of France. We all stayed a short while in Paris then travelled to the Riviera and went our separate ways from a station between Cannes and Nice. The parents continued their trip to Italy while we soon reached our destination, Antibes.

Our hotel was situated at the tip of the spit. From there we looked upon the spot where Napoleon once had come ashore returning from Elba. It was a delightful stay. How often we watched the incredibly beautiful sunset from our window. I never again saw such colors: at times the whole sky seemed aflame, then again little gold clouds appeared on a violet background which slowly changed to blue and then became light green. We gratefully acknowledged our good fortune in being able to see this almost daily. Not only in the sky did we find beauty — the earth too delighted the eye with its splendor. Magnificent red and violet anemones were blooming, as was the reddish-purple star anemone with black calyx. We rested under olive trees on our excursions which often passed through extremely interesting little old towns.

We visited Grasse where the famous perfumes are produced. To our surprise we looked upon mountains of violets, rose leaves, and orange blossoms, and the air was filled with the fragrance of these flowers. Wherever one looked there was beauty, including the yellow and light blue porcelain of Valori which was made nearby. More interesting than pretty were the army worms which crawled in long rows, one behind the other, moving along like a long freight train. The strange fact is that if you take one caterpillar ever so quietly even from near the end of the procession, the leader stops at once and the whole train rests. In the branches of the evergreens we saw thin webs in the shape of balls with young caterpillars. Nobody could answer our question, "Who spins these balls?" Only later in London in the zoological museum did we get our answer. The head of the insect division read to us that the little larvae get to work spinning their house as soon as they have crawled out of the eggs.

What a wonderful time we had in Antibes. We not only relished the splendor of nature but we also took an interest in the people, a handsome race. I remember a shepherd leaning on his staff, who presented a picture for a painter. He was chuckling to himself at our vain efforts to start a fire with matches that had gotten wet. He succeeded in starting our fire amazingly fast with a flintstone.

In the meantime it had become very hot in Antibes. We longed for the English climate and were glad when we were called back to England. There our life settled into its regular routine. The interesting piano lessons with Dannreuther were resumed with only a short break at Whitsuntide. I used this holiday to accept an invitation from Mrs. Napier Miles to her magnificent property, Kings Weston near Bristol. The whole living area, including two huge halls, was at ground level. Wide stairs led up to a square gallery and all the bedrooms opened onto this gallery. The son of the house was musically gifted. He had studied music with Draesecke in Dresden. Our common admiration for Richard Wagner and Therese Malten often provided the subject for our conversations. We discussed the individuality of the great singer, compared to others, who usually revealed with whom they had done their dramatic studies. With Therese Malten, everything was spontaneous. She did not act Isolde, she *was* Isolde. Watching her performance became an experience, and everyone who saw it instinctively felt the ennobling quality which emanated from her art. Napier Miles and his mother felt this deeply, and we spent lovely evenings dedicated to the memory of our days in Dresden.

The spring was particularly lovely that year, and after our afternoon tea under the big evergreen cedar in the garden, I would stroll further along and enjoy the evening cool on the beautiful large terrace at the end of the park. Mrs. Miles called this her old-fashioned garden. Here I found many of the flowers I had loved as a child: Maltese cross, larkspur, bluebells, monkshood, the large and simple rose Gallica — in short, a host of familiar blossoms which awakened childhood memories.

While in Kings Weston, I received a letter from Therese Malten with the sad news that my beloved friend, Count Alexander Keyserling, had died. She had read the notice in a German newspaper. Knowing of my close friendship with him, she wanted to spare me the pain of reading this news in the paper and informed me in tender words. The very next day I received the death notice, sent by friends in Russia. Count Alexander Keyserling had died of erysipelas, and in order to serve science, he had recorded the daily progress of this fatal disease in his diary, almost to the day of his death. His passing was a great loss for me, as it was for all who knew him. His grandson, Count Hermann Keyserling, inherited the wonderful estate Raykull, where fields and meadows, trees and flowers were a testimony to the departed's love of nature. All this has now been taken from Count Hermann by Estonia through expropriation.

My friends were very sensitive and left me alone much of the time, so that I could learn to cope with my sorrow among the abundant flora and with the spectacular view of the Bristol Channel.

In Lingfield I met Violet again. I have always been attracted by the opportunity to guide a maturing young girl into adulthood. Sometimes I saw their future like a carpet spread out before them, into which they were to weave their decisions and experiences. One of my young friends who was inclined to be melancholy once said to me, "my carpet is black, but I manage to weave some roses and forget-me-nots into it." I told her, the background was too dark, and she should try to unravel the black threads. This she did later on and succeeded in weaving in a lovely grey. In Violet's carpet everything was bright and clear. Just as she overcame difficulties then, she made her way with determination in later years. On one occasion I had reason to caution her, "You are right in what you are intending to do, but I can tell you beforehand that certain persons will be very upset. Are you willing to risk that?" "Then they will just have to be upset," she said very calmly. In this way she pursued her path through life unerringly, became a happy wife and mother and the center of a lively family circle. However, she did not have that family egotism which is limited, often with great sacrifice, exclusively to one's own family; rather, like a good fairy, she spread her benevolence in all directions.

After four happy years I left my now seventeen-year-old friend, who soon afterwards was to enter the adult world. However, only one year passed before she and her parents came to Dresden and visited me.

I settled into a very pretty garret in the Hotel Bellevue. Across the street, in the beautiful, old Catholic Hofkirche, I could hear the music of the High Mass on Sundays without having to go far. I especially enjoyed the Hasse "Te Deum" played on special occasions. Its exuberant joy was contagious.

I was eager to find a new position, but so far nothing suitable had presented itself. Then, one Sunday morning, I went, as always, to the reading room of the hotel to get the latest political news, when I happened to see the "Kreuz-Zeitung" on the table opened to the page with the advertisements. My eyes fell upon the notice, "Mrs. Dora de Cuvry is looking for a lady for several hours a day for the education of her half-grown niece." I immediately set out for the address and had myself announced to Mrs. de Cuvry. I was led into a tastefully furnished room, and a blond lady in her middle years but of youthful appearance entered. We felt a mutual liking for each other, and it was agreed that I would come weekdays from nine to one o'clock.

I moved to "Victoriahöhe" in Loschwitz where I rented a room with a beautiful view but a bed as hard as stone. But one gets used to anything! Whenever possible, I took my meals in the lovely garden.

It was most refreshing to walk in the cool morning air through the woods to the magnificent estate of Mrs. de Cuvry. In earlier days, the "Schillerschlösschen" (little Schiller palace) had stood here, a restaurant which had been a favorite destination for walkers from all over Dresden. Under the stately trees one had a charming view of the Elbe. In this spot Mr. and Mrs. de Cuvry had their beautiful home built according to their own design. Tragically, Mr. de Cuvry succumbed to an incurable disease soon after it was completed. His intelligent wife then became the energetic but charming mistress of the property. Not only in summer was the villa attractive; in winter the conservatory adjacent to the salon offered an almost magical surrounding. The lighting was so distributed that sitting under the large plants one imagined being in a garden in the orient. The lessons took place in a pleasant room upstairs with a view of the Elbe.

Since I had never acquired a diploma and could not teach my students in proper school fashion, it was my main goal to instill in them an interest in everything which gives life value. And I usually succeeded. Mrs. de Cuvry, in her charming manner, used to say; "You set the girls on their feet and say, now run!"

There was always much activity in the house, since Mrs. de Cuvry had a wide span of intellectual interests. In her home I met Paul Wiecke who is now director of the Dresden Schauspielhaus, and who was a frequent visitor to her home. His "Richard II" and many years later his marvellous presentation of "Ysbrand" by the Dutch writer Frederik van Eden are indelibly etched in my memory. I love to remember my teaching in Mrs. de Cuvry's home and, after work, visiting friends or walking in the woods. The crown of my days was when I received an invitation from Therese Malten. Often I listened to her improvisations at the piano in her wonderful music room where the walls were hung not with wallpaper but with the ribbons which once had tied the flowers presented to her, inscribed with passionate words of admiration and love. Sometimes it would get dark while she was still playing: Beethoven, Richard Wagner, Mozart, as well as modern composers. Beautiful modulations led from one to the other. I usually sat in a corner, and when she closed with the chorale; "A mighty fortress is our God," I became aware that I could never forget these hours. Everyday life took on a special glow, nothing remained grey on grey, after a visit with her. This music room contained the most precious souvenirs: gold and silver laurel wreaths and an exquisite silver set of armor with shield and lance which innumerable admirers had presented to her. One could sit there for hours and still not finish looking.

At one of these visits I asked the singer why she so rarely appeared at social occasions. She answered, "I have always hated coffee- and tea-parties, and, fortunately, never had the leisure for such a waste of time. Whoever has time for that kind of party is lacking work; and he who does not work seriously will wither like a flower without sun. In addition, I found that there is too much gossiping at these events. Gossip is the most dangerous poison. If one does not have any other topic of conversation one should gossip about oneself but not others."

I was fortunate in that my next position did not force me to give up these precious visits to the artist's home. The Countess Hohenthal desired a lady to give a year of music and language lessons to her almost grown daughter. Mother and daughter heard about me when they were spending a day in Dresden. I liked them both at our very first meeting and we decided that my engagement would begin in July.

My former student, Dora, was now in college preparing for her teacher's examinations. Her younger sister remained as "house daughter" with her aunt, Mrs. de Cuvry, in whose company she would have opportunity to advance her knowledge. With the prospect of frequent occasions to see each other, we parted joyfully. Life did bring us together often, and both sisters, who have been happy wives and mothers for a long time, are still my friends.

During my vacation I attended a memorable celebration, the twenty-fifth anniversary of Therese Malten's first appearance on stage. It was a festive and impressive event, but it ended in horror. *Tannhäuser* was being performed and her admirers had made her a gift of a solid gold crown for the occasion. Her Russian devotees had sent precious stones for it, and the jeweler Elimeyer had worked all this into a truly artistic gem. It had been the original intent to crown the artist as Elisabeth with this diadem at the end of the performance, but at the urging of many of her admirers, it was presented to her behind the closed curtain. When Elisabeth greeted the hall in the second act, the joyous applause did not want to end and Schuch had to put down the baton while the house, filled to every last seat, continued its "bravo" calls. After the third act, the ecstatic roar began anew. The curtain remained closed for a few minutes, and when it opened the stage was transformed into a sea of flowers. The enthusiasm of the audience knew no limits. There was screaming and shouting. Again and again Therese Malten reappeared, the darling of the audience. At last she came to say a few words. Quiet was established and she began, "My deepest thanks..." At that moment the stagehand, under the impression that the quiet meant that the artist was absent from the stage, let the curtain down and — what horror! it hit the singer. She rushed at once to her dressing room.

A large part of the audience was not aware what had happened and kept calling for her. Finally she appeared once more, a handkerchief over her bleeding face. Then her strength left her and she was quickly driven home in her carriage. The multitude in the square in front of the theater knew nothing of the accident. The joyous acclaim and the shower of flowers which accompanied the open carriage gave me, standing in the middle of the square, an eerie feeling. She suffered for a long time from the effects of this happening, and yet, one has to be grateful that she was not wearing the gold crown when the curtain dropped, since that could have been fatal.

Several days later I met my friends, the Semenovs, who were staying at the "Kurhaus" in Blasewitz for two months and had invited me to join them. From Blasewitz it was easy to check on the recovery of our dear friend, and Mrs. Semenov and I did this daily, while her husband pursued his scientific interests with his friend, the butterfly collector Bang-Haas. The great scholar was so absentminded that he once sat for two hours in the Goethe Garden, while we were expecting him for a rendezvous in the Schiller Garden. The time spent with my friends from St. Petersburg is among my most cherished memories. I have often discovered that nothing draws people closer together than a common admiration for someone else.

୶

In July I began my new employment with the Countess Hohenthal. I made the short trip to Eilenburg, where I was met by a carriage which brought me to the castle Hohenpriesnitz. It would more accurately be called a mansion. Embraced by blue wisteria which climbed all the way to the third floor, it presented a charming picture. Our rooms offered a lovely view over garden and park, and all the furnishings and decorations demonstrated the loving care of the Countess. It was a joy for me to see the friendly and kind expression in her blue eyes whenever she entered the room. She also had a great sense of humor, and when she read a Dickens novel to us in the evening, we would often laugh heartily. It was delightful to live here in such close touch with nature. After the excursions of the summer came the hunts. The participants gathered in the evening for lively discussions. The two older sisters of my pupil, Gerda, were real beauties, both very tall with handsome carriage. I was told that they were greatly admired at the court not only for their beauty but also for their unaffected manner. I once asked the Countess how she had succeeded in raising her daughters to be such unassuming, genuine persons. "I did not contribute much to that," she answered, "Believe me, life in the country is an absolute necessity in the upbringing of children. Here they do not hear the gossip and small talk so common in the cities. Animals and flowers are their companions and remain so in later years."

I remember an incident in the spring. Gerda and I were playing the overture to *Der Freischütz* four-handed, when the Countess called the children from downstairs, "Children, come out and hear the thrush singing!" All of us, including Gerda's two older brothers, came and listened attentively.

The time before Christmas was particularly delightful. Beginning on the first Sunday of Advent, every evening one more candle was lit on the Christmas tree, and we accompanied this ritual with singing. Often the three sisters would also dance together. I would play a Strauss waltz and the three lovely girls with arms around each other performed a graceful roundelay.

In this period, a thought came back to me which had occupied me often when I was a young girl. In those early days I childishly considered writing a book about attainable happiness. Of course, this topic has been written about in many different versions; however, in the midst of this charming family I realized again how happy people can be surrounded by the natural world, without any outside stimulation. Nature, with its rhythm of becoming and perishing, offers so much that is interesting, that it should bring, if not happiness then at least contentment to anyone who is not deaf and blind. I am reminded of an unusual woman whom I knew in Hamburg. She suffered from a spinal cord disease, was bound to her bed and had become totally blind. When I came to visit her one morning, she called to me already as I approached her room, "Imagine, I heard the nightingale last night." She was blissful, although not free from pain. There are now educational institutions in Germany where children are brought up in the country. Schnepfenthal was probably one of the first of these schools, but a large number has been established since then. Naturally, the children go home to their parents during vacations.

Fortunately I could occasionally attend musical performances in Dresden without missing any lessons. I left for Dresden immediately after my last lesson and arrived in time, before the first act, saw the whole performance, had dinner in the "Europäischer Hof" and headed back for Eilenburg at about 3 AM. I arrived in Hohenpriesnitz for breakfast and started my lessons punctually at 9 o'clock as usual. *Der Cid*, by Peter Cornelius, was given its local premiere during that time. Therese Malten sang the role of Ximene. An interesting feature in this performance was Therese Malten's portrayal of the Spanish role. She captured the dignity of the Spanish character not only in her appearance but also in her acting. The music also moved me deeply. Such special pleasures added spice to my life.

The spring seemed particularly beautiful that year in Hohenpriesnitz. The Countess' hyacinths and tulips bloomed profusely, the birds sang at the top of their voices, and we would sit in the park at the Mulde late into the evenings and enjoy being alive.

One evening I received a letter from Mrs. de Cuvry asking me to take on the education of two motherless young girls in the home of a Mr. Beckett in England. It was the time of the Boer war, and I refused the position for political reasons. A second letter came in which Mr. Beckett pleaded with me to accept the position and added that his daughters were to spend the coming winter in Dresden. Lady Bingham, my former student Violet, had influenced him make in making this plan. (She had married Lord Bingham when she was still very young; he later became Earl of Lucan through the death of a relative.) I decided to accept.

I spent one more beautiful summer month at Hohenpriesnitz. It was a joy to watch the games of the young people. The three lovely sisters had many visitors from Berlin. I still see them in their big straw hats, green bands blowing in the wind, taking part in the games. The two brothers also invited friends frequently. The oldest son, Count Lothar, was very charming. He began a career in the diplomatic service but died young in Paris from a serious but short illness. At one of my later visits to Hohenpriesnitz, his mother, sad but composed, showed me the beautiful gravestone designed by Wilhelm Kreis, which marked the last resting place of this son. Now she, too, is resting there. Death struck her not too long after her son. She suffered a stroke, and in that moment, so as not to frighten her husband, she whispered, "Say nothing to the Count."

The second son, who was always cheerful and amused everyone with his funny ideas, took over the estate and became a good husband and father. Countess Emmy, who was also happily married, died in the delivery of her second child; and Anna, Countess Turckheim, is head of a large family. Gerda, my pupil, is now Baroness von dem Busche and lives with her husband and children in Nicolassee near Berlin. The parting from this family who had become so dear to me was eased by the certainty that we would see each other often.

After only a few but very enjoyable days in Dresden I set out for London.

WITH THE FAMILY
OF LORD GRIMTHORPE

Upon my arrival I went to Mr. Beckett's apartment in London, where the whole family was staying at that moment. Mr. Beckett welcomed me very graciously. The oldest daughter, Lucille, was in the middle of a violin lesson. Her lovely dark eyes, brown hair, and pink dress were in perfect harmony as she came to greet me. After a short time the younger sister appeared. She had been shopping with her maid. Her greeting was so natural and graceful, and her pretty features expressed such openness and good will, that she immediately won my heart.

We stayed for only two days in this pleasant apartment. Several good portraits by old Dutch Masters made it particularly attractive for me. Our rooms were also very comfortable. Still, we were glad to move to the lovely country house not far from London. Mr. Beckett (who became Lord Grimthorpe upon the death of his uncle) was an exceptionally cultured man. Not only was he familiar with every newly published book, but he devoted himself enthusiastically to philosophical studies. He had spent some time in Japan, and had brought back many interesting objects. Japanese figures were placed throughout the garden. In the hall, at the foot of the stairs was a horrible looking warrior whose face was covered with a fearsome mask. In hopes of finding a friendly face, I once lifted his mask. The face that stared at me was so distorted with anger, rage, and hate that I quickly replaced the mask.

He also had brought exquisite embroideries and ivory carvings from Japan, so that the whole villa was like a museum. On weekends many visitors came here. One of them was Wilhelm Backhaus, the famous pianist, who enchanted us with his marvellous playing. He was also a great conversationalist and knew how to amuse the party with riddles and puns.

Among the Sunday guests was a Mr. Cust, an extremely attractive, intelligent man. He had just recovered from a severe case of pneumonia, which had been treated in St. Moritz. When the illness took a turn for the worse, the physician there thought it his duty to tell the sick man that he had only a few more hours to live. Mr. Cust's answer was, "I don't see the necessity of that." Indeed, the physician's prediction did not come true.

I really enjoyed these Sundays in the rose covered veranda, when I could listen to the interesting conversations of prominent people and occasionally participate. On one of these occasions arose that question with which I opened these memoirs.

Lucille took part in the lessons, but I was primarily occupied with Muriel, who was called "Moonie." This nickname seemed to suit the charming child so well, that I, too, called her nothing else.

During the fall I was alone with the girls for two months. Since they had the same interest in art and science as their father, my teaching job was very easy. We studied, played four-hand piano together, and took long carriage rides with one of the girls always holding the reins of the horses. When winter came, we moved to London.

Shortly after Christmas I traveled with my charges to Dresden and moved into an apartment in the Hotel Bellevue. Both girls made excellent progress in their piano and violin playing. Upon the recommendation of Adolf Stern, Dr. Otto Erler assumed the literature studies. It was a joy to sit in on these lessons, especially when Erler had "his moments." When he started to talk about Goethe or Kleist, he became excited. He would ask intriguing questions, such as, "Whom do you prefer, Penthesilia or Käthchen von Heilbronn?" The passionate Lucille called out at once, "Käthchen von Heilbronn!" But the delicate, graceful Moonie preferred Penthesilia. It seemed strange, but whenever charades or similar performances were presented, Moonie always chose to play the role of the villain. At a masked ball given by the wife of the prominent Dr. von Leyden in Berlin, she appeared as Ortrud.

Otto Erler had just finished writing his *Tsar Peter*. Before this drama appeared on stage, he introduced us to the actor, Paul Wiecke, who became known for his excellent representation of Alexei. What a wonderful evening! After dinner the two gentlemen read the roles of the play, and their animated conversation lasted deep into the night. After this introduction, we watched the drama with keen interest when it opened in Dresden. Erler had obtained the authentic Russian songs of mourning for the funeral of Alexei, which made a particularly deep impression on me. The preceding scene between Peter and Alexei, acted by Lothar Mehnert and Paul Wiecke, was deeply moving. We went home enthralled.

The lessons continued. During the last literature class with Erler, we mentioned our observation and puzzlement that Goethe had basically taken no notice of Kleist. Erler explained that, in his opinion, Goethe stayed clear of anything violent, while in almost every one of Kleist's dramas, some violent act occurs; for instance, Penthesilia goes to such excess in her passion that she bites a man.

When the time came for the sisters to visit their grandmother in Rome, I was to accompany them. We rode from Dresden directly through the St. Gotthard pass. Unfortunately, I caught a very severe cold, for which Mrs. Lee sent me to the sea. She had recommended the hotel "Delle Sirene" in Porto d'Anzio. To my dismay, I found it closed when I arrived there in the evening, and the other hotels in the area were also not open. Here I was, walking around the deserted streets with the porter, until I found a room in an old palace. I lay there for two days with lumbago and, in order to eat only real Italian food, I always asked for pasta for dinner. The third day I got up and found an "albergo" where I had the famous fish soup, served by a lovely Roman lady with such ceremony as befits a queen.

Since there was no point in staying in Porto d'Anzio I travelled to Rome the next day. I had an introduction to the painter Gerhard, a friend of Professor Hermann Schubert. He was a kind old gentleman who frequently accompanied me to the Forum and showed me the excavations. I often went to a church where two nuns in white and light-blue habits would kneel together before the altar for two hours and pray for forgiveness for sinners. On Sundays these nuns sang, and their song moved me deeply. I saw the Vatican with its magnificent paintings, and the Sistine Chapel. I admired the masterworks by Michelangelo and Raphael as I walked from one delight to the next. The grandmother, the sisters, and I were invited to Saint Peter for the procession of Leo XIII. The Pope blessed us all from his high seat. Fans made of ostrich feathers were carried on both sides of him. Then he conducted a High Mass at the altar and from above sounded the heavenly music of the silver trumpets.

I was also given entry to the Vatican garden. A papal servant showed me all the attractions, including the bench on which Leo

XIII sat daily with two cardinals. He even wanted to give me a potted plant as souvenir, but unfortunately I would not have been able to take it along on the return trip. Another unforgettable sight was the Colosseum at night in the moonlight. I have vivid recollections of my visit to the monastery, "Tre Fontane." It is now inhabited by Trappist monks. As is well known, they are not permitted to speak a word. Only the Brother who deals with the public has dispensation from his vow of silence.

The monastery is at the spot where the disciple Paul is supposed to have been beheaded. His head is said to have split into three pieces, and where each piece touched the ground a spring erupted. The three springs are set in marble and can be seen inside the church. I was told that the environment of this sacred place used to be so unhealthy that the pious monks, the former guardians of the shrine, were unable to remain and the monastery stood abandoned for a long period. Only during the last century, after the eucalyptus tree was introduced from Australia, were the monks able to return. This tree was planted throughout the swampy area because of its ability to absorb large amounts of moisture and for its effectiveness against fever. The environment improved, and from the eucalyptus the monks now make a delicious brandy which no visitor neglects to taste.

In Trastevere, a district of Rome on the other side of the Tiber, we visited the church of Saint Cecelia which was under the then world famous Cardinal Rampolla. He was a great connoisseur of art and commissioned beautiful mosaics for the church. Just as we were about to enter the church, he came out and greeted us cordially. His prominent head and forceful features pressed themselves deep into my memory. At the death of Leo XIII, he was one of the foremost candidates to become the new Pope, but his election was vetoed by Austria.

We made lovely excursions to Tivoli and visited the Villa d'Este. At that time the villa still belonged to Cardinal Hohenlohe, a noble, intelligent man. I had met him in Weimar when I was accompanying Baroness Rahden on her return trip from Davos. We had stopped there in response to an invitation by the Grand Duchess Katharina, who happened to be staying at the Thuringian residence. The Cardinal was a noble, intelligent man, and I followed his discourse with admiration. Grand Duke Karl Alexander was also present on that memorable evening, and I was so delighted that the Baroness commented with a smile the next morning, "Life at court agrees with you, doesn't it?"

The garden of the Villa d'Este with its tall cypress trees is indescribably beautiful. I was enchanted, walking through the arcades and taking in the view from the garden wall over the Campagna to Rome. In the palace itself I admired the paintings by Zuccaro.

Unfortunately, my cold had gotten much worse and Lord Grimthorpe, who had arrived in the meantime, insisted that I had to recuperate on Capri. We decided to meet again in Como, and I went to Capri by myself. The route to Naples passed through Monte Cassino. The Benedictine monks there are said to be great scholars and to have one of the best libraries. This monastery in its picturesque setting and with all its treasures has great attraction not only for Catholics but also for Protestants. An English lord who had lost all his money said to me in jest, "Now I shall become a monk on Monte Casino."

I stayed in Naples for two days. Early the first morning I went to the museum where I saw the objects found at Pompeii, including the famous baker's boy who had perished in the lava. I also visited the aquarium and watched with interest the fight of two lobsters. Afterwards, I mused how strange it is that it is generally much more interesting to observe animals who are fighting than those living peacefully together. The same holds for people. If we hear of a little quarrel, we start to pay attention. We hear of agreement and harmony and our interest wanes. — There were many other attractions in Naples. Above all, I could not miss going to Pompeii. My guide and I walked all alone through the narrow, deserted streets. A villa, the "House of Vettier," with beautiful frescoes, had been recently excavated. I was thinking of that day of horror when the burning lava reached the fleeing people. Along with the joy over the frescoes, I had a feeling of sadness when I left for Capri the next day.

A small boat took me to the big ship. The sea was stormy and the waves washed into the boat. I was so frightened that a sister of mercy tried in vain to calm me down. Even the big ship pitched terribly and could not dock in the usual place. For this reason there was no carriage to meet us and we had to climb a steep path to get to the hotel Quisisana. My room had a view not of the ocean, but of the lemon orchards, which were lovely too. Doctor Cuomo, the Italian physician, was a friendly, young man. He ordered me not to talk on my walks. Therefore, I had to decline all invitations by the other guests to join their outings. I went by myself, saw adorable gold-green lizards, and occasionally heard a native of Capri singing while he worked. Rarely did I meet another person. Once I came to a villa, hard against the sea. The door was open, the rooms empty, nothing was locked. I thought, I would not like to live here. You hear so much about the beauty of Italy, but right there, where the eye saw only the sea, nothing but sea, I did not like it. Give me a little house in the Black Forest or in Norway on a fjord, that would be more to my liking.

The hotel itself was very pleasant. There was much music making. The Neapolitans and their companions sang their songs in the evening. Doctor Cuomo's conscientious care cured me and I always remember him with gratitude.

Cured, I left Capri with its lemon orchards, red-blooming geranium bushes, and fire flies, and travelled as fast as possible to Florence. I could stay only a short time. The Florentine art treasures enchanted me and I was sorry to have so few days to devote to them. In addition, there were the charming villas with lovely gardens — and the historic connection to the Medicis. I told myself I would rather live in Florence than in Rome.

From Florence I proceeded to Venice. To sit in the Piazza San Marco in the evening was a special pleasure. I also enjoyed looking out the windows of my hotel, watching the gondolas on the canal and hearing Italian folk songs.

I would have liked to visit the "Palazzo Ventramin" where Wagner stayed at the end of his life. However, when I arrived there by gondola, the elegant attendant advised me that the Richard Wagner rooms were temporarily closed to the public. I was excited about Titian's "Ascension of the Madonna." On the other hand, I stood for a long time before Palma Vecchio's painting of Santa Barbara at the altar of the church Santa Maria Formosa. It became one of my favorite pictures.

In a big hotel in Como I rejoined Mrs. Lee and my two young friends. The surroundings were charming, but the formal dress expected in the evenings (many American and English visitors stayed at this hotel) was not to our liking and we were quite glad to move on. When we arrived in Paris we took lodging in the "Villa des Dames."

Lucille was to have her debut at her grandmother's in Rome the following spring and wanted to practice French conversation. The beautiful garden of our pension used to be part of the Luxembourg and the ladies-in-waiting lived in this little palace, hence the name. We stayed here for two months. The mornings were devoted to studies; in the afternoons my young companions played all kinds of running games with the sons of our landlady, who were of the same age. Even though the girls had been introduced to social life in their father's home, they had remained real children. A few times we attended the "Comédie Française," probably the best and most entertaining way to learn French conversation.

Our pension was the winter home of my dear Norwegian friend, Charlotte Jakobsen. In the summer, however, she had an apartment in the woods of Rambouillet, where the French socialist Auguste Comte had founded his so-called "Colony." It was his intention to move several families into the charming palace, once owned by a marquis, for communal living. This plan had to be abandoned because of the high cost. Instead, the followers of his idea settled into the workers' apartments in the woods. Each member paid down two hundred francs, which was refundable upon resignation. These apartments were in long, one-story buildings. My friend had her three rooms there, and belonged completely to this so-called "family." There were weekly meetings to take care of the common expenses. Artists, physicians, professors, etc. belonged to this community. We three visited my friend here a few times. It was rather inconvenient to get there, because one had to take the primitive mail-coach. Once arrived, however, one was rewarded by the beauty of the place.

In the fall we travelled to Yorkshire via London. Kirkstall, the country house of Mr. Beckett, was near Leeds, but the smoke of the industrial city fortunately did not reach us. The house was comfortably furnished. The living areas with music room and library were most inviting, especially when we returned from long carriage rides in the evening and the blazing fire in the hearth illuminated the prepared tea table. At such moments we would exclaim, "Isn't it beautiful here!"

Lucille was happy to return to Kirkstall the following spring after her triumphant debut in Rome. Ralph, too, the youngest member of the family and a delightful boy, was released from his school for a holiday. He was soon to enter Eton. Often we had visitors from Saturday till Monday. The theater in Leeds was not bad, and thus the vacation time passed very pleasantly. Summer turned to autumn, and each season brought its own charm and festivities. For Christmas I went home to Dresden and heard *Merlin* by Goldmark. This work fascinated me, because the character of the heroine is displayed differently in each of the three acts. It was always a celebration for me when I could enjoy such an artistic treat. It cast a glow over my work, to which I returned strengthened and refreshed.

While Lucille was making a second trip to Rome, I joined Moonie in London. Soon we received the news of Lucille's engagement to Count Czernin. The wedding was to occur very soon in London. In the meantime we had the joy of receiving the famous sculptor, Auguste Rodin, at our home. He was very interesting and so unassuming that we soon became friends. Before we parted, he pleased Moonie with the presentation of a pen drawing, a little masterpiece which he had created in our presence. He also invited us to visit him in his studio in Paris.

Mr. Beckett had a knack for making his guests feel comfortable in his home. I noticed this particularly when the Duke of Connaught and his wife were invited for luncheon one day. We were staying again in the lovely country house, the weather was pleasant, and the large table was set out of doors. During the meal the conversation was gay and uninhibited, and the ducal couple felt so relaxed that they stayed a long time. I was particularly interested in the Duchess. She was born a Princess of Prussia, daughter of Friedrich Karl, and we naturally conversed in German. She spoke at length about her mother, the once very beautiful Princess Friedrich Karl, who was now hard of hearing and suffering from an eye ailment. She told this with tender love and deep compassion. She herself was a very good mother, though rather strict. When they left, we had the impression that they had really enjoyed these hours.

The time for the wedding approached and Count Czernin came to England. He was a member of the Austrian embassy and a very congenial person. The wedding was celebrated in a Catholic church in London. Afterwards, the guests were seated around small tables and served a breakfast. The usual speeches and toasts were given and then the bridal couple left for their honeymoon. As is the custom in England, they were showered with rice as they left.

My student was now going to join relatives in the country for the hunting season. I myself travelled to Bayreuth, and again fell completely under the spell of *Parsifal*. Kundry was always an experience for me, and I felt her impact more deeply every year. From Bayreuth I went to Dresden to spend some precious hours in Therese Malten's garden, where her many friends had planted flowers and trees. It was a pleasure to have as my kind hostess the same person who had given such a gripping performance as Kundry. The Semenovs were also in Dresden, and we shared these musical pleasures and the visits to our friend in Zschachwitz. Mr. Semenov, the art connoisseur, led us through the art museum and enlightened us about the Dutch school of painting.

During this visit we also saw Gluck's *Iphigenia in Aulis*. Another year we saw Gluck's *Armida*, in my opinion one of the most beautiful operas. There is a particular melody in it which has impressed itself on my mind and which Therese Malten often used when she was improvising at the piano at dusk or even in the dark.

Too soon I had to part from all my dear friends. Duty called me back to Yorkshire. Mr. Beckett was travelling, but his brother, Mr. Gervase Beckett, who lived quite far from Leeds but had business there, would often stay with us during the week until Saturday. The evenings were usually devoted to literature. Mr. Gervase Beckett entertained us with his dramatic recitations of Shakespeare. Moonie's uncle had a wide knowledge of English literature, and we learned much from him. My student had matured to the point where her observations often gave the conversation an interesting turn.

This period came to an end when Parliament went back in session, and we returned to the apartment in London. I remember many stimulating discussions which we — Moonie, Mr. Beckett and I — carried on in the Chinese dining room. This little room was as comfortable as it was unique. The Chinese paintings on the walls transported us into a fairyland. Mr. Beckett was still in the House of Commons and often discussed politics with us. His family belonged to the Conservative Party, but he was so thoroughly liberal in his thinking that he publicly transferred to the Liberal Party. This was accomplished by simply stepping from the right to the left side and taking a seat there.

Now he was Liberal. Once he had to give a political lecture in Manchester, and he took us along so that we could witness the proceedings. I took a great interest in this, as in all political presentations. I was also intrigued by the luxurious hotel where we stayed. It almost reminded me of a theater. We sat in a gallery decorated with flowers and could watch those who dined below, while we were served the most delicious food to the accompaniment of lovely music.

About this time we received the news that Lord Grimthorpe, Mr. Beckett's uncle, had died. He was the designer of the wonderful clock and bell in the tower of Westminster, Big Ben. When he was elevated to the peerage, he assumed the name Grimthorpe. The children considered this quite significant, for they remembered the grim expression on his face when he tested Ralph in arithmetic during meals. Now Mr. Beckett received his uncle's title, and as Lord Grimthorpe he could not remain in the House of Commons but was introduced into the House of Lords as a peer. He invited us to attend the ceremony. We could not understand the speeches because we were too far away, but we could observe the curious procedure when Lord Grimthorpe stood before the "Lord on the Woolsack." (I was unable to discover the origin of this old English custom in the House of Lords.) He wore a traditional English costume consisting of a red coat and a strange hat, which he silently lifted and replaced three times — in a sense greeting the Lord Chancellor. Then, with his hat on, he walked ceremoniously to the right where the seats are located — somewhat elevated, inserted in the wall — and took his place. This ceremony appeared very comical and our urge to laugh was put to a severe test. Once at home, we released our pent-up laughter.

Again my young friend paid her annual visit to her grandmother in Rome where she would also see her married sister. Afterwards, we spent some time in Paris. When I met her at the railroad station I observed that she did not look well, even though she had had a delightful time. However, she seemed to perk up quickly and both of us were delighted when we received the news that her little nephew had been born in Italy. She now took lessons in French declamation from the splendid actor of the Comédie Française, Dehelly. His lessons were so interesting that we both looked forward from one lesson to the next. According to our promise, we also looked up Rodin in his studio. He had just completed the monument of Balzac which the judges refused because of its unusual concept. A bitter fight erupted in the world of art because of it. In my view, he had captured the thoughtful expression of one of France's greatest writers wonderfully, so I was not bothered by the insignificant details which had evoked the objections. When we visited his studio a second time, he was beginning a sketch of a girl praying. Whether he ever completed it, I do not know, but it was a most illuminating experience for us. Rodin said, "I want to show you my model." A very young girl in a blue gown appeared. She was not exactly beautiful but had very expressive features. She knelt down, and Rodin knew just how to elicit the expression he wanted by calling, "More intense!" It was as if her face became transfigured. After a few more similar suggestions given in a quiet tone, he said, "It is good." Then she rose and went modestly into the next room. We were deeply grateful to the great artist for giving us this intimate view of him at work in his studio.

A few days later we visited the museum in Cluny. It was of special interest for us because of the memorabilia relating to "Karl der Grosse," whom the French claim as their own "Charlemagne." Our interest in Montmartre was kindled when we saw the opera *Louise* by Charpentier, which represents the night life there in a most amusing fashion. This opera later became popular in Germany too. — Since we lived quite close to the Panthéon, we went frequently to this historic place. We also saw the oldest church in Paris, St. Génévieve, where sinners are promised forgiveness at the tomb of the saints for a certain number of "Ave Marias." We loved the modern paintings and art objects in the Luxembourg.

We did not neglect to visit my friend, Charlotte Jacobsen, in the Colony Rambouillet. In order to get better acquainted with this establishment, we decided to stay for several days. We witnessed a busy life. During the day, the men went hunting or fishing and returned with meat or fish, as needed. Vegetables came from the well-kept garden. Chickens, pigs and ducks were also raised. All meals were taken communally. In the morning, a big copper kettle with boiling milk was standing on the stove in the large kitchen, and everyone prepared his own coffee by mixing it with coffee extract; everything else was on the table. In the afternoons I strolled through the wonderful woods with my friends. The evenings were spent in animated conversation, making music, or playing cards.

After our stay in Paris we travelled to Kirkstall via London. Again I spent my vacation at home. I heard *Parsifal* in Bayreuth and met not only Therese Malten but also my English friend, Napier Miles. In Dresden I had the pleasure of seeing the Semenovs. Then I returned to England.

We enjoyed the winter, which we could devote to literature and music without distractions. Mr. Gervase Beckett visited us often. For the "Season" we moved to London and Lord Grimthorpe decided to give a ball for his daughter. Many daughters of the nobility were invited — including the Princess Patricia of Connaught. Some of them were real beauties. Winston Churchill, who is now an English Cabinet Minister, interested me particularly. He is the son of Lord Randolph Churchill who once played an important role in politics. We talked for quite a while. He expressed his regret that he had not studied classical languages and thought that Latin would have been of great value to him. At the table he sat next to Moonie and she enjoyed their conversation.

I had a brief, interesting encounter with the previously mentioned Mr. Cust. I was hurriedly crossing the room to arrange something, and he passed me going in the opposite direction, also in a great hurry. "Good evening. What can you tell me?" I said in passing. Without hesitation he replied at once, "The sky is high and wide, the clouds pass dark and grey. Behind them arched to infinity, enraptured, eternal blue." In a second we had raced past each other and I had experienced another flash of Mr. Cust's wit.

Supper was served downstairs around small tables. Afterwards there was dancing. It was early morning before the last guests departed. Lord Grimthorpe, Moonie, and I stood by an open window. Dawn was breaking and coloring the whole sky. A few night owls drove by in open carriages and waved to us. The city awakened and we went to sleep.

Another stay with her grandmother introduced Moonie to many German diplomats, among them Mr. von Bohlen-Halbach with whom she established a close friendship. Baron Ritter zu Gruenstein, later the Bavarian ambassador in Paris, also became her friend, and so she spent a very pleasant time in Rome.

THE END

With Moonie's debut my work as governess was completed, and it was time to part. We had come to truly love one another and I had to promise Lord Grimthorpe that I would return at once if I were needed.

I went to Mainberg to Johannes Müller, the comforter who stood by you when your heart was heavy. He looked at life from the bright side and inspired everyone to do his duty, while emphasizing the need to preserve one's uniqueness. He insisted that one must not be diverted from pursuing one's personal goals. Our conversations usually occurred in the vineyard where we walked back and forth. Below, the Main was flowing quietly, and along its shore the express train frequently zoomed by.

Just before I left England, Dr. Müller had done me a great favor. We had a friend in Herrnhut who had been deserted by her fiancé. Since everything became known in that small community, her mother wrote to us in desperation that she did not know what to do with her daughter. Moonie said at once, "We will send her to Dr. Müller." And we did. Within eight days the young girl was in Mainberg and her life took a new, wonderful direction. Müller, to whom all sentimentality was alien, came to her on the day when her wedding was supposed to have taken place and said, "I hear that this was to be your wedding day. I congratulate you on getting rid of this person. You are being expected at a boat down below. Go with the others and row along on the Main." The young girl later met a theology student at Mainberg, married him and became a happy pastor's wife and mother. In this way Johannes Müller has always tried to reconcile people with each other and to lead them to inner harmony.

Johannes Müller was already the father of a large family at that time. His wife, a beautiful blonde, was a typical German and as such, a passionate mother. Sounds of joking and laughing emanated from the house on the Main where Dr. Müller and his family lived. The Thursday evening dances, which I mentioned previously, were a real treat for me. I especially enjoyed watching Dr. Müller dance, executing some really artistic routines with his partner. What he emphasized for living he also expressed in his dancing. He considered rhythm the most important aspect. I found it particularly fascinating to observe the quadrille with its precise beginnings and the sudden stops at the end of the various parts.

Among the gentlemen, I met two Catholic priests. One was the court librarian in Vienna with whom I discussed his interest in Müller's aims. The other, whom I preferred, was a young Father from Bamberg, an extremely intelligent and farsighted man. I also got acquainted with two Protestant clergymen who were both liberal but drew opposite conclusions from their liberal theology for the direction of their lives. One told me that he could no longer remain a pastor and proclaim a dogma from the pulpit which he did not believe. The other said, " I consider my concept of Jesus to be correct, and that is a light which must shine, therefore I will not leave the church until I am thrown out."

I was more in sympathy with the latter stand, but each person has to act according to his own convictions, and anyone who had not done so before, would certainly learn it from Johannes Müller during a stay at Mainberg. Dr. Müller told us that he planned to move his establishment to Elmau because the climate in Mainberg was too mild for people who needed to be refreshed. "But what will those who called themselves 'Mainbergers' be named in Elmau? Perhaps 'Elmouths' or 'Elmice,'" he added laughingly.

∽

I settled into a simple room in the Europäischer Hof and intended by New Year's to find an apartment with my former maid. I had a small but cherished circle of close friends here. A real joy were the occasional visits of my nephew, Martin Dibelius, who had studied in Berlin and was a student of Adolf von Harnack. He too had been deeply moved by Therese Malten's art and beautiful voice, and he told me as well as her, that her influence had a lasting effect on him. His conversation was always greatly stimulating for me. He now returned to Berlin where he soon became "Privatdozent."

I also became friends with the sculptor, Kramer. Because of his great admiration for Miss Malten, he asked her permission to do her picture in relief. With her agreement he did so and it was placed in the Albertinum. Kramer had been in very poor health, but my cousin, the privy councillor Schmaltz, as his physician built up his strength so that he got better, married, and settled in Langebrück with his charming young wife. Both visited me frequently for tea and lively conversation in the Europäischer Hof. Kramer was working on a bust of Otto Ludwig at that time, and it was very interesting to watch its creation. The bust found a suitable home in the Bürgerwiese where even in winter the greenery presents an effective background.

At the opera I especially enjoyed Mascagni's *Cavalleria Rusticana*. This one-act opera was always paired with Leoncavallo's *Pagliacci* with Wedekind and Perron in the main roles. He sang the prologue beautifully. I have also heard Caruso sing it, but I always cherished the Dresden performance. The greatest praise, however, was won by Therese Malten's ideal representation of Santuzza in *Cavalleria*.

During my stay in Dresden, Holbein's Madonna from Darmstadt was brought to Dresden for a comparison with Holbein's Madonna here. The Dresden work was determined to be a copy. The Sixtene Madonna, however, a copy of which was also found later on, remains the crown jewel of the Dresden museum.

Naturally, I kept up a correspondence with my young friend, Moonie. At first she wrote joyfully about the hunts in which she participated once or twice a week. Then her tone changed and she told me that she was not feeling well. "Should I come?" I wrote back. "No, it is already a little better," was the reply. I assumed she had recovered and prepared for an artists ball where I wanted to come dressed as a fat cook, Therese Malten as a maid. Suddenly I received a telegram from London, asking me to come to my friend. I left the next day and traveled via Hook of Holland. Lord Grimthorpe was in Rome and according to his wish we stayed in England.

We chose Ventnor on the Isle of Wight for our sojourn. On our balcony we could enjoy the fresh sea breezes. A small pony buggy was rented for us, and we took daily rides around the island, often having our tea in little hotels right on the water. We had to go to London every three weeks to see the doctor, but we always returned happily to the island. My young friend loved to watch the activity of the ships and tugboats. We often visited the apartment of the coastguard. His son taught us the different colors of the ships' flags and the use of rockets in shipwrecks. He explained how the ropes are tied which serve to quickly pull shipwrecked sailors to shore. This young man owned a nice boat, and since we had confidence in him — and additional inquiries confirmed our judgment — I could entrust my charge to him for daily rowing excursions. Nevertheless, with my fear of water, I would sit on the beach like a hen who had hatched a duckling, especially nervous when the waves were high. The young man, who was totally at home on the water, would actually row up an oncoming wave and come down the other side without getting any water into the boat. Moonie was delighted by this maneuver and asked the seaman for repeat performances. Fortunately, this could only happen on stormy days which were rare occurrences.

We enjoyed not only the sea but also the land. The vegetation on the Isle of Wight is famous. I had expected to find rare flowers, which I did not, but the abundance of the plant world was surprising. For instance, on one of our excursions we came to a field of radiant blue. Here were the lovely bluebells which grow wild all over England, but nowhere in such profusion as here on the island. Another time, a pink band stretched along both sides of our path, created by a type of carnation. We often saw whole fields of the familiar, lovely white daisies. Sometimes we took long excursions, and so we visited Carisbrook Castle one day. We were shown the room in which Charles I of England was kept prisoner. He tried to escape through the window but was discovered and shortly thereafter executed on orders of Oliver Cromwell. Osborne, Queen Victoria's favorite place, we saw only from a distance. Lord Grimthorpe told us later that for Queen Victoria's funeral, large warships were lined up in two rows from one shore to the other, and the funeral boat carrying the earthly remains of the dead Queen sailed slowly between them while the other boats saluted and lowered their flags. This ceremony left a deep impression on him.

It was not nature alone that gave us pleasure. At the hotel we were introduced to a small group of people which we were pleased to join. At the head was a charming and cultured lady, Princess Salm-Salm, who took a special liking to my young friend. She invited us often, and we were usually joined by Mr. J. W. Cross, who had been married to the famous George Eliot. The marriage was very brief since the great writer died after only a few months. He often read English poems to us which he did with great feeling, and the discussions which followed always dealt with interesting topics.

When Lord Grimthorpe returned from Rome, he too came to Ventnor, lived of course in the same hotel, and added much zest to the little group. He did not stay long, but on one of our walks he saw a beautiful villa which had such great attraction for him that he immediately rented it. Before we would make the move, he wanted us to spend some time in Scotland. He and Ralph were going to join us. The physician in London gave us permission to spend a few weeks on the island of Skye. We went aboard on the coast of Scotland, and the "Lapwing," a real nutshell, took us across. It was stormy, we were on the Atlantic Ocean, and the waves kept coming overboard. A gentleman, who wanted to reassure me, said, "Don't worry, the captain is sleeping below in his cabin." This comment did anything but have the desired result. After this horrible crossing we landed safely in the harbor of the island. Even though it was raining, we proceeded to ride in an open carriage the considerable distance to the country house which Lord Grimthorpe had rented for us. Happily arrived, I was amazed to find such a comfortable house in so sparsely inhabited a region. Everything one could desire for human comfort was provided: electric lights, a bathroom, even the owner's three good servants. Naturally we often had delicious fish since the house was near a bay. My window looked out over the ocean. Our life here was very relaxed. The landscape had a particular charm, and we explored the region on our daily rides. The roads led over hilly and rocky terrain and then again along the shore. The gentlemen went hunting and fishing. They could shoot all kinds of birds, of which the Scottish grouse was particularly tasty. Once they returned from fishing with a very strange creature. It was a large fish with a triangular head and a long, skinny tail in the form of a spike. The natives of Skye ate this interesting fish, but we rejected it.

Occasionally we had visitors. One of Lord Grimthorpe's friends spent a whole week. On those occasions we would sit a long time at the table. One evening, after the last course, oysters rolled in bacon (angels on horseback), had been eaten, Lord Grimthorpe suggested that we should quickly, without much thinking, name persons from the past whom we would like to see. They could be historical or private persons. I have a faint recollection that I quickly named Shakespeare and Goethe. I have forgotten whom the other three wished to see, because Lord Grimthorpe played the trump: he named the Alpha and Omega — Christ. This put us to shame, but his next choice brought forth our laughter, the beautiful Helena.

He was an unusual person. There were many contradictions in his nature, and the readings he chose for us were extremely varied. Every day he read us some Spinoza, for he loved to philosophize. In the evenings he selected novels by old English authors who were anything but prudish.

In this way the two months passed most pleasantly. We had to prepare for our return and were glad that Lord Grimthorpe had rented the villa on the Isle of Wight. This estate had a lovely garden and a magnificent view of the ocean. To Moonie's delight, a telescope had been set up and she could watch the passing ships and identify them by their flags. One morning she woke me early to watch the big four-masted "Preussen." Unfortunately, this beautiful German ship sank not long afterwards.

Soon after our return to the Isle, Violet (still named Lady Bingham) visited us. She and Moonie had become close friends and her visit was a real gift for us. We took motor boat rides to Shanklin, had lunch there and returned again by boat. For me this was no great pleasure since the waves often washed into the boat. Mrs. Lee, Moonie's grandmother, came for a short while and then went to the baths at Dinard. We were going to join her, and I intended to take my vacation at that time, knowing that Mrs. Lee would like to spend some time alone with her granddaughter.

We had to travel to St. Malo, the harbor from which Dinard can be reached. We embarked in Portsmouth on a quiet evening. The harbor and the illuminated ships presented an impressive sight. Slowly we were gliding along. We would have liked to stay on deck all night, but I thought it wiser to get some rest. Suddenly the ship began to rock terribly and we could not stay below. Up on deck, one of the sailors pointed out the island of Guernsey where Victor Hugo, the writer of *Les Miserables*, spent the years of his exile. He has long since gone to rest from his politically stormy life. We now remained on deck and were relieved when we reached St. Malo. From here we went on to Dinard, where Mrs. Lee was expecting us.

After a few days I left for my vacation. I traveled via Paris to Dresden where I met my friends, the Semenovs. I left shortly for Berlin to consult the famous physician, Exzellenz von Leyden, about my young friend's illness. Upon his emphatic reply that he absolutely had to see her, I left immediately to bring Moonie to Berlin. On the way, I spent a few days in Paris and followed an invitation by Rodin to Meudon where he had established a museum for his works right next to his apartment. He showed me his marvellous work: the muse in the form of a young man presenting a golden apple from a tree behind him to Alfred de Musset. Then he called my attention to a woman's head leaning over a kind of basin. "Do you see the pain in this face?" he asked me. I answered, "I can feel it." Indeed, these not exactly beautiful features with half-closed eyes and clenched lips, which I believed to see trembling, expressed such intense suffering that I was on the verge of tears. This was my last visit with the great artist who passed on many years ago.

Dr. von Leyden decided that Moonie would have to reside in his clinic. The treatment he prescribed fortunately did not keep us from enjoying concerts and the theater. Moonie did not care for the opera; she revered Therese Malten's vocal and dramatic art so much, that the opera in Berlin did not appeal to her. Therefore, we attended the theaters, Deutsche Theater, Lessingtheater, and Kammerspiele, that much more. We saw Moissi as Hamlet and were spellbound. Moonie began lessons in declamation with Moissi. His teaching was fascinating. His recitation of Heinrich Heine's poem, "Die Wallfahrt von Kevelaar" was unforgettable. It was a special joy to become personally acquainted with Dr. von Leyden. He stayed with us for coffee after he had finished the daily visits to his patients. We enjoyed listening to him. His method of treatment consisted primarily in the diet he prescribed for his patients, apparently achieving great success with it. The Countess Shuvalov who had been given up by her Russian doctors, had been completely cured through his consistent and appropriate dietary regimen.

After Moonie completed the treatment in the clinic, we realized that it would be best to stay in Berlin near Dr. von Leyden and his assistant, Professor Dr. Lazarus. Both of them attended Moonie with concerned care, and so we did not return to England for the time being.

We attended Dr. Johannes Müller's interesting lectures in Berlin and had the pleasure of seeing him often at our home. He had developed a great liking for my friend, as did everyone who knew her. "To know her was to love her," as her sister-in-law once wrote to me.

We heard a wonderful concert given by Busoni. His playing was as sensitive as he was himself. Soon we became better acquainted with him and spent many hours in his home. His beautiful, blond wife was always the charming hostess, and his young admirers often gathered around the tea table and hung on his every word. His remarks were usually clever and funny. He was widely read, and his library contained the works of the great minds. Thus we had an interesting life in Berlin, graced by frequent visits from Therese Malten. We occasionally spent a few days in Dresden, for Zschachwitz continued to have a great attraction for us. The artist had taken Moonie into her heart and Moonie returned the feeling with love and devotion.

Moonie's condition now required that we move into the country, and we took up residence in a sanatorium by the Schlachtensee near Berlin. We had a veranda, shaded by firs and pines, where we often took our meals, and we enjoyed walks around the lake. This stay was very beneficial for my companion. Our friend, Dr. von Leyden, had become sickly and could not come so far, but his assistant, Professor Lazarus, filled in for him. The treatment was so successful that we decided to make our home in Berlin. By chance, an apartment near the "Tiergarten," with conservatory and all imaginable comforts, was available. Furnishing the new apartment was a pleasant diversion. Moonie was especially amused by the selection of the wallpaper, and we were delighted that we could decorate the walls of the large salon with original oil paintings: Leistikow's "Im Grunewald" and Schultze-Naumburg's "Rudelsburg und Saaleck" with the wonderful white cloud in the background. Now we were ready to receive guests. It was a joy to see my nephew, Dr. Martin Dibelius, and his wife frequently at our home for supper. He introduced us to the most important new works in music and literature. Sometimes he sang and played a whole opera for us at the piano.

Moissi continued his lessons and occasionally came for tea. Max Reinhardt was just producing Tolstoy's *The Living Corpse*, one of Moissi's best roles. In the scene where he is called to judgment, his entrance involuntarily reminded one of Christ. His magnificent rendition of this speech displayed his greatness as an artist. Among other friends who came to tea was Lola Artot de Padilla, the daughter of the once famous Désirée Artot who had married the Spaniard Padilla. She also invited us to her attractive apartment. She was very popular in Berlin, but her life was not easy. But then, does any artist have an easy life?

The Christmas season was delightful. To walk along the brightly lit streets and go shopping was just the thing for my young friend. During the holidays we gave a dance for the servants. Moonie had a very rich wardrobe, and she dressed the porter as a Venetian gondolier, his wife in Japanese costume, Mary, the maid, as a shepherdess, and the housemaid as a devil. We two took turns playing the dance music and had as much fun as the participants.

It was an enjoyable winter. Musical performances in Berlin and Dresden brought much variety into our lives. In the spring Moonie travelled first to England then to Rome. I accepted an invitation to attend the golden wedding anniversary of the Semenovs in St. Petersburg. Even though this was a celebration with their immediate family, they included me. It was a joy to see the celebrants so happy together, he eighty-five and she seventy years old. They had shared much joy and sorrow and were now surrounded by many children and grandchildren. The Tsar had added the name "Tian-Shansky" to his other titles in recognition of his scientific explorations in Asia. I saw many old friends in St. Petersburg, including some of the university people from the student kitchens. I visited Mrs. Abaza, whose appearance now reminded me of the portrait of Queen Luise. She was still interested in music and I could recommend a promising pianist to her. How many memories were awakened by this visit: Grand Duchess Helene, Baroness Editha von Rahden, Rubinstein, Dostoevski.

After these wonderful weeks I met Moonie again in Berlin. Dr. von Leyden and Professor Lazarus now sent us to Vichy, and

Leyden asked me to drink the water too, to keep my friend company.

We travelled by way of Montreux where we stayed in the hotel Eden directly on the lake. It was very beautiful even though the fog hid the "Dent du Midi" which I had once seen in the moonlight in all its beauty. After two days we continued to Vichy via Lyon. The trip was very tiring. We took rooms in the "Grand Hotel," which is conveniently located on the avenue leading to the spring and to the theater. Our physician, Dr. Chabrol, had been recommended by Exzellenz von Leyden who knew him personally. We found him to be an intelligent, likeable person. In the mornings we would walk with our cups to the spring. After we had drunk the prescribed amount and taken the walks which go along with the treatment, we went home for the delicious breakfast. Later we would make music or go for rides. We often rode to Montagne Verte. The road led through strawberry fields and was very pretty. At the top we had a view over water, woods, and fields, and could really relax and talk about the many things which were on our minds. In the evenings we were often invited by Dr. Chabrol for bridge games. This was quite useful for us, since the idioms of the language can also be learned during card games.

Dinner was at seven o'clock. We were amused that strawberries were served in little straw hats. After dinner we often went to the theater which was just five minutes away. The company of the "Comédie Française" played here, and the performances were most enjoyable.

After four weeks we returned to Berlin. The servants were really happy to see us, which made it a pleasant homecoming. We spent our time again studying history. We read Taine's interesting work *La Révolution*. We also read plays by Shakespeare, some of which we saw at the Deutsche Theater. Our beloved and revered Dr. von Leyden had passed on and, deeply saddened, we visited his widow.

Moonie still had not fully recovered and Professor Lazarus ordered another stay at Vichy. On the way we stopped in Paris and went to the "Comédie Française" of which we had become very fond. We saw a longer comedy followed by a one-act play. During the performance, the conversation on stage suddenly stopped and almost immediately an unnaturally bright glow spread over the stage. A panic arose among the audience, and the call "Incendie" was heard. Many hurried out. I got up and wanted us to leave, but my young friend in her wonderful, harmonious calm said, "Oh no, let us stay." Just then, one of the actors came on stage and told us that some scenery had caught fire but that it had already been extinguished. They completed the performance as if nothing had happened.

We found out that Mrs. von Rahden, née Jenny Weiss, the wife of a nephew of Editha von Rahden, lived in Paris. Naturally, we went to see her. She had suffered a tragic fate. Her husband had died in Braunschweig. She became an equestrian in a circus in Nice in order to support her father. One morning she awoke and asked the maid to draw back the curtains. "They are drawn back, the sun is shining brightly," was the answer. The poor woman was overcome with horror. She had gone blind overnight. It was discovered later that a kidney disease had caused her blindness. Now she and her father were living in Paris. She tried to eke out a living by giving Spanish and German lessons. It was touching to see how her old father took care of her, dressed her, etc. She had a beautiful voice, trained by a friend to enable her to participate in the musical soirées in private homes. She did this once, but the invited guests declared it was dreadful to hear a blind person sing. So she had to forego this means of earning some money. We felt terribly sorry for her. She had worked very hard. She told us how gratified she was that she had been able to support her governess until her death and, above all, that she had succeeded in having a monument erected on her husband's grave in Braunschweig. The Countess Levachov, whom I knew from St. Petersburg, assisted her. We could not help but smile when Jenny von Rahden responded to our inquiry, what she would like, with, "I love to eat lobster." This wish was easy to satisfy. The war kept us from hearing any more from her, but I recently heard that she is no longer alive.

We again had a pleasant stay in Vichy. Dr. Chabrol had become our friend and counselor. Since he had been in Germany, where he became acquainted with Leyden and Lazarus, he wanted to expand his knowledge of German and we had a reciprocal arrangement with the two languages.

Following the treatment in Vichy, a rest in the Engadin was prescribed for Moonie. First we rode to Zurich and stayed two weeks. It was delightful to take the boat to the other end of the lake, see the grave of Ulrich von Hutten, and then glide slowly back by the light of the evening sun. Not far from Zurich, up on the Green Hill, we saw the former Wesendonk property and next to it the house where Richard Wagner spent those poetic days when he was consumed by his love for the lovely Mathilde Wesendonk. We had good friends in Zurich with whom we made several excursions into the surroundings. In St. Moritz we had a breathtaking view from our room onto the Rosegg glacier, which sometimes had a bewitching beauty in the glow of the sunset. Lord Grimthorpe and Ralph, Moonie's brother, joined us at the hotel. Moonie was delighted to have her brother there. Brother and sister had a very close, lasting relationship. Ralph was a great mountain climber and ascended most of the peaks near St. Moritz. The young people would often row on the lake. I believe that the Engadin is the most beautiful part of Switzerland because it combines mountains and water. Lord Grimthorpe had to leave us soon, but Ralph stayed longer. When it began to get cold in St. Moritz, we looked forward to our cozy, warm home in Berlin.

The coming winter was particularly enjoyable as we met old and new acquaintances. Dr. Krupp von Bohlen was an occasional visitor with his pleasant wife. One time we discussed education. "When my children reach a certain age, I do not want blind obedience from them. I always explain the reason why I require certain things from them," he said. This view was debated at length. His visits were always stimulating. Another frequent visitor was Mr. Harvey from the American embassy. With him we usually played bridge after tea. Thus the years passed.

One time, when Ralph came for a visit after he had been sledding at Engelsberg I decided to give the brother and sister some undisturbed time with each other and went to Klein-Welcke for three days. The widow of Pastor Hans lived here. Pastor Hans had been the preacher at the Herrenhut colony in St. Petersburg during my time there, and I had admired him very much. He was an excellent preacher and his stimulating lectures had given us great pleasure. He had remained my friend until his death. His daughter was the young woman who had once sought and found consolation in Mainberg at Johannes Müller's.

When I returned, Moonie and Ralph were full of enthusiasm about the days they had spent together. They had been to the Grunewald and to the theater. They had eaten at Kempinsky's. In short, I had succeeded in my purpose. Next, Moonie's sister came to Berlin with her three boys. Lord Grimthorpe came too, and at Christmas time Moonie's brother-in-law, Count Czernin, as well. The Christmas tree and the presents were set up in our large music room. I can still see Moonie playing with her nephews under the tree. After Count Czernin's departure, we often had the children with us. Another little brother was born at the end of January.

In the spring Lucille left us and returned to her home. We made many excursions to the lovely Grunewald and often extended our walks from one lake to the other. Our veranda was like a flower garden. Here we spent the afternoons and evenings reading. We were sitting here one afternoon, and I was reading Tolstoy's *Resurrection* to Moonie, when our maid rushed breathless into the room with the words, "The crown prince has been murdered!" We assumed it was the German crown prince and jumped up in horror. Later we found out that the Austrian successor to the throne, Franz Ferdinand, and his wife had been murdered in Serajevo. While we were appalled, we did not anticipate the dreadful consequences. We were still quite happy the next Sunday when our friend from Zschachwitz came in response to our invitation. However, during the outing we had planned for the afternoon, the newspaper vendors were shouting, "Extra, Extra!" The special edition reported that the Emperor had cut short his trip to the north. We were understandably upset, and when we took our visitor to the train that evening, everything was in confusion.

We now experienced the excitement of the first days of the war. We heard the Emperor speak to the people from the balcony, and caught the enthusiasm. Soon afterwards, we were at the Schlesische station, waving "good bye" to the soldiers who were leaving for the front. Hardly was the train out of the station, when a voice called, "Silence! Lord Goschen has requested his passport." This was a terrible blow for both of us. My young friend was overcome with sorrow at the thought that her country was now the enemy of Germany, the land she had come to love, and I experienced the same feeling. A painful parting lay before us. At my request, General von Haxthausen received us and granted permission for me to accompany Moonie to Holland. The train left Berlin on September 23, 1914. In Vlissingen, I stayed the night in her stateroom and then we said "farewell." As the ship slowly disappeared from sight, I had no idea that I would never see Moonie again.

In order to stay in touch with my friend, I remained for a while at my niece's in Holland. She lived in Wageninen, not far from Doorn. From here we, who had been so suddenly separated, could easily correspond. It was different once I returned to Germany. In Germany one was not permitted to receive or write any English letters, and in England the situation was reversed. Therefore, my nephew in Holland acted as translator. English cards were translated into German and sent to me, and my German cards were translated into English before they went on to England.

My first job now was to clear the apartment in Berlin which occupied me for quite a while. Mrs. von Helmholtz was a kind and comforting friend during this period. It was not easy for me to leave her, but I had decided to settle in Dresden and I had to part from her and my other friends in Berlin.

In Dresden I took a room in the hotel "Europäischer Hof" and from there looked for a pension. The war laid a heavy hand on Germany and on me. The hope for an early end to these days of horror was an illusion which vanished in a cloud.

The following summer I accepted an invitation by my niece to come to Zurich. Here I met the Busonis again. This intelligent and prominent man had become quite active here in exile. He and his family lived in a lovely apartment on a hill, and a group of friends gathered daily around his table at tea time. Just as in Germany, Mrs. Busoni was again the charming hostess. Busoni expressed his longing for Germany to me. Fortunately, his wish to return was eventually fulfilled, and he could move back into his lovely home after the war. He, too, is no longer among the living, but this important person and great artist lives in my memory,

Back in Dresden, I settled into a pension where I enjoyed receiving guests and returning their visits. Following an invitation to Weimar by Baroness Helene von Taube, born Countess Keyserling, I stayed with her for several weeks.

This visit gave me comfort and consolation in my sorrow, for in the year 1916 my beloved young friend, Moonie, had spread her wings and flown to her eternal home.

Mrs. von Taube was particularly interested in birds and observed them in truly scientific fashion. In front of her window was a board with food. We sat at some distance armed with opera glasses and studied the behavior of the different birds. A hawfinch had much trouble with the upbringing of her three sons; we called them Ishmael, Jacob, and Esau. Esau did not want to touch the nuts, but the mother was persistent. Beautiful woodpeckers showed up too. Time went incredibly fast during such observations.

We often went to see Mrs. Elisabeth Förster-Nietzsche on the days when she received guests. She lived in a lovely villa outside Weimar. Already at the entrance we were greeted by mementoes of her deceased brother, which the sister preserved reverently. She was always glad to see us. I once asked her about the friendship between her brother and Richard Wagner which had such a sad end. "You are right," she said, "Wagner suffered deeply at this break, which, as you know, my brother initiated; but my brother had no choice." It is only natural that the sister would take the side of her brother, while my sympathy belonged to Richard Wagner. I will always remember this lively little woman with her diverse interests. Unfortunately, I no longer get to Weimar since Mrs. von Taube moved to Munich with her son, the writer Otto von Taube.

In the summer I visited my niece in Holland who had been widowed and had moved "with stoves and hearth" as is the custom in Holland, to a house of her own in Heerde. Here was a camp for interned Germans. I became acquainted with several gentlemen from the camp, and they invited us to little theatrical productions. I also met two ladies who were Christian Scientists. One of them was a "healer" and rode her bike past our house several times a day. She often stopped to tell us of the successful cures of her patients. The other one, the rich daughter of a landowner, brought us strawberries and asparagus. I must admit that the members of this sect display remarkably sunny dispositions. For this reason it is delightful to associate with them. They are also extraordinarily generous and help one another.

After my return to Dresden I contracted erysipelas on my feet and had to stay in the hospital for ten months. Since I had a private room, the time passed very pleasantly, except for the pain associated with this disease. The enforced solitude was good for me. I could get in touch with my inner self and was really at peace when I was cured and moved to my new, pretty apartment in the Marienheim in Dresden where I still live.

ఌ

On June 18, 1923, it had been fifty years since the eighteen-year-old Therese Malten had sung Elsa for the first time as a newly engaged member of the Court Opera in Dresden. This anniversary became a special celebration for her and all of Dresden. Her box was decorated with garlands of flowers. When she entered, the overflowing audience rose and greeted her with enthusiastic applause, so that it was impossible to start the performance. Again and again the house paid homage to her, and many a tear was shed in remembrance of all she had given us. As she stood there in her white gown, arms spread out for her final greeting, the music critic, Eugen Thari, said to me, "She reminds me of Elisabeth receiving her guests on the Wartburg. How beautiful she still is!" Such days remain in the memory, and when I sit in my quiet room, these remembrances appear and brighten the present.

When I expressed my congratulations to her at this celebration, she said, "In my thirty years on the stage I have never had any unpleasantness with my colleagues and, above all, I have never put my nose in things which did not concern me."

I spent the next two years in satisfying, quiet activities, interrupted by short trips to Lübeck and Hamburg. A high point in the evening of my life was Therese Malten's seventieth birthday on June 21, 1925. She wanted to observe it in quiet retirement.

However, the serenade intended for the evening of her birthday she finally accepted a few days later in the morning. She stood in the midst of the red geraniums on the steps of her veranda, the sun shining through her silver hair; in front of her stood the singers in a semicircle with flags and banners, singing their beautiful choruses with obvious excitement. Countless demonstrations of admiration and respect came to her on her day of honor. I doubt that there was ever another artist who was still so loved and honored thirty years after leaving the stage.

It sometimes seems to me now as if Therese Malten is high on a mountain top taking a bird's-eye view of the past and the present. I recently told her of an unpleasant encounter where I thought I had not been treated with due respect. She said, "Times change, and we have to adjust to the new ways and learn afresh. One is never too old to learn afresh."

Now the chain is closed. Many of its links were jewels, some of which unfortunately are missing now. But among those which remain are several which brighten and beautify the evening of my life. The brightest light, however, comes from her to whom I dedicate these pages and who gave me the name "Sunday's child." And so I close with the words of Lynceus, the lookout (Goethe, *Faust*, Part 2. Act V.):

> *Ihr glücklichen Augen,*
> *Was je ihr gesehn,*
> *Es sei wie es wolle*
> *Es war doch so schön!*
>
> *You fortunate eyes*
> *of all you have seen,*
> *whatever it was,*
> *beautiful has it been!*

Susanne Schmaltz died in Dresden on January 31, 1934, at 95 years of age.

Susanne Schmaltz at 90 years

SELECTED ANNOTATED
BIOGRAPHICAL INDEX

Krupp von Bohlen, Gustav v. Bohlen Halbach, married the eldest daughter, Bertha, of Friedrich Alfred Krupp - 3rd generation of the German steel magnates. 206

Kshesinsky, F. I., character dancer, unrivalled in mazurka, born in Warsaw, 1823. Ref.10 91

Lassen, Eduard (1830-1904) Belgian composer, settled in Weimar, succeeded Liszt as conductor of the opera. 121

Lavroskaia, Elizaveta Andreevna (1845-1919) Russian singer, contralto 80

Leo XIII, Pope (1810-1903) Pope from 1878 to 1903 183-184

Lind, Jenny (1820-1887) Swedish soprano "The Swedish Nightingale." 8, 15, 41-43, 164

Liszt, Franz (1811-1886) pianist, composer, conductor, after 1869 he divided his time between Weimar and Rome. Became Franciscan, Abbé Liszt in 1865 .... 63, 121-122

Ludwig I, (Louis I) King of Bavaria (1786-1868) great patron of the arts; Munich owes him the two Pinakotheken, Odeon, the University and Glyptothek. Died in Nice, February 28, 1868. .... 55, 162

Lvov, Princess, the "High Stewardess" in the employment of the Grand Duchess Helene. 69. 81

Malten, Therese - Therese Müller - (1855-1930) German soprano. Debut in 1873 at the Hofoper in Dresden as Pamina in the *Magic Flute.* Her debut was so impressive that she was given a contract for life. She became the leading Wagnerian soprano of her generation, and Wagner himself considered her the best Kundry. She made great efforts on behalf of Wagner's music and introduced his operas in Petersburg and Moscow to tremendous acclaim. Her guest appearances in Holland and England were equally triumphant.Ref.6 ....
.... 150-156, Chapters 9, 10, and 11.

Maria Alexandrovna, Empress (1855-1880), Maximilienne Wilhelmine Marie, daughter of Grand Duke Ludwig II of Hesse, wife of Tsar Alexander II. 79, 106

Maria Feodorovna, Empress (1758-1828) aunt of Grand Duchess Helene, born Princess Sophie Dorothea von Württemberg, wife of Tsar Paul I. 74

Maurice, Charles (1805-1896) Founder and Director of the Thalia Theater in Hamburg. 13

Meier, Camilla and Franziska members of Brahms' Women's Chorus. Excerpts from Franciska's diary, relating to Brahms' Women's choruses were published. Ref.7 and 11 .... 11-12, 15

REFERENCES

1. *The Russian Empire 1801-1917,* Hugh-Seton-Watson, Oxford University Press 1967

2. *My Life Vol II.* Richard Wagner, authorized translation from the German New York, Dodd Mead and Company 1911

3. *Great Soviet Encyclopedia,* McMillan 1983

4. *Biography: Duse,* William Weaver, Harcourt Brace Jovanovich 1984

5. *Aus dem Leben, Zwei Novellen von Carmen Sylva,* with an introduction by Paul Lindenberg. Philipp Reclam jun, Leipzig

6. *Die Musik in Geschichte und Gegenwart,* Vol 8, Barenreiter, Kassel Basel London New York, 1960

7. "Jahrbuch der Gesellschaft Hamburger Kunstfreunde" 1902

8. *Das treffende Zitat,* Karl Peltzer, 3.erw. Auflage, Ott Verlag Thun und München 1957

9. *Autobiography of Anton Rubinstein 1829-1889,* translated from the Russian by Aline Deleno, Boston Little, Brown, and Co. 1890 Republished 1970, Scholarly Press

10. *A History of Ballet in Russia, 1613-1881*, Cyril W. Beaumont, C W Beaumont, London 1930

11. *Brahms and His Women's Choruses* by Sophie Drinker, Published by Sophie Drinker under the auspices of Musurgia Publisher, 1952